# Critics, Ratings, and Society

# Critics, Ratings, and Society

## The Sociology of Reviews

Grant Blank

ROWMAN & LITTLEFIELD PUBLISHERS, INC.
Lanham • Boulder • New York • Toronto • Plymouth, UK

ROWMAN & LITTLEFIELD PUBLISHERS, INC.

Published in the United States of America
by Rowman & Littlefield Publishers, Inc.
A wholly owned subsidary of The Rowman & Littlefield Publishing Group, Inc.
4501 Forbes Boulevard, Suite 200, Lanham, Maryland 20706
www.rowmanlittlefield.com

Estover Road
Plymouth PL6 7PY
United Kingdom

British Library Cataloguing in Publication Information Available

**Library of Congress Cataloging-in-Publication Data**

Blank, Grant.
    Critics, ratings, and society : the sociology of reviews / Grant Blank.
      p. cm.
    Includes bibliographical references and index.
    ISBN-13: 978-0-7425-4702-5 (cloth : alk. paper)
    ISBN-10: 0-7425-4702-7 (cloth : alk. paper)
    ISBN-13: 978-0-7425-4703-2 (pbk. : alk. paper)
    ISBN-10: 0-7425-4703-5 (pbk. : alk. paper)
    1. Social choice. 2. Criticism—Social aspects. 3. Consumers—Attitudes. 4. Critics.
I. Title.
HB846.8.B6 2006
302'.13—dc22                                                                   2006011575

Printed in the United States of America

♾™ The paper used in this publication meets the minimum requirements of American
National Standard for Information Sciences—Permanence of Paper for Printed Library
Materials, ANSI/NISO Z39.48-1992.

# Contents

# List of Figures and Tables

## FIGURES

## TABLES

# Acknowledgments

Since this book is, in part, about the independence of authors and potential conflicts of interest, I should disclose my affiliations. Among the corporations that I mention, I currently own stock in Microsoft and SPSS. As part of my consulting work, I have worked for and been paid by SPSS and Systat. I have received other products—usually free manuals, software, or meals—from BMDP, Manugistics, and SAS Institute. At *Chicago* magazine, the *Chicago Tribune*, and the *Washington Post*, interviews with restaurant critics took place over a meal. They were working meals in several senses.

My first debt is to the reviewers, editors, product makers, and readers whom I interviewed. The book could not have been completed without their time and interest. Their names are listed in appendix A. Their contribution to this project was immense, and I thank them all. I owe a special debt to Dennis Ray Wheaton, who contributed immensely to my understanding of restaurants, dining, and restaurant reviews. Ted Stevenson is due special thanks for his help with computer software and hardware reviews.

I received help from many who read and commented on parts of the book, or who shared their expertise with me. I would like to thank Rebecca M. Blank, Wendy Bokhorst-Heng, Fay Booker, Daniel Thomas Cook, Andrew Dornenburg and Karen Page, Penny Edgell, Steven Ellingson, Jack Fuller, Richard Goldstein, Mary Conklin Gomberg, Jennifer Lynn Johnson, Marvin A. Jolson, Mary Ellen Konieczny, Johannes Kuttner, Harriet P. Morgan, Andrew A. Norton, Daniel Norton-Middaugh, Lorayn Olson, Deborah Popely, Lynn Rapaport, David Reynolds, Leland Wilkinson, and Jolyon Wurr. Virginia Bartot, Martha van Haitsma, Marilyn Krogh, and Stuart Michaels were part of a study group that provided valuable support in the early days of this research. Several students worked on the book at American University: Lori

Goode, Margaret Emma Holland, Amy Mennerich, Andrea Miller, and Jami Obermayer. Presentations at the Workshop on Culture and Society at the University of Chicago greatly improved several chapters.

Leland Wilkinson and Ruth Van Demark loaned their lovely house in Truro on Cape Cod, where I wrote initial drafts of chapters 1 and 3. Jennifer Lynn Johnson first used the word *connoisseur* to describe restaurant reviewers.

My dissertation committee has been continued to be a resource: William L. Parish, chair, Andrew Abbott, and Wendy Griswold. I thank Andy and Wendy for their constructive comments and encouragement in all of our interactions. I am particularly grateful to Bill Parish for his support of this project from the time it was only a fuzzy glimmer.

Petra Carter Blank has been a joyful distraction since February 23, 2000, as has Mara Porielle Blank since January 27, 2004. Denise Carter-Blank supported this book in many ways. I owe her an enormous debt. I dedicate the book to her in recognition of all the ways she has enlivened and enriched my life.

*Chapter One*

# What Are Reviews?

In the arts, the critic is the only independent source of information. The rest is advertising.

—Pauline Kael, *New Yorker* movie reviewer
(quoted in Cooper 1973: 96)

On February 24, 2003, Bernard Loiseau, one of France's greatest chefs and owner of an extraordinary restaurant, La Côte d'Or, shot himself in the head with his hunting rifle. He had recently been downgraded by the Gault-Millau restaurant guide from nineteen points to seventeen (out of a possible twenty) and many blamed the review. "Two points in one shot. That's not a judgment, that's an attack!" said former chef Andre Daguin. Loiseau had become famous for his radical version of nouvelle cuisine that he called "cuisine de jus" and had first been awarded three stars by Michelin in 1991. The stars represent the top award from France's most important restaurant guide, the Michelin Red Guide. Of the 9,000 French hotels and restaurants in the Red Guide, only about 25 restaurants receive the top award. The far more important Red Guide retained his three stars; however, *Le Figaro* had published rumors that his third star might be in danger. Paul Bocuse, the originator of nouvelle cuisine and the first chef to receive the Legion of Honor, said, "Gault-Millau took away two points, and, along with two or three press articles, that is what killed Bernard." The world of French haute cuisine was changing and Loiseau's cooking was attracting less attention; fusion cooking was the new rising fashion. Loiseau felt he was losing status and the mechanism that transmitted that pressure was a restaurant review.[1]

Reviews are a mechanism through which social status is made publicly visible. They can make reputations: Loiseau first drew widespread attention

1

when a Gault-Millau review said he was a culinary genius. In more mundane areas, reviews can make or break the balance sheets of restaurants: Loiseau's restaurant first became profitable when Michelin awarded it a third star. The strength of a good review can help justify a bank loan; creditors can ask for their money back after a bad review. High review ratings become proud emblems of identity for employees, owners, managers, and customers. Reviews are a mechanism through which pressures are transmitted to audiences, to cultural creators, and to producer organizations.

Restaurants are only one area where rating systems are important. Books and movies, theater and opera, computer software, appliances, and cars are a few of the other areas where reviews can have a major impact on audiences, profits, and reputations. Given their power it is not surprising that ratings are widespread throughout contemporary society. *Consumer Reports* currently has over 16 million readers. Zagat's book of New York restaurant reviews alone sold 650,000 copies in 2002 (Aikman 2003), plus Zagat's sells books of restaurant reviews in forty-five other cities worldwide. *PC Magazine*, which reviews personal computers, had a 2003 circulation of over 1.2 million and over 6 million readers.[2] These examples illustrate the large audiences that read reviews.

Why do people read reviews? Consider the alternatives: The availability of diverse information sources means that some people never read a review; "ask a friend," "ask a salesperson," or "read an ad" are time-honored solutions. Many, however, find these solutions undesirable. Friends may not have relevant personal experience; their experience may be out of date or too narrow; you may not trust the quality and reliability of their advice; or you may not like their taste or style. Advice of salespeople and advertisements suffers from a serious conflict of interest. The party giving the advice will benefit if you follow its recommendation. This weakens the credibility of ads.

These cases describe a general problem afflicting many information sources: The quality of information is uncertain because they lack a broad perspective, or because they are biased and self-interested. People often value a broad, unbiased source of information. Consequently, many search for a source that is not self-interested but is still capable of evaluating a wide range of alternatives and recommending a course of action. This search guides many toward reviews.

I received a lesson in the power of reviews early in this project when I was visiting a software company. I was sitting in on a perfectly ordinary, slightly stuffy business meeting that would decide on the features to be added in the next version of their flagship product. The current version of the software had recently received a major, largely positive review in an influential magazine. During the discussion I made a passing reference to the review and, suddenly, the whole meeting broke wide open. Everyone started talking. Everyone had read the review: most had read it so intensely that they could quote whole sentences verbatim. They had opinions, many were angry or frustrated, above all, they really, *really* wanted to talk about it. I sat back, amazed, while animated conversations went on all around me. That these employees reacted so openly in the presence of a researcher who was taking notes testifies to the intensity of their preoccupation. By my watch it was fifteen minutes before the chair could redirect the meeting back to the task at hand.

Later I would see similar responses to reviews. What these moments had in common was striking, intense emotion. It seemed like an overreaction to about 750 words of often dry text. I was puzzled. After that first incident, back in the chair's office, I asked, "I thought that was a positive review. What happened in the meeting?" He sighed heavily and said, "you can be more detached. Those reviews are *so* important to us. They can change our sales, our marketing, our product development plans; they have a huge impact. But we can't do anything about them. We have almost no influence. We never know what they are going to say until we read them." Another person from the meeting pointed to the review to explain his anger "Look at that sentence! He's wrong! We can do [that]! I spent two weeks writing [the computer code] myself. Now everyone will think that we can't."

"But it was a good review. He liked [your product]. Isn't that what's important?" I asked. "Besides," I continued, "what's one feature? Your marketing literature says you can do it. Won't you get the word out?"

The company president, standing in the office doorway, said, "Our brochures are right and marketing will get the word out. . . . The reality is that when there is a conflict between our literature and the review, people probably believe the review."

This struck me as the core reason why this review was powerful: The review had credibility. When there was a conflict, the review was more credible than the alternatives. The puzzle was, why? Why did readers believe the review? Why was it so powerful?

Despite the powerful emotions aroused by reviews and despite their millions of readers, I found that the study of reviews and rating systems has been neglected in sociology. Most of the limited prior work has been studies of individual cases or review genres. This is the first book to address reviews as a general phenomenon. Looking broadly at reviews reveals how they influence stratification, economic sociology, and culture. While I use case studies— especially, restaurants and software—I argue that they represent broad categories of reviews. Their muscle is a result of the fact that they are credible. The mechanisms of credibility, therefore, are central.

## CREDIBILITY AND REVIEWS

To see why credible reviews deserve sustained sociological attention, it is helpful to compare reviewers and gatekeepers. The roles of reviewers and gatekeepers are often confused.[3] A key characteristic of gatekeepers is that they occupy a position of formal authority in an organization or a process. They are like reviewers in that they evaluate the suitability of items brought to them; however, gatekeepers are not sought out for information; they give permission. They can allow the item to proceed or, if they deem it unsuitable, they can stop it. Gatekeepers have the administrative authority to make their decision final. Gatekeepers have been studied extensively since Kurt Lewin coined the term in 1947. Many cultural processes have multiple gatekeepers. Paul Hirsch (1972) described the many editors, producers, and company executives responsible for gatekeeping in movies, books, records, and other areas of popular culture. Academic journal editors are classic gatekeepers. If they reject a paper, the author has little recourse and the paper will not be published in that journal. When editors decide what to publish and what to reject, they act as gatekeepers; for example, see White's (1964) classic study of a newspaper editor.[4] Gatekeepers may explain their decisions, but they don't have to convince authors that their decisions are correct.

Reviewers must convince. Although they are often members of formal organizations, reviewers have no formal authority and the decision to follow a reviewer's advice is strictly *voluntary*. Reviewers must convince readers to follow their recommendations; they rely on persuasion. This fact has far-reaching consequences for almost every aspect of reviews. It influences the actions of reviewers, product makers, and publishers. For example, reviewers pay self-conscious, explicit attention to the rhetorical characteristics of their text that help persuade readers to believe them, and audiences are alert for evidence of biased or distorted information. Reviews are an appropriate site to study the construction of credible information because credibility is so central. The persuasive mechanisms of rhetoric, methodology, organization, and culture are more self-conscious, more open, and more visible.

The concept of credibility has a history stretching back to Aristotle. More recently, credibility has been extensively studied in communication research under the name "source credibility."[5] Early empirical studies were summarized and synthesized in 1966 by McCroskey, who published a definitive article complete with measurement instruments.[6] He found credibility to be composed of two dimensions, which he called authoritativeness and character. *Authoritativeness* refers to the perceived competence of speakers; do they know what they're talking about? Do they provide reliable information?

*Character* refers to the intentions or good will of speakers; are they truthful? Are they on the listeners' side?

This is a helpful start, but this research stream has two limits.[7] First, without exception it studies the credibility of speakers, not written text. Text is sufficiently different from speech that the applicability of this research stream is limited. Further, communication research is based largely on designed experiments using college students. The use of experimental studies removes institutional embeddedness and with it many sociologically interesting issues. Real-world reviews exist in social institutions. Real-life credibility judgments take account of the institutional context. To address these issues I develop a theory of credibility as a product of the institutional context.

The *Oxford English Dictionary* defines *credible* to mean "capable of being believed." Credibility is usually defined as the capacity to elicit belief. "Capacity" and "belief" link the producer and the audience of a product. Credibility is therefore an inherently relational concept. In this sense, the construction and reception of credibility are always social processes. There are two sides to credibility: an audience side and a production side. The key point of the source credibility research is an excellent starting point: the character and competence of each reviewer are central to readers' judgments of credibility. This research can be extended by asking both audience and production questions: How do readers actually judge character and competence? What is the process? What evidence do they use? How do reviewers promote their own credibility? What arguments do they make? What evidence do they put forward? The goal is a theory encompassing both audience judgments about credibility and reviewer's attempts to create credibility.

To answer these questions we first need to be clear about what we study. Since this is the first book about reviews and rating systems, it is particularly careful to define and describe the major actors involved in the systems of production and reception.

## THE SOCIOLOGY OF REVIEWS AND RATING SYSTEMS

Since this is a book about reviews, it is of interest to "review" the small literature on reviews. Two themes are relevant: the influence of reviews on sales, and highbrow-lowbrow differences.[8] By far the most common research topic is influence on sales. All writers believe that reviews have a significant influence on the popularity of cultural products; they disagree about the circumstances. Coser, Kadushin, and Powell (1982) give examples of book reviews that have had a major impact on sales, but they suggest that book reviews only matter in the absence of a major marketing campaign by the publisher. Burns' (1972) London theater informants believe that reviewers have the power to make or break a play. Coser, Kadushin, and Powell's informants also suggest that even a negative review can increase sales and a positive review has a larger effect. Shrum's (1991, 1996) study of attendance at the Edinburgh Theater Festival concurs. White and White (1965) also agree, arguing that the primary role of art critics and private art galleries in France is to connect artists with an audience of private collectors who are potential buyers. Mulkay and Chaplin (1982) argue that Jackson Pollock's success as an artist was closely tied to the activities of a small group of critics and gallery owners. Goodlad's (1971) London informants believe that positive reviews have no effect but negative reviews can kill a play. Sorenson and Rasmussen (2004) use the highest-quality data—comprehensive data from Nielsen BookScan—to look at the effect of reviews in the *New York Times Book Review* on sales of 175 hardcover fiction titles. They found that even negative reviews increase sales but positive reviews have a much larger impact. The impact of reviews is particularly important for new authors. To summarize: These studies find that reviews are influential, but not under all circumstances.

Research on the difference between high and popular culture has yielded ambiguous results. Levy (1988) found only minor differences in highbrow and lowbrow newspaper theater reviews. Shrum (1991) found that review evaluations have an impact only for high-culture genres, like theater. Lang (1958) found no differences for theater, books, and movies, but found that reviewers in mass and elite publications use different criteria in reviews of television. The inconsistency of findings echoes the results from the single-genre literature that the high culture versus popular culture distinction is far from being universally important.

What is most striking about the literature on reviews is how small it is. There are less than twenty studies, mostly empirical, and there is little theoretical work. The topic most often addressed is the influence of reviews on sales. Only four or five articles treat other topics. This is not a coherent literature in the sense that papers reference each other and a body of well-established findings is understood. Further, no studies address the larger institutional context in which reviews are embedded.

To expand and extend this literature, the study of reviews needs a broader empirical and theoretical base. Much of this book is devoted to that task. In particular, I describe the organizational forms within which reviews are produced, how audiences receive reviews, and the impact of systems of reviews on the larger social world. The goal is to connect reviews to their institutional and organizational base and thereby to connect them to theoretical and empirical concerns of the sociology of culture and sociology in general. To do this we need to be clear about what is a review and we need a distinctive vocabulary to distinguish the actors.

Some reviews are private, like employee performance evaluations. The reviews studied here are published and thus are public. Specifically, by *reviews* I mean public summaries and evaluations that assist readers to be more knowledgeable in their choice, understanding, or appreciation of products or performances.[9] Although reviews take many forms, what matters is that there is a summary and an evaluation. Reviews answer two questions: What is it? Is it any good?[10]

To help clarify the core characteristics of reviews, it is useful to distinguish reviews from news articles and columns. News reports summarize an item that interests readers. Reviews differ in that they do not just summarize; they also evaluate. They summarize the qualities of an item for an audience and they evaluate the extent to which the item meets a purpose for the particular audience. Newspaper and magazine columns are typically written by a person who blends information and personal opinion to interpret recent events for readers. Some columnists like Jerry Pournelle of *Byte* or Bill Machrone of *PC Magazine* often discuss products, sometimes to call readers' attention to deserving products, sometimes to warn readers to stay away from bad products, often to report their personal experiences with products that may interest readers. To the extent that columnists mention products, their mention tends to be a description of their personal experiences with a product and to lack the formal weighing of evidence and comparison of alternatives that are typical of reviews.

Reviews may be seen as a matter of publishing the reviewer's private taste. A glance at the letters pages of many publications shows disagreement about the criteria used in reviews and the outcomes of reviews. Lack of consensus is not surprising, but more is going on than conflict over idiosyncrasies of taste. Reviews are produced by institutions with institutional memories and sets of standard operating procedures. The production process strongly influences the content of the review that is published. Further, people's choices are influenced by the standards of a specific time and place. As Lieberson (2000:7) says, "it is a matter of individual choices operating within the context of social influences." As a result of these social and institutional influences, choices have systematic patterns.

The larger institutional and organizational context is the rating system. Much of the focus is on the reviews themselves, but we keep the larger system in view by identifying two different rating systems, called *connoisseurial* reviews and *procedural* reviews. Connoisseurial reviews rest on the unique skills, sensitivity, training, and experience of a single reviewer, a connoisseur. Procedural reviews are based on the results of tests—well-defined procedures—that allow reviewers to rank the performance of a product compared to similar products. These two rating systems organize both production and reception.

To speak clearly about the actors in a rating system, we need a consistent vocabulary. "Reviewers" evaluate the product, write the review, and receive byline credit for the published review. Reviewers may be a single individual or a team of as many as eight to ten people. I use the words *reviewer* and *critic* interchangeably. Synonyms for review are *evaluation* and *rating*. To simplify awkward sentence construction, I refer to reviews as being "published," "written," or "read," even though this always includes reviews in other media, such as those viewed on the Internet, heard on the radio, or watched in person or on television. *Published* means "made available to the public," which is exactly my meaning, regardless of the medium through which publication occurs.[11] Similarly, references to the review "text" include oral presentations by a speaker, in person or via media. The organization that publishes the review is the "publisher." Publishers include both the editors and publications where the reviews are published. The editor is the principal liaison between the publisher (as an organization) and the reviewer and is directly responsible for assuring that the review is acceptable to the publisher.

Reviews are the cultural object under study. In standard sociological usage the item being reviewed could also be called an object. To avoid confusion, I refer to the item under review as the "product" even though I use this term more broadly than the more common, strictly economic meaning. I do not intend to imply any economic reductionism. This sometimes leads to unusual wording, as when I refer to a concert as the product of a symphony orchestra. This wording is consistent with describing the review as the result of a "production process." Production is used in a broad sense, to refer to all stages of the production process; this is consistent with the usage in the production of culture literature. It is also consistent with referring to the organization or person creating the product as the "product maker." This category includes people involved in retail sales and marketing of products. For many products a key person in the product maker organization is often the marketing person who has direct personal contact with the reviewer. "Audiences" are the final consumers, listeners, viewers, or readers of the review. Reviews have multiple audiences. Three important audiences include the users or potential users of the product, product makers, and other reviewers.

This language yields four major actors: the reviewer, publisher, product maker, and audience.[12] The actors are analytic categories. All four actors have to cooperate for the review to happen. The review only emerges as a joint product of the interactions between the organizations and the individuals who staff them. In this sense, the actors in a review form a system. The rating systems have a core process: they present actors with choices drawn from a set of socially structured alternatives. Choices are not presented in an even-handed or neutral way; they are differentially rewarded or punished. Thus, in order to understand this environment, we have to look at the institutional patterns that shape the incentives and penalties imposed on each of the actors. One goal is to discover, clarify, and explicate the social mechanisms through which the rewards and penalties are made real to the actors. I collected data from all four of the actors in each system and I frequently discuss the same issue from multiple points of view, particularly in the case studies.[13]

## CULTURAL EVALUATION

Evaluations are central to reviews. Cultural evaluation seems underappreciated: it is not seen as a distinctive, stand-alone literature and no summary has been published.[14] Therefore, a brief digest is appropriate here.[15] Previous work can be divided broadly into two approaches: research across several genres and research within a single genre.[16] Cross-genre research includes important theoretical work such as Bourdieu's *Distinction* (1984) and DiMaggio's (1987) paper on art classification.[17] A theme of this literature is that cultural categories are created and sustained by social groups in order to enhance their prestige or power. Successful institutionalization of a genre occurs when a social group is able to create a separate intellectual space and find the necessary economic resources to create permanent supporting institutions. Most often the social group being studied is the upper class and the primary cultural category is high culture. *High culture* encompasses both the classification of certain works as especially distinctive and refined (e.g., high-culture versus popular-culture novels) and also the classification of whole genres as superior (e.g., opera and painting). Bourdieu is particularly concerned to show how the privileged classification of entire genres is a key component in the reproduction of class inequality. Dominant classes (and class fractions) have succeeded in classifying their cultural genres as legitimate high culture. They use the status classification of genres to help them maintain their status, measure their distance from other classes, exclude lower-status classes, and recruit or exclude people from prestigious occupations. DiMaggio's (1982a, 1982b) articles on the creation of high culture and the development of supporting nonprofit organizations by elites in Boston and New York during the late 1800s is the model empirical study of this research stream (see also Beisel 1990; Corse 1997; DiMaggio 1992; Levine 1988).[18] A strength of this literature is its emphasis on the organizational field required to support cultural classification (DiMaggio 1991), particularly the field supporting high

culture. DiMaggio explains (1992:47) that high culture "in this sense has less
to do with the content of art than with the kinds of barriers—both cognitive
and organizational—that are built up around it."[19]

For our purposes, the most valuable idea in this literature is its emphasis on
the need for institutional support to sustain intellectual distinctions. Since reviews evaluate cultural products, studying reviews is one way to study the
creation and maintenance of cultural distinctions. In published reviews, publishers are a key supporting institution. They must find resources to pay for
the buildings, staff, and programs needed to produce reviews. The importance
of formal institutions should not obscure the fact that the ultimate source of
all resources is always an audience.[20] Even in advertiser-supported media, advertisers are willing to place ads because of the readers they reach. Publications where reviews form an important component cater to an audience interested in reading the reviews. This may seem like an obvious truism but it has
been problematic in the history of reviews.

The impact of audiences is easiest to see at the origins of reviews. Reviews are a relatively new cultural innovation and both audiences and publishers have had to discover their value. The fact that audiences provide resources and, therefore, their interests strongly influence content is so central
that it is worth pausing briefly to illustrate the point. A discussion of two examples follows.

There was a first modern American restaurant review. On May 24, 1963,
*New York Times* food editor Craig Claiborne originated modern American
restaurant reviews when he wrote brief reviews of three restaurants including
star ratings (Claiborne 1963). His initial reviews were short (about one hundred words each) and unsigned. He began weekly reviews without a lot of
thought and without any overall vision of the importance of reviewing. Even
his autobiography, written in the 1980s, spends little space describing them.
No one, certainly not Claiborne himself, anticipated the enormous response
of *Times* readers. Within a few years he would become "the man who could
make or break restaurants" (Manville 1968). Nor did he anticipate that he was
creating the new cultural role of restaurant reviewer. The *New York Times* has
published weekly restaurant reviews continuously since 1963, and they have
spread to hundreds of other newspapers.

In 1984 *PC Magazine* published its first large comparative review of software; an enormous comparison of sixty-eight databases published over seven
issues (volume 3, numbers 11–17). Editor Bill Machrone's commentary
makes clear that *PC Magazine* was surprised by the magnitude of the audience response. He says, "Was [Project: Database] on target? From the response we have gotten from manufacturers and readers alike, the answer is an
overwhelming 'yes.'" (1984:81). This comprehensive, laboratory-based,

comparative review was so successful that it became *PC Magazine*'s trademark. Comparative reviews made *PC Magazine* the dominant personal computer magazine during the late 1980s and 1990s (Armstrong 1994).

The popularity of reviews surprised publishers and motivated them to make reviews a permanent part of their publications. This underscores two points. The first is that reviews are published because audiences are interested. By buying and reading publications, audiences provide the resources needed to conduct and disseminate reviews.[21] Second, the discovery that reviews are valuable cannot be taken for granted. Reviews are valuable under certain circumstances that are explored throughout the book, especially in the last two chapters.

The majority of studies of cultural evaluation focus on single genres. The most frequently studied genre is novels (Corse and Griffin 1997; de Nooy 1988, 1989; DeVault 1990; Griswold 1987a, 1992; Gross 1969; Ohmann 1987; Sorensen 2004; Sorensen and Rasmussen 2004; Watt 1957); in second place is music (Binder 1993; Bryson 1996; Dowd et al. 2002; Dowd and Byler 2002; Peterson 1978; Santoro 2002); followed by a smattering of other studies that cover film (Allen and Lincoln 2004; Baumann 2001), gastronomy (Ferguson 1998), housing décor (Halle 1993), science (Shapin and Schaffer 1985), and theater (Shrum 1991, 1996). By focusing on a single genre, these studies become case studies. Most studies cite the cross-genre literature (usually Bourdieu or DiMaggio) to provide theoretical context. The most common context links the genre to high culture or to a canon so that Bourdieu's and DiMaggio's theories of high culture can be applied. Following Bourdieu or DiMaggio, these studies emphasize characteristics at the level of the organizational field. Concern with the field of a single genre dovetails closely with the prevailing emphasis on structural aspects of the production of culture (DiMaggio 2000). There are few better ways to enhance the importance of a sociological case study than by arguing that it shows how important characteristics of a social field influence stratification. Although the cross-genre theorists generally ignore the single-genre work, there is a nice symbiotic relation where single-genre studies appropriate portions of the cross-genre theory.

In spite of this complementarity, these two literatures disconnect at several points. One is a sharply different approach to stratification. The research across genres ranks the prestige of different genres but is almost entirely silent about status within genres. Genres are treated as black boxes and there is nothing about the processes by which prestige and status are awarded within genres, or about the nature or shape of the within-genre stratification system. In other words, it offers no theory about the internal stratification of genres. Research within single genres cannot compare prestige across genres but it has at least the potential to describe how individual cultural products are evaluated within a genre. However, it has generally not done this. Since most within-genre research uses the cross-genre theory, this theoretical weakness of the cross-genre literature may be one reason why many single-genre studies use simple binary stratification systems, often a canon and a residual category for everything else.[22]

High culture has been extremely important historically, but recent single-genre work suggests that the distinction between high and popular culture has eroded, thereby questioning much cross-genre theory.[23] Art is classic high culture, but Halle's (1993) study of home décor suggests that art consumption does not mark social boundaries. He concludes (p. 198) with a strong statement about the current evidence: "Above all, the link between involvement in high culture and access to dominant class circles . . . is undemonstrated."[24] Not only are there questions about the continued importance of high culture, but once one moves beyond the realm of high culture other processes seem more important. More recent work suggests that the scope of cultural competence across many genres—high, low, and in-between—is most important for high status (e.g., Bryson 1996; Peterson 1997a; Peterson and Kern 1996; Erickson 1996). Since relatively few studies have been completed of non-high-culture genres, there is no clear answer to the question of how their social processes differ.

These two literatures take different approaches to change in cultural evaluations. The cross-genre literature tends to stress the reproduction of existing classes. To the extent that this literature deals with change it tends to tell a story of how elites defended their privileges by creating new cultural categories (e.g., high culture in DiMaggio [1982a]; or vice in Beisel [1990]). Bourdieu has a theory of change in the status of social groups, but he applies it mostly to show that change doesn't occur: elite groups defend their status so the overall class hierarchy remains static. By contrast, several of the single-genre articles describe how the rise or decline of social groups is linked to changing cultural evaluations; for example, Corse and Griffin's (1997) study of the changing status of Zora Neale Hurston in the context of rising recognition of black novelists, Dowd and Blyler's (2002) study of the structural factors that facilitate or hinder the success of black musicians, Peterson's (1978) sparkling study of change in country music, and Shapin and Schaffer's (1985) study of the rise of empirically minded scientists. The single-genre literature seems to have much more interest in changing evaluation.

The single-genre literature stresses two topics relevant to this book. First, this work clearly shows that evaluative judgments are not based on the immutable qualities of the text, art, or music genre. Instead, evaluative judgments are influenced by the social characteristics of institutions, cultural practices, and actors. These in turn influence the content of the evaluation of the product. This point about the social construction of culture is, of course, made throughout the sociology of culture and is one of the themes of this book.

Second, when evaluators can use a strong, existing discourse the evaluation is more powerful. Powerful discourses are linked to existing theories of the genre; in film, for example, auteur theory has played an important role in the construction of an artistic field (Baumann 2001) and in the valorization of individual films (Allen and Lincoln 2004). Media writers use certain frames that resonate with particular evaluations of heavy metal and rap music in Binder's (1993) fine study. Discourses also play a major role in standardizing the components of a category, defining its boundaries, and publicizing models. They transform the original sensual mode—auditory, gastronomic, or visual—into an intellectual activity (Ferguson 1998). Discourses are linked to particular communities both of producers and audiences (Binder 1993). Discourse communities may generate different discourses about the same product, depending on their social situation and their interests (Griswold 1987a). Reviews play a role in these discourses; indeed, the studies of discourse often use reviews as their data (e.g. Baumann 2001; DeVault 1990; Griswold 1987a). Reviews then can help define the nature and boundaries of cultural categories. Public reviews speak to more than just a single discourse community; they speak to an entire field, which contains multiple audiences (Ferguson 1998). The importance of discourse is echoed in the persuasive power of credible reviews.

The single genre research tends to study situations where the actual evaluation process is comparatively unproblematic and simple. Typical examples include Allen and Lincoln's (2004) study of the "implicit criteria" for inclusion in the American Film Institute and the National Film Registry, and Dowd et al.'s (2002) study of symphony orchestra canons. In these cases the product is unambiguously in or out: Films are either included or excluded, symphonies are either performed or not. The researchers have data only on what products are included and the structure of the fields of film and orchestras, respectively. This is consistent with the prevailing emphasis on field-level characteristics in the production of culture literature. In both cases there are no middle categories. Both "hierarchies" consist of just two levels, as simple a hierarchy as is possible. The field-level emphasis in both studies means that they have little to say about how evaluation actually occurs. What is missing is the evaluation *process*. Given their field-level data and theoretical interests, these studies have no way to gain access to that process. It requires more detailed, lower-level data describing the evaluation of specific products.

The biggest weaknesses of the single-genre work stem from its case study approach. The conclusions of each study tend to depend on the characteristics of that specific cultural category, and the extent to which findings generalize to other genres is often unclear. For example, Corse and Griffin's (1997) fine case study of the changing reputation of Zora Neale Hurston's novel, *Their Eyes Were Watching God*, describes issues of changing criteria used in evaluation, social groups that supported the evaluations, and the characteristics of the text itself. The study takes a broad-brush perspective on how the evaluation occurred: the criteria are derived from the interests of the groups involved, not from a detailed analysis of the process that generated the evaluation. Griswold (1981) points out that genre imperatives are an important influence on literature. Without more comparative work across genres it is impossible to know the extent to which the findings from research in a single category are due to the imperatives of that genre or to more general characteristics of cultural evaluation. Since most work is narrowly focused on specific high-culture genres, it is particularly unclear how the results may generalize to non-high-culture genres or to other categories of cultural consumption. There are no studies of commercial genres. No one has attempted to synthesize the field.

Since evaluation is an extremely common cultural act and it is directly related to the core sociological concern of stratification, one would expect to find a wide range of research. The existing research is important but, considered as a whole, the striking fact is that there is so little. Of course the sociology of culture is a young specialty and that point could be made about many topics, but this literature is particularly scattered and difficult to use.[25] Bourdieu, DiMaggio, Corse, Dowd, Griswold, and others provide useful information but their work is not directive. Most research consists of case studies of single genres, and the majority of those focus on books and music. These works generally do little conceptual development. As a result, issues related to how to evaluate cultural work have not been explored. There is no review article. Excellent work has been done but much of the potential terrain has not been explored. Consequently, there is a lack of basic data contextualizing the process of cultural evaluation and a lack of concepts to help understand evaluation. This book begins to remedy these weaknesses.

## GOALS AND METHODS

The study of reviews can broaden our understanding of cultural evaluation. Reviews are a subset of cultural evaluations but they have unusual characteristics that make them powerful. Prior studies of reviews emphasize their impact on sales; in fact, the impact of reviews is far wider. Reviewer's evaluations create and highlight inequality. In contrast to scholarly articles by literary critics or film scholars, reviewers perform their task frequently, often on a weekly or monthly schedule. They reach millions of readers interested in an extremely wide variety of cultural products. In some cases they create boundaries and distinctions where none existed; in all cases they hold up distinctions to public view. By publicizing them, discussing them, and describing their criteria, reviews generally make distinctions far, far more public and accessible. And they do this all by the force of their own persuasion. For these reasons, reviewers occupy a strategic position, yet this social role remains largely unstudied and not well understood. How do they go about their work? Where do their criteria come from? Are there systematic biases, emphases, or omissions? Since sociology places great emphasis on understanding the concrete forms, functions, conflicts, ideologies, and processes through which work is accomplished, these are major omissions.

Despite having millions of readers, reviews have received little sociological attention. One goal is to bring reviews to the attention of a wider sociological audience. The book explores some of the ways in which the study of reviews can be fruitful empirically and can teach us about neglected portions of contemporary society. It examines the characteristics of review texts, the production of reviews, audience responses, and the effects of reviews on the larger social world. The book also suggests that the study of reviews can shed light on some current theoretical concerns. Through this I hope to indicate the value of studying reviews to other sociologists.

Cultural evaluation in general has not been widely studied. In contemporary society, I suggest, evaluations are far more important and far more widespread than most sociologists recognize. This point can be made via the study of published, widely available reviews. Establishing the importance of evaluation in the contemporary social world is the special goal of the last two chapters.

A third goal is to develop a broader understanding of cultural evaluation by studying the characteristics of reviews as a whole. Here this research makes several unique contributions. It begins systematic work on concepts useful for understanding evaluations. These concepts help describe the process through which evaluations occur. In addition, prior research has neglected audiences other than elites and products other than high-culture or popular-culture products.[26] By contrast, I want to find out what reviews have in common without regard to the product under review or the audience. We will have a much clearer understanding of reviews if we understand the salient characteristics they all share. An important part of this broader understanding includes extending the study of cultural evaluation to include commercial genres. We shall see that apparently different reviews in fact have much in common.

Fourth, reviews are a research site where credibility and trust are particularly important issues. Most of what we know is not based on personal experience. We all depend on secondary sources of information, but no one has the time or resources to verify it. In modern society, where much of our information comes from mass media, the credibility of secondary information is central. How do people evaluate the information that they receive? This issue—the construction of credibility—is a core problem of reviews. A goal of this book is to improve our understanding of the social processes used to create and receive credible knowledge. In short, it studies the processes through which people answer the question, "How do you know for sure?"

Finally, one of the first things a researcher discovers about reviews is that there are no published accounts of the processes whereby reviews are produced. This is a serious omission, since everywhere in the cultural evaluation literature sociologists start from the premise that institutions should be contextualized specifically in terms of structure, recruitment patterns, professional training, and rewards, and more generally in terms of time and place, and relationships to related institutions. This book supplies the first published accounts of the context of review production and reception.

Studying cultural evaluation requires balancing two issues: breadth and depth. The goal of understanding similarities among all kinds of reviews requires a broad study. The goal of supplying an institutional context for reviews requires an in-depth study. My methodology resolves this conflict by multiple, carefully selected case studies. The results illustrate the value of a research design more sophisticated than single-genre case studies.

The use of case studies is a result of my personal experience as a reviewer (e.g., Blank 1993) and editor of reviews (e.g., Blank 1986). These experiences made clear that many significant aspects of review production take place behind the scenes. To talk adequately about reviews requires understanding nonpublic processes. This does not imply a gossipy, backstage examination that reveals the tawdry "truth" hidden behind the public façade of reviews. On the contrary, after studying reviews my overall conclusion is that the public face of most reviews is largely accurate (and I discuss conditions when it is not). Rather, the point is that most of the contingencies, processes, and decisions that influence the final published review happen out of public view. Case studies give me the ability to describe those nonpublic events.

Case studies are ideal for a micro-level examination of how reviews work in actual practice: the interactions of the actors, and how and why the actors make certain choices. Furthermore, the structure of incentives in the system of reviews restricts the range of variation of many variables so that they tend to vary together. Case studies that focus on the "nodes" in the property space where there are nonempty cells can obtain an accurate description of the entire system with an economy of research effort. To obtain the necessary breadth, I used a theoretical sampling strategy: choose cases that are as *dissimilar* as possible. One major, largely unexplored disjuncture in the sociology of culture is the split between the arts and consumer products. As my primary case studies I chose fine-dining restaurant reviews for the arts and software reviews (especially statistical software) for consumer products.[27] I supplemented these cases with less detailed studies of cars, computer hardware, books, movies, and the Internet. (See appendix A for a full description of the methodology.) Choosing these two primary cases offered a significant methodological advantage: restaurants and statistical software seem almost totally unlike each other. They differ in so many dimensions: arts-oriented versus consumer-oriented, a performance versus a product (plus software is such an unusual, ephemeral product), buyers' experience based on personal interactions with the product maker versus sold by third parties and operated out of the presence of the product maker, among others. By finding common elements in such dissimilar cases, I would better understand the characteristics shared by *all* reviews.[28]

Since these cases are not random sample surveys, they cannot tell us about things like the distribution or frequency of review-reading among the population, or among various standard social categories like generations, classes, genders, races, or ethnic groups. I was careful to include people from different races, genders, and classes in my interviews. Interviews were completed with thirty-eight people involved in review production and thirty-three review readers, plus I conducted three focus groups with a total of twenty-two review readers. I found review readers in all parts of society: Farmers read reviews of tractors, fishermen read about casting rods, millionaires read art reviews. As these examples imply, the subjects of the review reflect the interests of particular groups. When, for example, the American Film Institute produced its list of the 100 best films (Wilmington 1998), *Ebony* magazine wrote about the best black films (Ebony 1998). Although people of different races, genders, classes, or ages read about different products, they all read reviews. Reading reviews seems widespread. I do not make arguments about the race, ethnicity, age, or class of review readers; consequently, when I quote interviewees I do not identify them by their age, race, or other characteristics.

## CHAPTER OUTLINE

Since credibility is a core issue for reviews, I begin chapter 2 by outlining a theory of credible reviews. The theory suggests that two different rating systems produce credible reviews. I call these systems *connoisseurial* reviews and *procedural* reviews. Chapters 3 and 4 are the first published ethnographic case studies of rating systems. They supply heretofore unavailable basic data about the institutional and social environment of review production, publication, and audiences. Chapter 3 describes connoisseurial reviews of an arts performance: fine-dining restaurant reviews. Chapter 4 describes procedural reviews of a consumer product: computer software reviews, especially reviews of statistical software. These chapters are primarily descriptive, providing extensive, detailed information about the context in which reviews are conceived, written, published, and read.

Having established the fundamental social and institutional environment, we are prepared to systematically compare the two rating systems. Production and reception are so closely related that they cannot be neatly separated, but chapter 5 emphasizes production issues. It compares the organization of production, resource requirements, the affinity between certain products and certain types of reviews, and the ways that different texts produce different audiences. This chapter also contains a graphical study comparing the ratings produced by connoisseurial and procedural reviews of the same product.

What impact does the connoisseurial-procedural distinction have on the reception of knowledge? Chapter 6 explores some implications of reviews for the sociology of knowledge, especially credible knowledge. Prior studies of credible knowledge have been done in the sociology of scientific knowledge. This chapter summarizes and extends prior work by suggesting ways in which credibility judgments are related to the connoisseurial-procedural distinction. The chapter emphasizes that credible knowledge is socially created and it spells out some of the mechanisms through which the production environment influences the content of the knowledge that emerges. From a reception point of view the connoisseurial-procedural distinction helps us understand the different ways that knowledge spreads beyond the local context in which it originated. Thus, the connoisseurial-procedural distinction improves our understanding of both the production and reception of knowledge.

These five chapters, 2 through 6, describe the relationships between reviews, products, product makers, and audiences. The final pair of chapters broadens the scope of the book to consider how reviews help shape the larger social and cultural world, with particular emphasis on issues of interest to the sociology of culture. Chapter 7 considers reception of reviews in the context of stratification and inequality. By assigning products to categories, reviews make cultural boundaries public. By publicly evaluating and comparing products and performances, reviews make stratification into a cultural hierarchy explicit and public. Public boundaries and hierarchies are important for people seeking to achieve or maintain their status as cultural omnivores. The chapter discusses the implications of these hierarchies for Bourdieu's theory of habitus, cultural distinction, and cultural capital. Reviews open up access to critical cultural distinctions to anyone willing to read them. This unlocks a door to individual mobility. I argue elites will find it difficult to monopolize control over cultural capital in any field where reviews are common. In those fields status based on distinction may be weaker, possibly nonexistent.

Chapter 8 considers the impact of rating systems on culture and society in general. This chapter links two themes of the book: credible knowledge and review-created status hierarchies. It begins by describing the importance of transparency in hierarchies. Credible, transparent hierarchies help audiences sort through the complexities of contemporary society. Specifically, they help audiences make choices. How do people make choices in a complex society? We have the tools to construct a sociological theory of choice. A simple economic theory of choice—based on prices—is much better known, so the chapter contrasts it to this sociological theory. Particular attention is given to the conditions under which the sociology of choice dominates considerations of price. These are the conditions where culture constructs markets. The chapter concludes by summarizing the value of a sociology of reviews and rating systems and discussing how it can improve our understanding of contemporary society. Reviews produce status rankings and they link to the core of sociology: the study of inequality and stratification. Reviews are powerful because audiences use the status inequalities to help them navigate their way through contemporary life. Technological developments like the Internet are reducing the importance of physical distance. As a result, status distance is becoming more important. Thus reviews have become an ever more important component of contemporary society.

Since good and bad reviews are such emotionally intense subjects for authors and other product makers, readers may naturally wonder if there is anything here about what produces the good evaluation or the bad. Sadly, I have nothing to say about the outcome of the evaluation. I can't tell authors how to get better reviews for their books; I can't tell other product makers how to improve the reviews of their products. If you think about it, the actual evaluation of a product is probably not something about which one can generalize. This book discusses issues such as the evaluation criteria, how the evaluation will be conducted, how the results will be presented, and how starkly the results will compare different products. These are issues where general patterns are apparent. But a positive or negative evaluation of a product depends on its idiosyncratic characteristics and no general statements are possible.

# NOTES

1. The material in this paragraph is drawn from Betts 2003; Echikson 2003a; Mariani 2003; Miller 2003; Parseghian 2003; Smith 2003. The most complete discussion is Echikson (2003b), who quotes Bocuse. The Daguin quote is in Adler (2003).

2. Uncredited data are from Mediamark Research Inc.'s Spring 2003 report of magazine subscriptions and readerships available at www.mediamark.com.

3. For example, Caves (2000) refers to critics as gatekeepers; he means reviewers. Another example, Mulkay and Chaplin (1982) describe the activities of art reviewers; however, Crane (1992) summarized Mulkay and Chaplin's argument as a description of gatekeepers. In fact, Mulkay and Chaplin describe reviewers, not gatekeepers. National Science Foundation peer review panels function as gatekeepers since all grant applications must be peer reviewed and a low rating from a panel guarantees that a grant application will not be funded.

4. But see also Whitney and Becker's (1982) critique of this study.

5. A second stream of research is in the sociology of scientific knowledge literature. Since it is linked to the sociology of knowledge, it is summarized and discussed in chapter 6.

6. Source credibility is usually defined somewhat differently than my subject; a typical definition is "the attitude toward a source of communication held at a given time by a receiver" (McCroskey and Young 1981, 24). The difference is that this definition is broader and more general; it refers to "the attitude," while my focus is on the extent to which the review is believed, that is, on the evaluation of the review by the reader. I am not concerned with other elements included in the attitude of the reader. It is nonetheless close enough that the research is relevant.

7. I summarized the most relevant portions of this research stream. Later researchers add more dimensions; for example, Berlo et al. (1969) and Leathers (1992) add "dynamism." During the 1970s McCroskey and associates conducted a series of studies that concluded there were five dimensions to source credibility: competence, character, sociability, composure, and extroversion (McCroskey and Young 1981). Leaving aside minor issues of changing terminology, since this study only concerns text, many characteristics of speakers—such as composure, dynamism, extroversion, or sociability—are not relevant.

8. There is also some research that compares the social groups from which reviewers and audiences are drawn. Gans's (1999 [1974]) theory of taste cultures suggests that critics are typically members of middle and upper-middle taste cultures and the criteria they apply reflect middle- or upper-middle-class standards, even when their audience is lower class. Wanderer (1970) compared moviegoers' ratings in *Consumer Reports* with film critics' evaluations and found that they agreed. He suggests this result occurs because the critics and the moviegoers belong to the same upper-middle taste culture.

9. See Adler and van Doren (1972) for a similar, though not identical, view of reviews.

10. Because I study public reviews, I do not discuss the important topic of scientific peer review. Because peer review is private and unpublished, its production and

audiences are different than the public reviews that are the subject of this book. Further, since there is nothing voluntary about peer review, peer reviewers are actually gatekeepers. For the same reason, I do not discuss various administrative reviews undertaken for reasons of legal accountability. The restriction to public products or performances excludes topics like student test performance, academic degrees, and other personal achievement awards and prizes. These are noteworthy topics, and they are evaluations, but they are not reviews in the sense that the term is used here.

11. A review of the literature summarizes: "There is no evidence of consistent or significant differences in the abilities of different media to persuade, inform, or even to instill an emotional response in audience members" (Neuman 1991:99). Therefore, combining different media into a single reference called "text" loses little.

12. Related distinctions are made by Gans (1999:7) and Clark (1975:198).

13. As a primarily qualitative, ethnographic study of the social institution of reviews, this book follows the tradition of other studies of institutions such as Coser, Kadushin, and Powell's (1982) study of book publishing, Faulkner's (1983) study of Hollywood composers, Gamson's (1998) study of talk shows, Gitlin's (1985) study of prime-time television, Grazian's (2003) study of Chicago blues bars, Peterson's (1997b) study of country music, Schudson's (1984) study of advertising, and many others.

14. Curiously, the review literature is largely disconnected from the literature on cultural evaluation. Some studies of cultural evaluation—such as DeVault (1990) and Griswold (1987a)—use reviews as a methodological tool to provide access to the norms and values of groups or society as a whole. Baumann (2001) studies movie reviews to understand the changing status of an institution: films. Although a few cultural evaluation papers mention reviews (e.g., Ferguson 1998), studies of cultural evaluation do not focus on reviews.

15. This is only a brief digest. A more complete survey of relevant literature would include the literature on boundaries (recently reviewed by Lamont and Molnar 2002), the literature on commensuration (recently summarized by Espeland and Stevens 1998), and others.

16. By *genre* I mean a category that is bounded by a distinctive style or content, and the associated audience expectations. The term *genre* originated in the arts, but it can be used elsewhere; we can think of restaurants or software as cultural genres. Genre works on multiple levels: music is a genre, but so are rock 'n' roll and country.

17. Interestingly, Gans's (1999 [1974]) well-known theory of taste cultures and publics, though widely cited, has had little theoretical or empirical impact on cultural evaluation (but see Wanderer [1970] for an exception). Its argument favoring cultural democracy against Frankfurt School criticism is outside the mainstream of sociology of culture. Griswold's (1986) study of Renaissance revivals also covers multiple genres; while well known in the sociology of culture, it is not usually cited by studies of cultural evaluation. Griswold is discussed below.

18. In literature, *genre* refers to a type of authorial expression, interpretation, and the associated audience expectations (Hirsch 1967), however, it can be applied on more than one level. This uncertainty influences how research in cultural evaluation is classified. For example, if Binder (1993) is a study of one genre, music, then it belongs below with other studies of a single genre. If it is a study of two genres, rap and

heavy metal, then it belongs above with studies of multiple genres. Similar questions exist for Bryson (1996), Griswold (1986), and Shrum (1991). Although individual articles may move to another category, the fundamental conclusions about these two literatures do not change.

19. This approach has heightened awareness of the importance of cultural boundaries and boundary maintenance, spawning a large literature (e.g., Lamont and Fournier 1992; a recent review article is Lamont and Molnar 2002). This literature suggests that boundaries are established and sustained when they serve the interests of important actors. One cultural contribution of reviews is that they create new boundaries and publicize existing boundaries between cultural categories. This directs our attention to the interests of the four actors in the review. Parts of the paragraph referenced by this note follow Dowd et al. (2002).

20. This is the theory of resource dependence. The most important source of resources are audiences of customers and investors, see Pfeffer and Salancik (1978) for a thorough argument.

21. This does not imply that audiences *determine* the content of reviews. Content is influenced by a large number of factors. The case studies describe these often-conflicting influences in detail.

22. Two exceptions: Corse (1997) and Shrum (1991) collect data on both high and popular culture. Corse compares the shape of the literary stratification in Canada and the United States.

23. See Bell (1973) for an early version of this argument; see Gans (1999) for a counterargument.

24. The data supporting the cross-genre work is scanty. Bourdieu (1984) has only survey data, which is not well suited to address issues about fields. DiMaggio (1987) is a theoretical article, laying out a series of hypotheses for later testing, and it contains no data at all.

25. The closest the field comes to core research is Bourdieu's *Distinction* and DiMaggio's (1987) article on art classification, and these have limited value to single-genre research; furthermore, their value declines rapidly when one moves away from researching high culture. The cross-genre area is difficult to research because it requires data on multiple genres and their relative status. There is no easy way to collect this kind of data; furthermore, the payoff is unclear. One problem is that there is a lack of model cross-genre research exemplars. DiMaggio's studies (1982a, 1992) of the development of high culture in the United States supply a model for historical research; they are less useful for contemporary studies. The best contemporary work is the interesting but underappreciated book by Sarah Corse (1997), who used college course syllabi as her data source for canonical literature and best seller lists for popular literature. Corse has not been a good model for other work because it is not clear either how the idea of using syllabi might be applied to a more diverse set of genres other than literature or to areas where categories like high culture and popular culture are not necessarily the most important concerns. Furthermore, she can't compare the relative status of different genres. A third model could be Griswold's (1986) study of Renaissance revivals. In many respects it is the most sophisticated treatment of cultural evaluation available. Its distinctive feature is attention to evaluation on multiple

levels, from the personal motives of the theater manager, the current and historical conventions of the theater, the characteristics of the field of London theater, and the larger social environment of Great Britain. Despite its theoretical and empirical sophistication it has been largely overlooked, I suspect, because Griswold is uninterested in comparing the status of different genres, so the book does not dovetail well with the theoretical agenda set by Bourdieu and DiMaggio.

26. Exceptions to the focus on elites include Binder (1993) who studies journalists, Bryson's (1996) use of national survey data, and Griswold's (1987a, 1992, 2000) studies of West Indian and Nigerian novels.

27. Although the distinction between the arts and consumer products is helpful in other contexts, it turns out not to be a useful way to think about reviews, but I didn't know that when I started.

28. Although not the most common approach, there is a stream of cultural analysis that examines a wide range of actors in a given field, and not a subset of the canonical or the best known. Books like Becker's (1982) *Art Worlds*, Griswold's (2000) study of Nigerian novels, and White and White's (1993) study of nineteenth-century French painting ably show the strengths of this approach. My admiration for this work helped push me toward greater breadth in this study.

*Chapter Two*

# Toward a Theory of Credible Rating Systems

A restaurant review reader says:

> I like reviewers who write rich, detailed descriptions of spices, textures, [and] flavors. That tells me they are sophisticated and sensitive food critics. . . . I feel like these reviewers know what they are doing.

A computer video card review reader:

> My games push the limits of all the current video systems. I want video card reviews with comparative tests of the speed of major subsystems. . . . They have to have real comparative data. I wouldn't take any other review seriously.

Both people describe how they decide to trust reviewers, but they explain the basis for trust in very different ways. One talks about "rich, detailed descriptions"; the other wants "comparative tests." One common explanation claims this is a result of differences in personal taste. Or we could attribute it to differences between restaurants and computer video cards. I argue that much more is going on than differences in taste or product categories. These are not simple differences; behind them lie two different approaches to reviews, supported by different forms of social organization, and each claims credibility based on a different logic.

## REVIEW FRAMES AND AUDIENCES

To understand audience response to reviews we need a theory of the interaction of media and readers. There are two approaches to understanding media.

By one approach, media simply report events. Media organizations are transparent; they record and transmit events to audiences without changing or editing them. An alternative argument notes that events don't come with labels telling what is and is not news. Media organizations have to decide what events qualify as news, how to report them, and how prominent they should be. Recent research on media supports the second view. Two facts stand out. First, reporting is strongly influenced by media practices. The standard operating procedures of the media influence which events they report and what they emphasize. In the language of media research, media "actively construct" events (Gans 1979; Lester 1980; White 1964). Gamson and Modigliani (1989) give an example: Journalists tend to accept explanations from established organizations (particularly government organizations) as authoritative. Another example: available space in publications tends to be fixed—most reviews are restricted to less than one thousand words—and this limits their content.

Second, audiences do not act simply as passive message recipients; instead, they actively construct their own meanings from the text. However, media supply the classifications and metaphors that audiences use to construct meaning (Iyengar and Simon 1993; Zaller 1992). Media do not supply the detailed content of audience views so much as a broad perspective or cultural lens (Geertz 1973) and a collection of more-or-less-standardized metaphorical tools and categories for audiences to use as they interpret events. There is tension here: the structure embedded in reviews encourages certain interpretations, but audiences use the review for their own ends. In later chapters we see repeated examples of how reviews interpret and encode reality, and how audiences reinterpret and decode it in different ways. To understand the way this works we examine how media discourse operates to frame audience perceptions. We briefly describe frames in general and then concentrate on the operation of frames in reviews.

Drawing from Goffman (1974:21), Snow et al. (1986:464) define frames as "schemata of interpretation" that enable individuals "to locate, perceive, identify, and label" events.[1] Frames select certain aspects of reality and make them more salient in the text. This directs audience attention toward those selected aspects and away from other aspects. The selected salient aspects suggest the meaning of an event by connecting it to certain causal interpretations, moral evaluations, problem definitions, or prescriptions for action (Entman 1993). Frames are most influential when they are so well understood that they can be evoked with a single catch-phrase, story, or metaphor. Frames work by linking text to the mental information-processing schemata of audiences. Both elements work together. The characteristics of the text (e.g., catch-phrases, symbols, or metaphors) trigger the schemata that help readers organize events into easily understood classifications, patterns, and hierarchies (Entman 1991, 1993; Gamson and Modigliani 1989).

Reviews supply frames to help audiences understand products. The core task of review frames is to explain how products and attributes can be interpreted so that audiences connect them to personal uses, needs, and desires. Frames are not the same as the evaluation criteria used in the review; frames are broader and more general. An example of a well-understood review frame is a review of several products that concludes by making one the winner by awarding it the title "best product." Frames are powerful because they connect the text to audience actions. For example, the text award "best product" implies the action "this is the product to buy." Audiences, however, are not limited to the frames embedded by the publisher. They may reinterpret frames to support their own agendas. Two examples illustrate how audiences incorporate their agendas into reviews. First, a reader says:

> I usually don't buy the exact product that *PC Magazine* recommends. . . . The value of the reviews is that they tell me what features to ask about when I talk to salespeople or to look for in sales literature.

A reader describing book reviews explains that he looks for an answer to the question:

> Does the book sound interesting? Whether the reviewer liked it or not isn't so important. I want to know whether *I* would enjoy reading it. [Emphasis in original.]

These do not exhaust all possible ways readers understand reviews; they simply illustrate two of the many different ways that review frames can be used. The link to credibility comes from the fact that not every reviewer offers an equally credible framing.

Up to this point we have treated credibility as a single, unitary phenomenon. This turns out not to be sufficient: all actors recognize more than one way to frame credible reviews. For reviews, I found two different frames. Frame theory emphasizes the catch-phrases and metaphors in the text that trigger mental schemata that audiences use to interpret events. This emphasis gives little weight to the characteristics of the organizations that produce frames. In the case of reviews, organizational characteristics are extremely important. Review frames are part of larger structures that I call "rating systems." The following section describes these systems by analyzing the logic of the review text, audience reception, and the social organization of review production.

## CREDIBLE RATING SYSTEMS

Reviewers and editors work together on review after review, but the other participants—the product makers and audience—are less stable. To stabilize the expectations and roles of these part-time participants, reviews take a consistent character, a frame that is easily recognized and understood by everyone who either produces or reads reviews. Consistency means that many elements of the review are regularly found together. I refer to the consistent collection of common elements as the rating system.[2] Rating systems incorporate frames, but they are broader. In addition to the standardized metaphors, stories, and mental schemata of frames, rating systems also include standard forms of organization around which the roles of the participants are defined. The roles provide appropriate goals as well as mechanisms for reaching those goals for all of the actors in the review: reviewers, editors, product makers, and audiences. Review organizations that incorporate the same rating system have similar core tasks, taken-for-granted ways of doing things, and styles of audience reception. Thus, rating systems are stable social systems and this has strong implications for the production, content, and interpretation of reviews.

A particular rating system can be thought of as the short answer to the question, "Why is this review credible?" I discovered two different answers to that question. I refer to them as *connoisseurial reviews* and *procedural reviews*. These are my terms, although they draw on the words and images used by reviewers, editors, and audiences.[3] They serve as a kind of a metaphor for the primary characteristics of each rating system. The two rating systems incorporate the idea that the production of a credible evaluation is the core task of a review. Beyond that, they differ sharply on how they achieve credibility: their arguments follow different logics, they have characteristically different texts, they are created by different social organizations, and they are read differently by audiences. The rating systems are analytic constructs and all actual reviews are mixtures of the two systems.

## CONNOISSEURIAL REVIEWS

One of the first things one might notice about reviews is that they seem extremely diverse, as diverse as the products that they review. In particular the criteria that reviewers use seem to be very different across different product genres. Consider the following examples that will stand in for many others. Readers in these examples are describing what they look for to assure themselves that they can trust the review. A movie review reader:

I like to see comparisons to other films, other directors, and other actors; historical materials like that. A thoughtful, well-written comparison . . . illuminates the review. There is no better way to convince me that this is someone who knows his stuff.

A book review reader:

> The subjects that I know well seem to have certain . . . central issues. . . . I want to know how a new book contributes to those issues. I look for the reviewer to summarize what the book says about them and how the book fits with other current work. . . . The reviewer shows me he's good by writing a lucid, accurate summary and—more important—a clear statement that relates the book to the current issues in the field.

Such examples can easily be multiplied across many product categories. On their face, these product genres seem very different. Even within genres there is great diversity. Books alone display enormous variety in broad categories like fiction, nonfiction, self-help, children's, or poetry. Reviews are equally varied. Reviewers make diverse arguments for and against the quality of each book or other product. They demonstrate credibility in different ways in different categories. Each product category seems to have its own criteria.

On a very straightforward level the reviews seem different. Where is there common ground to compare them? When we listen to people describe their reasons for believing a reviewer we are working at a level of fine-grained detail. To do a comparison, we need to step back and ask, what do these reasons have in common? When we step away from the low-level detail we find that there is a single characteristic shared by these reviews: The reader depends on the skills, knowledge, talents, or experience of a single reviewer who gives an expert opinion.

These reviewers make the same basic argument regardless of the product under review: "Believe my review because—for this product—I am a particularly well-informed, experienced, and knowledgeable person. I am a connoisseur." Central to these reviews is the refined judgment of the reviewer, so they appropriately are labeled *connoisseurial reviews*.

Connoisseurial reviews, then, are a particular method for producing reviews. The key to the method is dependence on the ability of a person—a reviewer—who, because of unusual talents, extensive experience, or special training, has developed a refined sensitivity with respect to a certain product genre.

It is worth pausing to remember that regardless of the argument that the reviewer makes, an audience has its own perspective. The audience may read the review in many ways; there is no reason to assume that the connoisseurial reviewer's intended message is the message that the audience receives. Many critics are fully aware of this. Here is how Roger Ebert recommends reading his film reviews (1994:885, emphasis in original):

> A good critic should provide enough of an idea of a film so that you can decide if you'd like it, whether or not he does. (I once got a call from a reader who asked what I thought about Ingmar Bergman's *Cries and Whispers*. I said I thought it was the best film of the year. "Oh, thanks," the reader said. "That doesn't sound like anything *we'd* like to see.")

Even if the audience chooses to follow exactly the reverse of the reviewer's recommendation, it still depends on the one reviewer, the connoisseur.

Connoisseurial reviews are widespread. Craig Claiborne's restaurant reviews in the *New York Times* were predominately connoisseurial, as are other restaurant reviews like those by Ruth Reichl in the *New York Times* or Dennis Ray Wheaton in *Chicago* magazine. Other products often reviewed using connoisseurial methods include books, theater, dance, music, movies, and many performance reviews. Figure 2.1 contains an example connoisseurial review from the *New York Times Book Review*.

The first thing to notice about connoisseurial reviews is that they are almost entirely text. Many reflect the limits of space in magazines and newspapers; they are frequently limited to 500 to 750 words. However, some, especially certain book reviews, are thousands of words. Their textuality represents more than just a statistic about length or words. They are written in the sense that a novel or an essay is written and because of this they can be understood according to their literary qualities. They are measured by the criteria of good writing. They can be analyzed according to the sequence, depth, or emphasis that they accord to the various elements in the review; in other words, using standard criteria that measure the qualities of narrative text. As such their first goal is to interest and hold their readers. Ruth Reichl made the link between connoisseurial reviews and other forms of literature explicit in some of her early restaurant reviews for *New West Magazine*. She attracted readers by writing restaurant reviews embedded in a love story and a story about discovering one's roots, among others (Reichl 1980a, 1980b).

There are almost as many ways to approach a connoisseurial review as there are reviewers. Indeed, one of the characteristics of this kind of review is its flexibility, which makes it easy to adapt to many different settings. This is one reason it is so widespread. Nonetheless, there are some general qualities that are common to almost all connoisseurial reviews and reviewers. The character of the textual descriptions is that they have the ability to show readers the complexities and nuances of the product under review. This potential may not be fulfilled, but it is clear that in the right hands connoisseurial re-

# Let's Review

*A composer surveys the critics who may (or may not) have transformed the face of classical music in America.*

**MAESTROS OF THE PEN**
*A History of Classical Music Criticism in America.*
By Mark N. Grant.
Eric Friedheim, consulting editor.
Illustrated. 374 pp. Boston:
*Northeastern University Press. $37.50.*

By Dana Gioia

"PAY no attention to what the critics say," the composer Jean Sibelius remarked. "No statue has ever been put up to a critic." The irascible Max Reger expressed himself in more earthy terms. "I am sitting in the smallest room in my house," he wrote to a critic. "I have your review in front of me. Soon it will be behind me."

Seldom do composers publicly extol the virtues of criticism, but how many would want to practice their craft in a society without it? Criticism is a powerful, enlivening and necessary cultural enterprise, but it is also a mostly ephemeral one. Great music endures, often gaining resonance and clarity with time, but even the best criticism fades. Few reviewers, except for composer-critics like Hector Berlioz or Hugo Wolf, are read 50 years after their deaths.

One virtue of Mark N. Grant's "Maestros of the Pen" is how vividly it re-creates the charm and authority of many forgotten reviewers. Taking material from hundreds of sources, including defunct 19th- and early-20th-century newspapers, Grant has assembled a lively narrative history of this neglected field. His scholarship (assisted by Eric Friedheim) is formidable, but more remarkable is the zest and personality with which he presents it. Engaging and often amusing, the book is serious, but without a whiff of pedantry.

It surveys, digests and analyzes over 200 years of American music criticism. Given the volume's manageable length, there are many notable omissions. The book discusses mostly New York and Boston critics, with only a few passing glances at writers elsewhere. It ignores academic musicology and concentrates solely on newspaper and magazine critics, sometimes following their careers into radio, film and television. There is little coverage of Italian opera criticism beyond the enthusiastic musings of Walt Whitman. The treatment of contemporary critics is also spotty. Grant, himself a composer, seems to prefer his subjects safely dead. "Maestros of the Pen" also excludes most criticism of recorded music. Consequently, it fails to address the decisive ways in which recording technology has altered the experience and dissemination of music. These omissions might have undermined the book, but Grant handles his chosen concerns with such intelligence that potential objections become mere qualifications. This may

not be a comprehensive history, but it is consistently cogent and thoughtful.

Grant focuses mostly on individual critics. Examining the lives and opinions of nearly 50 major music journalists, from 19th-century Transcendentalists like J. S. Dwight to contemporary neoconservatives like Samuel Lipman, he uses careers as lenses to view broader cultural developments, and he has a natural gift for the biographical sketch. He concentrates on two eras, which he calls the First and Second Empires. The first was the Gilded Age, from the end of Reconstruction to World War I, which saw the rise of music reviewers as a professional class of critics. Commanding immense readerships in daily newspapers, these cultural mandarins dominated the flow of information and ideas in a way not equaled before or since.

With obvious relish, Grant portrays the oversize personalities of the New York critics once nicknamed the Old Guard — power brokers including W. J. Henderson, H. T. Finck, Richard Aldrich, H. E. Krehbiel and James Gibbons Huneker. The imperious and argumentative Krehbiel typified the cultural eminence of these critics. He was so popular that The New York Tribune put his name in electric lights on Broadway. A man of immense girth and even larger ego, he was frequently mistaken for his friend President William Howard Taft. Krehbiel never corrected the mistake.

Grant's favorite among the Old Guard is the prolific and profligate Huneker. Now almost forgotten, he was once the most influential arts reviewer

in America, covering music, literature, theater and the visual arts, while also writing fiction. Fueled by a dozen or more daily bottles of Pilsner, Huneker published half a million words per year and still found time to chase divas, hold court at Lüchow's and practice Chopin. Helping move American arts from puritan provincialism to cosmopolitan sophistication, Huneker became the model for later culture czars like H. L. Mencken. For Grant, Huneker serves as a representative figure of a vanished intellectual authority, a magisterial critic who understood music's importance to general culture.

The "Second Empire" begins in 1940. With fewer daily papers, the individual reviewer had more influence, and print culture was already losing ground. The dominant critics included Olin Downes, B. H. Haggin, Henry Pleasants and Alfred Frankenstein. But for Grant the Second Empire was the reign of Virgil Thomson, whom he nominates as America's greatest music critic. The composer may have catnapped during many concerts he reviewed, but he wrote about them with brilliant alertness during his remarkable 14-year stint at The Herald Tribune. He typifies the composer-critic of high standards, discerning taste and refreshing candor.

Interwoven with Grant's engaging chronicle of writers is a speculative study on the nature and impact of criticism. Several questions run through the book. Do critics play a significant role in music history? Do they influence the practice of composers or performers?

Does critical opinion shape the enduring canon of classical music? Should critics move beyond informed reportage and evaluation into advocacy? To his credit, Grant tries less to answer these difficult questions than to explore them — without forcing broader generalizations.

He offers some persuasive examples of the role of critics in fixing the classical canon. Most of the Old Guard, for example, were ardent Wagnerians. While their enthusiasm did not create Wagner's American vogue, their nearly religious piety helped perpetuate the singular piety in which operagoers still hold the composer. Grant similarly documents Olin Downes's tireless advocacy of Sibelius, which established the Finnish composer as a major figure in American concert halls.

But I was more often struck by how impotent even the most eminent critics were in shaping posterity. Classical music is an international collaborative enterprise involving not only critics and composers but also conductors, instrumentalists, singers, teachers, impresarios, publishers and listeners. No critic can change any aspect of musical culture without assistance from their own constituencies. The Old Guard, for example, detested the early modernists. Krehbiel called Arnold Schoenberg's music "excreta," and Huneker confessed that "If such music making is ever to become accepted, then I long for Death the Releaser." Yet Schoenberg's serial atonality soon became a trans-Atlantic orthodoxy, which has only recently collapsed. Likewise, few American critics endorsed Mahler as either composer or conductor. Not even his untimely death at 50 sated the reviewers who had hounded him out of New York. Krehbiel tastelessly denounced Mahler in his Tribune obituary, and four decades later Downes still declared the Seventh Symphony "detestably bad" and the Fifth "vulgar music." Yet the championship of conductors like Bruno Walter, Otto Klemperer and Leonard Bernstein gradually created a huge cult for the composer.

Grant's tone is elegiac. He sees the present as "an embattled time for classical music." There are fewer papers with fewer critics writing ever shorter and less demanding reviews. Music criticism has become increasingly cut off from larger cultural concerns. The invigorating tradition of composer-critics like Thomson and Deems Taylor has nearly vanished. Reviewing rock is more lucrative. "The baby boom," he comments, "is the first generation in American history whose mandarins are not occupied with promoting the cultural good of classical music."

But, as his own study documents, classical music has always been in trouble in America. Problems just change from one generation to the next. We may have fewer critics today, but we have more orchestras, opera companies and festivals. Recording and broadcasts have vastly enlarged the variety and availability of classical music. Perhaps all we need to reinvigorate criticism is a few books as good as this one. □

*Dana Gioia, a poet, writes about classical music for San Francisco magazine.*

**12** January 24, 1999

**Figure 2.1. Connoisseurial Review:** *New York Times Book Review*
Source: Gioia 1999:12

views can explore subtle issues in the intellectual and material complexities of the product.

A further characteristic is that connoisseurial reviews offer the opportunity for comment on both the nature of the individual work as well as the larger currents and themes in which it is embedded. The text of a connoisseurial review supplies context for understanding the product. The ability to move back and forth between the product and its larger context and environment is one of the strengths of connoisseurial reviews. This is one way in which connoisseurial reviews are oriented toward the larger society rather than the individual.

Finally, we can ask, what is the ultimate point of connoisseurial commentary? Why write it? Why read it? Connoisseurial reviews are only worth producing or reading if they have some sort of impact. The impact can be on readers or on product makers or both. In this sense, underlying connoisseurial reviews is the reviewers' and readers' faith in the power of text to illuminate and transform our lives. Although connoisseurial reviews may be written in solitude, as an attempt to change the world they are a fundamentally social activity.[4]

These characteristics have implications for reviewers as well. Connoisseurial reviews can be very demanding. One important attribute of a good connoisseurial reviewer is the ability to write well. Good writing implies energetic, forceful prose that readers will listen to and be persuaded by. Like all good writing, connoisseurial reviews are personal statements. They comment on the ways that a product touches the reviewer personally. They are of wider interest only if the reviewer is someone who occupies a position or role that is of broader interest. This brings us back to where we started: connoisseurial reviews are written by connoisseurs, people who—because of their knowledge of details, technique, or principles—are uniquely qualified to write about the product. Because of the significance of the author, connoisseurial reviewers can attract media attention and become celebrities, like Pauline Kael on films, Craig Claiborne on restaurants, or Clement Greenberg on modern art.

Since connoisseurial reviews are personal responses, the personal agenda of the reviewer may intrude. The agenda may be self-conscious where the reviewer evaluates a product positively or negatively according to how well it corresponds to the point of view of the reviewer. Academic and intellectual battles are fought in part via book reviews. The agenda may be unselfconscious, simply reflecting the fact that the reviewer has had certain experiences and not others. A reviewer who has had different experiences would write a different review. The agenda of a reviewer is often more personal. Reviews offer opportunities for career advancement, for reaching a new and different audience, and for showing readers how good the reviewer really is (either as an analyst or a writer or both). The editor who assigns the review often pays attention to the possible agendas of each potential reviewer. This is usually one of the most important criterion governing the selection of a reviewer.

The pervasiveness of the personal perspective of the reviewer is both a strength and a weakness of connoisseurial reviews. It strengthens the credibility of the review when the reviewer is someone an audience respects as an authority. The review offers readers an opportunity to read a sophisticated evaluation and match their response to the response of someone who is widely respected. It is a weakness when it descends to one-sided, biased evaluation. Reviewers in this situation can easily become knee-jerk predictable. Any knowledgeable person knows what they are going to say as soon as it is apparent how the product matches the point of view of the reviewer. It is then unnecessary to actually read the review.

One complexity of connoisseurial reviews is that the genre has a number of practical limitations. The statements in the preceding paragraphs may describe the ideal of a connoisseurial review more than they describe the nitty gritty practical realities that reviewers face. Like reviewers, we cannot ignore practical issues. It is one thing to respect intellectual complexity; it is quite another to do so in less than one thousand words. Concerns like brevity, cost, and publication deadlines inevitably force reviewers to be selective in what they describe and to oversimplify. In this environment, some qualities of the review work against others. Energetic but selective descriptions can seem like overconfident or arrogant oversimplifications, hence losing the very readers that a reviewer sought to interest. And, few readers will find themselves influenced by five hundred words on, say, a dance performance; especially if written quickly by a reviewer on deadline. But suppose a longer essay was written, would it accomplish more? Not necessarily: reading five thousand words requires more commitment and may therefore attract fewer readers. Readers won't be influenced by the review that they didn't read. The point is that the content of connoisseurial reviews is strongly influenced by the limitations of publication and of readership.

Connoisseurial reviews occupy one end of the continuum of credibility. There is an alternative form of reviews that makes a different argument for credibility.

## PROCEDURAL REVIEWS

Readers may trust reviews for entirely different reasons than the personal perspective of the reviewer. Consider the following examples, again chosen from many similar statements across a diverse collection of products. A *Consumer Reports* reader:

> I used to be frustrated by how hard it was to get decent information about products like dishwashers or stoves. . . . I wanted something concrete, not some swirly lifestyle ad. Consumer Reports does objective tests. They give me a feeling of confidence that I know what I'm buying.

An information technology manager for a corporation says:

> The only way I know to get reliable numbers is to actually do tests. I'll give you
> an example. We just finished some tests to help us decide what monochrome
> network printer we are going to buy: mostly speed tests like text printing, graph-
> ics, and multiple copies. We found that printers with about the same [speed] rat-
> ing from the manufacturer differ by more than 50% in actual tests. This is typi-
> cal of most products.

There are many examples like this. The criteria for a good product seem diverse: objective tests and reliable printer speed. Appliances and printers are
different products. On a very straightforward level these reviews seem different. The reviews use different criteria because each review is tailored to the
product under review. This is, of course, true of any review, and it means that
across product genres, reviews are very different. We cannot directly compare
them.

However, if we again step back from the detailed criteria of any single review, there is a common theme underlying all these reviews. The common
theme is that readers depend on explicit tests to evaluate a group of products.
Notice the two parts of this theme. First, there is a group of products that in
some sense form a single category. In the examples above, the groups are
dishwashers, stoves, and printers. Second, in the review itself, readers look
for performance tests. For someone confronted with a group of products and
a feeling of insufficient information, the tests supply crucial data. A reader explains the logic: "Since every product is tested the same way, you can compare the results and you can tell which one is the best."

These comments contrast sharply with the connoisseurial reviews discussed above. Here no one mentions the reviewer. No one is looking for a
"personal response" to a product. The information technology manager
quoted above explains:

> We do careful comparative tests under conditions as realistic as possible. What
> justifies all the time and expense of the tests is the surprises. I have spent my ca-
> reer working with computers and networks, talking to salespeople, reading the
> trade mags, and going to conferences. Even with my experience, I have been
> surprised again and again by the test results. Many, many times the tests saved
> us from making mistakes.

Unlike a connoisseurial reviewer she does not depend on her personal response. In fact, she is explicit that, despite all her experience, her personal reaction has proven less reliable than comparative tests. Since they don't depend on an expert, these reviews are credible for different reasons. The
interview continues:

*Question*: You find your opinions are that unreliable?

Reliable opinions are based on the results from carefully measured tests. Of course, you have to choose the right tests and you have to know what to measure. That is what I know how to do. After I've done it I have a lot more confidence that I know what I'm talking about. After I see the test results it's not just my opinion anymore.

This respondent has had to defend her actions and logic in corporate meetings and so she has thought them through better than most people. Although the reasoning here is more articulate than most, the conclusion in the final sentence was echoed again and again by respondents: they rely on these reviews because they aren't opinions.

For many people this seemed self-evident to the point where interviewees sometimes became irritated when I kept using words like *opinion* in what they considered the wrong context. A typical response was the man who told me (using the exasperated tone and simple sentences often used in explanations to small children): "Why do you keep saying 'opinion'? This isn't my opinion. The tests proved it. It's true."

The tests transform opinions into facts. They transform something personal and subjective into an impersonal, objective reality. This transformation is the core of the credibility claim of these reviews.

In contrast to connoisseurial reviews, these reviews claim credibility because reviewers' judgments are not involved. Instead, reviewers apply certain procedures to measure the performance of the product and then they report the resulting scores. Human beings have no role other than tabulating the results. The procedures are purely mechanical; hence, the product seems to be speaking directly to readers without the possible biases or idiosyncrasies of people to distort in the evaluation. Because the results of these reviews depend on carefully following systematic procedures, they can be described as *procedural reviews*.

Procedural reviews are an alternative method for producing credible knowledge. The key to this method is the procedures. They are a set of mechanical operations that are applied to a product. Mechanical, in this sense, means that the operations are designed to reveal the performance of a product automatically, uninfluenced by people's perceptions, emotions, or biases. As the product carries out these operations, its performance is measured. Based on the measurement, a score is assigned to the product. When a group of products are tested, their scores can be compared and the products can be ranked. The primary result of the procedures is a set of tables containing performance scores and ranks. Consumers Union makes this logic explicit. It strongly insists that it "does not do reviews. We merely perform tests and report the results"

(Arons 1997). Despite their insistence, I use the word *reviews* to characterize what Consumers Union does. In any event, this argument only applies to CU articles on products like appliances or cars. It does not apply to products where CU does not apply tests, like its movie reviews or mutual fund recommendations.

Procedural reviews are also common. Like connoisseurial reviews, a diverse collection of products is reviewed using procedural methods. Examples include *Consumer Reports* reviews of appliances, Morningstar Mutual Funds reviews, and the features tables and performance tests in *PC Magazine*. Computer hardware reviews are typically procedural reviews. Figure 2.2 contains an example of a procedural review of tires from *Consumer Reports*. Notice particularly the "Notes on the Ratings" information in the upper left corner of the page that describes procedures Consumers Union used to test the tires.

The first thing to notice about procedural reviews is that a single review usually evaluates multiple products from a single product category. Procedural reviews almost never review a single product; they are explicitly comparative. While a comparison of 5 to 10 products is typical, some procedural reviews are enormous. *Byte Magazine* occasionally reviewed over 100 products in a single review, for example its review of 126 printers (Fox et al. 1993). Some of Zagat's city guides review over 1,000 restaurants, for example, the 2003 New York City Zagat's (Zagat and Zagat 2002) needed only 191 pages to review 1,924 restaurants.

Second, notice the author. Even a review of a small number of products does not have an author in the sense that a connoisseurial review does. Unlike connoisseurial reviews, a single named expert does not write procedural reviews. Instead, they are often composed by a writer who is working as part of a team. Procedural reviews are better described as being authored by an organization rather than a person. Most procedural reviews require many people for their production: someone to design the test plan (often an editor or a technical consultant), technicians to conduct the tests, clerical workers to assemble and tabulate the results, writers for the introduction, "how we tested," and other sidebars, all coordinated by an editor. In effect, in procedural reviews the reviewer is not a separate actor; reviewers and publishers become identical. Thus, only the three remaining actors—the publisher, product maker, and the audience—play independent roles in procedural reviews. Unlike connoisseurial reviewers, the people who do the tests and write about the results are not authors in the literary sense; they are more like technicians. They usually have certain training and technical skills, but they are often interchangeable with others having the same skills. They can even be anonymous without influencing the credibility of the review. In sharp contrast to authorship in connoisseurial reviews,

**Notes on the Ratings** These tires are logical replacements on vehicles such as the Jeep Grand Cherokee (which we used as our test car), Ford Explorer, Chevrolet C/K pickup, and Ford F-Series pickup. We bought standard-load, on/off-road tires in size P235/75R15. Prices are the estimated average, based on a recent national survey.

We tested for stopping distance on dry pavement from 60 mph (the average was 139 feet). On wet pavement, we tested from 40 mph with the Jeep's anti-lock-brake system (ABS) working (average: 72 feet), and then we repeated the tests with the ABS turned off (average: 93 feet).

To see how well the tires grip during both wet and dry cornering, we drove around our skid pad faster and faster until the Jeep could no longer hold its circular path. We also drove around our one-mile handling circuit, where we evaluated how well the tires responded to the steering and how well they warned the driver as they were about to lose their grip. And we drove on each set of tires for several hundred miles on a variety of public roads so we could evaluate the tires' steering response and ride comfort under normal driving conditions.

We checked rolling resistance—how long it took the Jeep to coast down from 40 mph, and how fast it was going at the end of a specified distance. The farther it rolled, the better the fuel economy should be. We recorded and analyzed the noise level inside the car on both smooth and coarse pavement at 30 mph. And we've listed each model's treadwear rating—a rough indicator of tire life.

## Sport-utility/pickup-truck tires: Overall score

P F G VG E

- Dunlop Radial Rover
- Michelin LTX M/S
- Michelin LTX A/T
- Cooper Discoverer
- Kelly Safari SJR
- Bridgestone Dueler APT
- General Grabber AP
- Goodyear Wrangler Aquatred
- Firestone ATX II
- Goodyear Wrangler Radial

## RECOMMENDATIONS

These tires were impressive. They could corner and brake almost as well as the all-season performance tires we reported on last year, except in one test: braking on wet pavement with ABS. In that test, even the best model in this group performed no better than the worst model in the all-season performance-tire group. Surprisingly, despite their aggressive tread designs, the light-truck tires weren't much noisier.

There wasn't all that much difference, overall, from the best to the worst tires in this group. Nevertheless, several models stood out. The Dunlop Radial Rover, A Best Buy, performed the best in all our braking tests and among the best in cornering and handling. It rode well and had good steering feel. And at an average price of $83, it's relatively inexpensive. For most light-truck owners, we see little reason to consider any tire model except the Dunlop.

We tested two Michelin models. The LTX A/T ($114), an on/off-road tire, behaved well overall. The LTX M/S ($105) is designed more for on-road use; we included it to see the difference. Not surprisingly, the M/S was the most like a passenger-car tire, quiet and comfortable. And it performed well in wet braking and wet cornering. But the two Michelin models earned the same overall score in our tests.

Finally, we were surprised that the Goodyear Wrangler Aquatred ($120) didn't excel in our wet-pavement tests, and that the Goodyear Wrangler Radial ($100)—a very big seller—was the worst of the group.

## CAN'T FIND A MODEL?

Call the manufacturer. See page 64.

### Dunlop Radial Rover ($83) A Best Buy

Slightly outperformed the rest in braking, and among the best in dry and wet cornering. Safe and responsive handling and a comfortable ride. Highest treadwear rating in this group.

**Braking:**
60 mph, dry pavement .....137 feet
40 mph, wet with ABS........69 feet
    wet without ABS .............87 feet
**Cornering:** dry pavement...........◐
    wet pavement .........................◐
Handling ........................................◐
Noise: smooth road ....................◐
    coarse road..............................○
Ride ...............................................◐
Rolling resistance .......................◐
Treadwear rating ...................440

### Michelin LTX M/S ($105)

A good wet-weather performer with ABS, and very comfortable—softer and quieter than the others.

**Braking:**
60 mph, dry pavement ......142 feet
40 mph, wet with ABS........71 feet
    wet without ABS ...........96 feet
**Cornering:** dry pavement ...........◐
    wet pavement ............................◐
Handling .......................................◐
Noise: smooth road .....................◐
    coarse road...............................○
Ride.................................................◐
Rolling resistance .......................◐
Treadwear rating ....................400

### Bridgestone Dueler APT ($85)

A performance-oriented tire, with a noisy, harsh ride. Very nimble and responsive, and second best in wet and dry braking. But doesn't grip as well as some on the wet skid pad. Worst in rolling resistance. Available only from Sears.

**Braking:**
60 mph, dry pavement .....137 feet
40 mph, wet with ABS........70 feet
    wet without ABS ..............90 feet
**Cornering:** dry pavement...........◐
    wet pavement ......................... ○
Handling .......................................◐
Noise: smooth road ....................◐
    coarse road..............................◐
Ride.................................................◐
Rolling resistance .....................○
Treadwear rating ....................300

### General Grabber AP ($84)

Cornered well on dry pavement, adequately on wet. Responds fairly slowly to steering. Reasonably quiet, but ride is only so-so.

**Braking:**
60 mph, dry pavement ......138 feet
40 mph, wet with ABS........72 feet
    wet without ABS ...............95 feet
**Cornering:** dry pavement ...........◐
    wet pavement ............................○
Handling ........................................◐
Noise: smooth road ....................◐
    coarse road...............................○
Ride.................................................◐
Rolling resistance .......................◐
Treadwear rating .......Not available

**Figure 2.2.    Procedural Review: *Consumer Reports* Tire Ratings**
Source: Consumers Union 1996:38.

*Consumer Reports* argues strongly that the anonymity of its reviewers en-
hances the credibility of its reviews.

Not only do procedural reviews not have an author; they don't *need* an author in the literary sense. In principle, any qualified person, including any
reader, can do the tests. Interested readers can perform their own tests by following the detailed descriptions of procedures like recipes. Some organizations, like Ziff-Davis, publisher of *PC Magazine*, *eWeek*, *PC Computing*, and
other magazines, use their tests as a marketing tool to enhance the visibility of
their publications in the industry. They make their specialized tests available
for a nominal distribution charge. Anyone can order their current benchmark
software for Windows PCs, Macintoshes, networks, servers, and laptops from
the eTesting Labs for five dollars per CD-ROM. A lot of people want to do their
own tests; as of June 2003, the eTesting Lab (2003) claims to have distributed
about 20 million copies of its benchmarks! Publicly available tests supply a
persuasive argument for the credibility of the reviews. One respondent echoed
many others as he explains why he believed *PC Magazine* reviews.

> You've got to trust them. [pause] Well, I mean, actually you don't have to trust
> them exactly. You can get their tests and run them yourself. I mean I've never done
> it, but I looked at their [eTesting Lab] web site. So I know that I could do it. I think
> that if they are willing to let me have their tests they must be honest. It shows their
> confidence that they are willing to give me the same tests that they use in print.

In addition to a different kind of authorship, procedural reviews are different from connoisseurial reviews in a number of other ways. First, procedural
reviews contain relatively little text. They are composed largely of numbers
that give relevant attributes of the product and the results of the tests. These
numerical results may be extensive, sometimes extending for pages. The
numbers are the carriers of the evaluation.[5] The text is secondary; it is there
to explain the numbers. Thus, the text is usually limited to an introduction to
the product category being reviewed, a conclusion that often summarizes the
characteristics of the best product (the winner of the review), and a section
with a title something like, "How we tested." This latter section is a description of the testing procedures that the reviewer followed.

Second, the most common presentation of the numerical results is a series
of tables. The tables are usually arranged so that each row contains a relevant
product attribute while each column contains one of the products in the review. The cells contain the test results for a particular attribute of a product.
This format simplifies comparison. Readers can compare the performance of
all products on an attribute by scanning a single line.

Given extensive results organized into this kind of table, readers may have
difficulty understanding or interpreting the numbers. To make the meaning of

the numbers clear to readers, procedural reviews usually try to summarize them in several ways. First and most important, they often aggregate the numbers into an overall score for each product. The overall score gives reviewers the ability to rank order the products and declare an unambiguous winner, a single best product. The overall scores arranged in rank order are usually a featured result of the review; the table appears prominently near the beginning. The winner may also be discussed in a special sidebar that explains why it is superior. This product is often given a special designation such as "Editors' Choice" or "Best Buy."

Third, the review often draws attention to certain numbers or other characteristics that are more noteworthy than others. By highlighting certain elements, the review helps readers extract meaning from the complicated array of numerical data. For example, here is how Morningstar Mutual Funds describes the value of their no-load fund reports (Morningstar 1999):

> All funds are not created equal. To help you sort through all the choices, our analysts give you candid evaluations written in plain English, not financial jargon. We highlight key statistics, tell you what the manager's done, and let you know where a fund stands.

Especially when a large number of products are being reviewed, procedural reviews often explicitly recognize that different audiences have different needs. *Consumer Reports* awards "Best Buy" designations based on a combination of performance and price, explicitly recognizing that many of its readers will not buy top performance at any price. Many *Consumer Reports* readers are more attracted to a product with acceptable performance if it is much cheaper. *Byte Magazine*'s review of 126 printers (Fox et al. 1993) recognized 9 major categories of printers—including workgroup network printers, CAD printers, and portable printers—and 27 subcategories. In a striking example of multiple audiences, Zagat's categorizes its restaurant listings into no less than 47 different categories, recommending restaurants for audiences ranging from the formal ("jackets required") to the trendy ("cigars welcome").

Finally, procedural reviews claim credibility because their procedures are mechanical and objective, in the sense that they do not depend on human judgment. The reviewer does nothing more than witness the performance of the product and print the scores in a convenient table for the reader. As the reader has probably already recognized, this is a rhetorical position rather than a strictly accurate description of procedural reviews. There are two areas where judgment enters a procedural review. First, there is the question of which tests to perform. We don't need to assume any deliberate attempt to alter the overall results. This is a matter of emphasis and framing: any review emphasizes certain characteristics of a product over others. Other reviews produced by other organizations may have different priorities. The second place where judgment usually enters the review is in the weights that are used to construct the overall score that determines the rank order of the products. The weights determine how much importance individual components have in the overall score and, hence, influence the comparative rankings of products. Again, this is usually a matter of emphasis: some reviewers believe that certain characteristics are more important than others and they weight accordingly.[6] Despite the claims of their proponents, procedural reviews are, in fact, socially constructed.

## CULTURAL EVALUATION AND SOME QUALIFICATIONS

The cultural evaluation and review literatures have been almost exclusively concerned with connoisseurial reviews. The limited range of connoisseurial reviews has limited research conclusions in at least three ways. For example, the idea of a "canon" is probably linked to certain characteristics of connoisseurial reviews, especially the emphasis on personal response of reviewers, which may emphasize reputation. It is not clear that procedural reviews would produce a canon. Procedural reviews tend to have a strong commitment to the most recent results. An editor explained:

> We reread our previous reviews but we are guided entirely by the results of our testing.
>
> *Question*: Would you give a product a break?
>
> That's really not the way we operate. Product reputation counts for something. But if the numbers come out against the established product, we see this as important news. . . . The story of an unknown company that produces a superior product is a powerful idea. . . . We *like* telling that story. [Emphasis in original.]

A consequence of the exclusive focus on connoisseurial reviews is that the criteria, review process, and rating systems have been largely invisible. This fact has strongly influenced the research. A major preoccupation has been to infer the criteria used (e.g., Allen and Lincoln 2004; Dowd et al. 2002; Gray 1997; Griswold 1987a; Shrum 1991; and others).[7] Further, many topics have been neglected; for example, there has been little research into how evaluators are chosen, only one study of characteristics of evaluators (de Nooy [1988] on judges for literary prizes), nothing on how interactions among various actors influence the evaluation process, and little on how audiences perceive evaluations (Corse [1997] and Griswold [2000] discuss some audiences) or when they find evaluations credible. The connoisseurial-procedural distinction helps to fill some of these gaps. Although not everything can be done in a single book, I hope to make progress toward a further understanding of evaluations.

Two qualifications may help readers understand what these two rating systems mean for editors, product makers, and audiences. Although I've described connoisseurial and procedural reviews in ways that highlight their differences, it is important to realize that real reviews are never so pure. Real reviews mix both connoisseurial and procedural elements. For example, even book reviews—among the most consistently connoisseurial of all reviews—often include procedural characteristics, like the length and the price of the book. Financial reviews, for example mutual fund ratings and computer hardware reviews—both strongly procedural reviews—include texts to help readers interpret the tables of numbers and rankings.[8]

There is no long-term historical trend. Connoisseurial reviews are not necessarily "bad" or "outdated" and procedural reviews are not necessarily "modern" or "better." There are probably more procedural reviews now than there were years ago, but most of this may be attributed to the development of technologies that make procedural reviews easier and more reliable; for example, cheap computers and telecommunications reduce the cost of collecting and summarizing data. Computers and telecommunications have enhanced the ability of all reviewers—both connoisseurial and procedural—to distribute reviews. Connoisseurial reviews are not going away. They have advantages that procedural reviews can't touch: they are fast, inexpensive, and often good enough. Both rating systems have their strengths and weaknesses and both will coexist for the indefinite future.

The preceding discussion of rating systems and audiences has been abstract and decontextualized. To bring it into sharper focus, the next two chapters are case studies of the institutional structures and relationships that support the conception, construction, publication, and reception of the reviews produced by each system. They present the social and cultural context of production and reception informed by the theory outlined in this chapter. Chapter 3 considers connoisseurial reviews using the case of fine-dining restaurants. Chapter 4 considers procedural reviews using the case of software, especially statistical software. The goal is to reach an empirically grounded, in-depth understanding of reviews that later chapters can use to elaborate theory.

## NOTES

1. In the case of reviews, audiences are not attempting to understand events; they focus on understanding products and their attributes, and relating them to their personal interests. This difference is not theoretically important.

2. Portions of this paragraph and the next follow Becker (1999).

3. Although the idea of a connoisseurial rating system is my own, many authors describe reviewers as connoisseurs (e.g. Eisner 1985; van Rees 1989). There is also a connoisseurship model of evaluation research (Scriven 1999).

4. Portions of this paragraph follow Dickstein (1992). Much of Dickstein's book, *Double Agent: The Critic and Society*, can be read as a sophisticated description of the historical and contemporary activities of connoisseurial reviewers. I found it stimulating and I have incorporated it into this section, although it is hard for me to point to exact sentences or paragraphs where Dickstein's ideas are present.

5. Keep in mind, however, that the numbers do not make a review procedural. The key characteristic of procedural reviews is the careful attention to the procedures used to produce rankings. Several connoisseurial reviews use numbers, most notably Robert M. Parker Jr.'s wine ratings, ranging from fifty to one hundred. They are connoisseurial reviews attached to a number scheme. Parker says his work "is simply taking a professional's opinion and applying some sort of numerical system to it on a consistent basis" (quoted in Echikson 2004:93). This sort of number system is like the stars used by the Michelin Red Guide, Claiborne, and other restaurant reviewers but more fine-grained.

6. The ways in which different organizations choose and use the tests and weights would be a fascinating topic for sociological study. There are ways to turn both the choice of tests and the choice of weights into procedural issues. *InfoWorld* did this in the 1990s when it used reader surveys to determine what characteristics to test and which are most important. To my knowledge, it was the only publication to do this; all others rely on editorial judgment.

7. Research has been carried out at an unnecessary arm's length. For example, Baumann's (2001) fine study of changing movie review evaluations depends entirely on content analysis, when interviews with past and present reviewers could answer his questions much more directly and easily. A similar comment applies to Allen and Lincoln (2004).

8. As we see in chapter 5, however, there are strong pressures for one system to predominate.

# Chapter Three

# Connoisseurial Reviews: Restaurants

A convincing case can be made for the cultural omnipotence of the drama, music or dance reviewers, but all this pales into *pâté* alongside the awesome power of the nation's true tastemakers . . . the food critics.

—*New York Magazine* 1968:2

Let's be clear about the object of the critic's scrutiny; what is a restaurant?[1] There was a first restaurant, opened in Paris in 1766 by a man named Mathurin Roze de Chantioseau. The establishment was named after its primary product; an intense bouillon broth called a *restaurant*, or restorative. Restoratives were believed to be exceptionally easy to digest and particularly good for people with pulmonary problems. They were a popular fad among health-conscious Parisians at the time. The health focus explains the development of many key characteristics of restaurants: personalized service to treat individual maladies, menus that allowed patrons to make the choices to treat their personal problems, and wide hours of service since patrons in fragile health might need restoratives at any time. Their original audience of consumptive men soon expanded to include women, who were believed by the health authorities of the time to be vulnerable to weak chests and digestive problems. Their wide hours of service and individual table service made them attractive to travelers. Other restaurants soon followed, and by the 1780s, they had evolved into something like their modern form; offering a menu of dishes at fixed prices, available at all hours, by waiters serving diners sitting at individual tables.[2]

This chapter describes how restaurants are evaluated and how audiences understand their evaluations. The connoisseurial evaluations studied here are not the only way that restaurants can be reviewed. I discuss another type of

43

restaurant reviewing in chapter 5. Since this is a case study it discusses actual restaurants, primarily in Chicago (although I also discuss some New York restaurants and I use New York reviews written by *New York Times* reviewers Craig Claiborne and Ruth Reichl; I also interviewed Phyllis Richman in Washington, D.C.). The problem is not that the Chicago restaurant scene is atypical; on the contrary, my interviews suggest that restaurant reviewing operates identically in Chicago, New York, Los Angeles, Washington, D.C., and other large cities. Chicago has an intense restaurant culture with an enormous variety of cuisines and types of restaurants, and an active set of restaurant reviewers. The variety and complexity of the Chicago restaurant scene is mirrored in reviews. For an analyst this is ideal: almost any kind of review and any kind of review situation has occurred and is available for study. This aligns the case study with reviewer activities: Most restaurant reviewers cover single metropolitan areas.[3] Specific Chicago restaurants and reviewers are less known to readers from other metropolitan areas. I try to minimize this problem by putting restaurant names in footnotes. Inevitably it is impossible and undesirable to avoid all mention of specific restaurants. To help readers keep the major players in mind, table 3.1 summarizes the major publications, restaurants, and restaurant reviewers.

**Table 3.1.     Restaurants, Publications, and Restaurant Reviewers**

*Chicago* magazine: Glossy monthly Chicago city magazine. Each month it publishes reviews of two restaurants by Dennis Ray Wheaton. It also publishes restaurant listings: a list of about 154 of the best restaurants in Chicago with 70–100 word capsule reviews. The May and November issues usually contain a special collection of reviews of the best new restaurants in Chicago. Currently published by the Tribune Company.

Claiborne, Craig: *New York Times* food editor, 1958–1972. Food writer for the *Times* 1974–1988. He originated modern American restaurant reviews with a series of weekly restaurant reviews that began on May 24, 1963.

*Lettuce Entertain You Enterprises:* Widely regarded as the most successful Chicago-based restaurant management company. As of 2004, it runs some 34 restaurants in the Chicago area. It has been successful in a striking variety of restaurant genres. Restaurants include Everest, Papagus, Brasserie Jo, Big Bowl Café, Wildfire, and The Pump Room. See Wheaton (1995) and Alva (1994) for comments on Lettuce's success.

Wheaton, Dennis Ray: *Chicago* magazine chief dining critic since 1989. Nominated in 1999 and 2001 for a James Beard Award for Magazine Restaurant criticism. 1987 Ph.D., Sociology, University of Chicago. A key informant for the restaurant review case studies.

Zagat's: A best-selling series of books of restaurant reviews. The reviews are based on a survey of diners who submit numerical ratings of décor, service, food, and a short textual comment on each restaurant. Originally only in New York, they currently cover 45 metro areas. The 2003 New York Zagat's reviews over 1,900 restaurants in about 190 pages.

The chapter has five parts. It begins by describing the characteristics of restaurant reviews. The next four parts follow the arc of a restaurant review from conception to reception, describing how restaurants are chosen for review, what happens when reviewers eat in a restaurant, and how the review is written and published. The chapter ends by considering several audiences who read the review. Throughout the chapter I try to contextualize reviews in terms of institutional structures, professional standards, rewards, patronage, or other support.

We begin by asking, what is a restaurant review? In one sense, a restaurant review is much like any other connoisseurial review; in brief, it is a description and evaluation of the experience of eating in a restaurant. Restaurant reviews emerged very soon after the emergence of restaurants. Starting in 1803, in eight issues of *L'Almanach des gourmands* (The Gourmets' Almanac), Grimod de La Reynière described the food establishments of Paris and passed out bad grades and compliments. The best way to understand the characteristics of a connoisseurial restaurant review is in the context of an actual review. Figure 3.1 contains an example, a review of a Manhattan sushi restaurant named Kurumazushi by Ruth Reichl, published in the *New York Times* on October 6, 1995 (Reichl 1995b).

Three characteristics of the review merit notice. First, the review describes several elements of the dining experience separately: the atmosphere of the restaurant, the service, and the food. It recommends several dishes; many reviews warn readers away from some dishes. The primary emphasis is on what makes the food good, that is, on the description and evaluation of food. Although not necessary and not typical, this review is a story in the sense that it has a narrative and characters with plot development: the review is embedded in a narration of a woman being taught how to eat and appreciate sushi. The critic's job, if done right, should give readers the feeling that they have already been to the restaurant, says *Chicago* magazine restaurant critic Dennis Ray Wheaton.

Second, the reviewer accomplishes this in fewer than one thousand words, so the writing is very lean. The review is an intense, condensed description and evaluation of the reviewer's experience.

Third, several details of the evaluation are further summarized in the box in the upper right corner. The famous and controversial stars, directly under the restaurant name, are the summary evaluation. Reviewers say that many readers look only at the stars. The right-side column in the box explains the meaning of the star ratings, and a one-sentence summary of the criteria used: "Ratings reflect the reviewer's reaction to food, ambiance and service, with price taken into consideration." The left-side column in the box contains details of address, hours, credit cards, and handicapped access. It also summarizes the

# Restaurants | Ruth Reichl

**A dubious sushi tyro without a safety net manages to get both lucky and converted.**

"Sushi?" said a dubious voice on the other end of the line. "Must we? I've never tried it."

That is not the answer I'd been hoping for; introducing your friends to sushi is an awesome responsibility. But when trendy restaurants like Match, T and Judson Grill start serving sushi and others like Blue Ribbon sprout actual sushi bars, it is time to take a look at tradition. Which brings me to Kurumazushi, one of New York City's most venerable sushi bars.

"But," my friend's voice dropped to a whisper, "what if I don't like it? Can I eat something else?"

This, I had to admit, was a problem. Kurumazushi, like the classic Japanese restaurant it is, serves only sushi and sashimi. There are no noodles, no teriyaki, no tempura. I hedged a bit. "The fish is so fine," I heard myself saying, "that any person who likes to eat as much as you do ought to appreciate it." I could feel her wavering.

"It's very expensive," I urged. "It might cost $100 a person, and I'm paying."

That did it.

Still, when I arrived at the restaurant she was standing in the deserted bar looking crestfallen. "It doesn't look particularly fancy," she whispered loudly, disappointment dripping from her voice. She stared accusingly at the plain wooden counter and the glass case filled with fish. Just then all the men behind the bar let out a boisterous chorus. "Hello!" they boomed in unison. My friend jumped. "Hello!" a waitress in a long Japanese robe echoed more softly. "Would you like to sit at the sushi bar?" She led us to seats in front of the proprietor, who gave us a gentle smile.

Toshihiro Uezu arrived in New York City in 1972 to work at Saito. Five years later, he opened his own restaurant, developing a loyal following long before the current craze for sushi. At night he serves a mostly Japanese clientele, but during the day most of the seats at the sushi bar are occupied by Americans. Nobody knows better than Mr. Uezu how to introduce people to the pleasures of sushi.

"The toro is very fine tonight," he began.

"Omakase," I said, "we are in your hands." And then I added that my friend had never tasted sushi.

He smiled broadly as if this were a pleasure and turned to say something in Japanese. The man beside us swiveled in his seat, looked at my friend and said, "You are very lucky."

And so she was. "First," Mr. Uezu asked, "sashimi?"

The answer to this was yes; serious sushi eaters always start with sashimi. Mr. Uezu set a pair of boards in front of us, heaped them with shiny, frilly green and purple bits of seaweed and began slicing fish. Next to him an underling was scraping a long, pale green root across a flat metal grater.

"What's he doing?" my friend asked.

"Grating fresh wasabi," I replied. "Very few places use fresh wasabi, but the flavor is much subtler and more delicate than the usual pow-

dered sort." The man scooped up little green hillocks and set one on each board. Beside them Mr. Uezu placed pale pink rectangles of toro.

I showed my friend how to mix the hot wasabi with soy sauce and dip the edge of her fish into the mixture. She picked up a slice of the fatty tuna and put it in her mouth. She gasped. "I never imagined that a piece of fish could taste like this," she said. "It is so soft and luxurious." She liked the rich, cream-colored yellowtail almost as well. Then Mr. Uezu put slices of fluke on our boards; we dipped them into a citrus-scented ponzu sauce, admiring the clean, lean flavor of the fish.

"Spanish mackerel," said Mr. Uezu, holding up silver-edged slices of fish as the waitress set down dishes of ginger-scented sauce. The mackerel had an amazingly sumptuous texture, almost like whipped cream in the mouth. "It just dissolves when I take a bite," my friend said, amazed.

"Now sushi?" Mr. Uezu asked.

"Yes," my friend said. "Yes, yes." She was clearly hooked.

"One piece each?" Mr. Uezu asked. "In Japan we always serve sushi in pairs, but I like to serve sushi one piece at a time so you can taste more." His hands hovered over the fish in the case, selecting Japanese red snapper, crisp giant clam, small sweet scallops. "Can I use my fingers?" whispered my friend.

"Yes," I said. "But be sure to dip each piece into the soy sauce fish side first; it would be an insult to saturate the rice with soy and ruin the balance of flavors."

Raw shrimp as soft as strawberries was followed by marinated herring roe, which popped eerily beneath our teeth. Gently smoked salmon gleamed like coral. Then Mr. Uezu pillowed some sea urchin on pads of rice.

"It looks like scrambled eggs," my friend said. She took a bite. "I think," she said finally, groping for words, "that this is the sexiest thing I've ever eaten. Let's stop now."

"You must have a little green tea ice cream with red bean sauce for dessert," the waitress behind us said. "Mr. Uezu makes it himself. He makes everything."

Of course, we had to have that. It was barely sweet but very appealing. My friend looked down at the Christmas-colored dessert and said, "Who would have thought I'd find myself liking raw fish and bean sundaes?" And then she was struck by an awful thought:

"It's not always this good, is it?" she asked accusingly.

I had to admit that it is not. There is nothing flashy about Mr. Uezu, and his restaurant has a deceptive simplicity. But after eating at Kurumazushi it is very hard to go back to ordinary fish.

Toshihiro Uezu, the owner of Kurumazushi, serving customers at the sushi bar.

Stephanie Berger for the New York Times

## Kurumazushi
***

18 West 56th Street, Manhattan, (212) 541-9030.

Atmosphere: Spare sushi bar with a few simple tables.

Service: In contrast to many traditional sushi bars, Kurumazushi is welcoming to people who do not speak Japanese.

Recommended dishes: Sashimi, sushi, red bean sauce with ice cream.

Hours: Noon to 2:30 P.M. and 5:30 to 10 P.M. Mondays through Saturdays. Closed Sundays.

Price range: Appetizers $5 to $15, entrees $25 to $45, desserts $5.

Credit cards: All major cards.

Wheelchair accessibility: Sushi bar is down a few small steps.

**What the stars mean:**

| | |
|---|---|
| (None) | Poor to satisfactory |
| ★ | Good |
| ★★ | Very good |
| ★★★ | Excellent |
| ★★★★ | Extraordinary |

Ratings reflect the reviewer's reaction to food, ambiance and service, with price taken into consideration. Menu listings and prices are subject to change.

Past reviews. Hundreds of Times restaurant reviews are available on line from @times, an arts and entertainment guide on America Online. Software and information: 1-800-548-5201.

**Figure 3.1. A Connoisseurial Review: Ruth Reichl's Review of *Kurumazushi***
Source: Reichl 1995b

atmosphere, service, and recommended dishes. In most other restaurants it would include a summary of the wine list, sometimes it includes other noteworthy aspects of the restaurant like noise level (e.g., Reichl 1997a). Not all connoisseurial reviews contain summaries like this, although almost all restaurant reviews contain some version of a summary; usually it is less detailed than the *Times* summary.

With these three characteristics of restaurant reviews in mind—dining experience description, review brevity, and brief summary—the basic organization of this chapter follows the path of a connoisseurial review from conception through dissemination to reception by two audiences: restaurateurs and readers.[4]

## HOW ARE PRODUCTS CHOSEN?

Since connoisseurial reviews usually evaluate one product, how the product is chosen is important. The reasons why a restaurant may be chosen for review are many and diverse. The first thing to recognize is that most restaurants never receive the attention of reviewers. The most important category here is chain restaurants. Chains include the obvious fast food restaurants like McDonald's, Pizza Hut, or KFC. They also include the midscale and upscale restaurants like Denny's, Red Lobster, Outback Steakhouse, or Cracker Barrel. The central characteristic of chains is that every unit in the chain produces products that look and taste the same. Chain restaurants' need to guarantee diners a standard product in every unit requires that they train cooks in standard procedures using standard ingredients in standard amounts. Although there may be some regional variations, menus are standardized across the chain, which limits them to ingredients obtainable in quantity anywhere in the country, or ingredients that can be obtained at a central site, frozen (or otherwise preserved), and shipped anywhere in the country. Their need for cost control encourages them to design simple, straightforward dishes so that they can be prepared by relatively unskilled, low-paid people after brief training. Chains simplify cooking. The key reason why reviewers are not interested in chains is that they use cooks, not chefs.[5] In this sense, cooking in a chain restaurant resembles industrial production. Industrial cooking uses interchangeable workers in a simplified, standardized, and routinized environment. Since anyone who has dined at one restaurant in a chain has dined at them all, chains aren't usually interesting to reviewers.

There are three exceptions to these statements. Chain restaurants are sometimes reviewed when the first units appear in a metro area. Many readers are curious because they have heard the restaurant name but they have no personal experience; they are newsworthy and review-worthy. This is especially true of upscale chains like McCormick and Schmick's seafood. In this respect the first unit of an upscale chain is like the other categories of reviewable restaurants discussed in the following paragraphs. A second exception is chain steak restaurants. They can serve very high quality food using standardized recipes. Chefs are not required in order to properly cook steak, so high-quality steak restaurants are an exception to the rule that restaurants that are reviewed are staffed by chefs. Finally, chain restaurant dishes are sometimes included in "best hamburger" or "best pizza" reviews. They are included to answer the question, say, how do standardized chain restaurant hamburgers compare with more expensive hamburgers from other restaurants. This is the exception that proves the rule.

The other category of restaurants that does not receive much attention is small restaurants run by independent proprietors, like sandwich shops, lunch counters, and pizzerias. Small restaurants like this may serve food to a clientele that is completely satisfied because the location is convenient or the restaurant is a gathering place for neighborhood friends. Such restaurants do not aspire to serve noteworthy food and they won't be reviewed.

Thus, the restaurants subject to review serve food that calls attention to itself. They are run by food experts, chefs, who usually specialize in a single cuisine. Chefs are independent operators who use a handmade, real-time, one-unit-at-a-time production technology; craft production, not mass production. Craft production technology defines a category of restaurants often called "fine-dining" or "white tablecloth" restaurants. These characteristics are shared by products that are typical subjects of connoisseurial reviews, such as books, art, live performances, or movies. There are connoisseurial reviews of mass-produced products as well; for example, automobiles and computers.

In this category, how are restaurants chosen for review? In the first place, reviewers maintain a mental list of restaurants that are, in some sense, "important" to their readers. Important restaurants are visited, reviewed, and revisited on a more or less regular basis. Every city has a collection of restaurants like this. Some are restaurants known to provide a peak dining experience: Charlie Trotters in Chicago, the Inn at Little Washington near Washington, D.C., or Lespinasse in New York. Restaurants come and go but chefs often stay; when a well-known chef leaves one restaurant and goes to another, the food at both restaurants may change and, if either had been reviewed before, they will be reviewed again.[6] When important chefs open restaurants they will be reviewed. Thus, when Wolfgang Puck opened his Chicago Spago everyone in town reviewed it. Some restaurant development organizations are known for producing high-quality restaurants on a regular basis, Lettuce Entertain You Enterprises, for example. Every new restaurant that Lettuce Entertain You opens will be reviewed (except, again, the clones). Reviewers use standard journalistic criterion: they review restaurants when they are a matter of public interest. These are restaurants that readers learn of from other sources. Most of his reviews, Wheaton says, are of "new restaurants that diners are curious about. They want to know if they are worth a visit."

New restaurants are reviewed after a short delay: Most reviewers allow them time to get the startup glitches out of their cooking and serving routines. Although some sources report waiting as long as eight months (Shaw 1984:296), reviewers in Chicago seem to wait about six to eight weeks. By waiting for the restaurant to stabilize its performance, reviewers ensure that their experience is similar to a diner's.

Existing restaurants are reviewed on a somewhat irregular basis as time allows and memories are jogged. No one uses a formal system to identify restaurants for review. Reichl (1985) describes how she chose the 10 restaurants she visited during one week. She visited one new Italian restaurant because a wine importer had made it sound interesting. Other restaurant visits are described with phrases like "It reminded me" and "I have been meaning to revisit"; at least two of the restaurants are chosen for convenience. The remaining restaurants are chosen because she has heard about them and some event prompts her to visit. This gives the overwhelming impression of accident and chance. That impression is partly true, but more than just accident is going on. From my conversations with major reviewers it is clear that they sit at the center of a network of information sources. Wheaton is an example. His editors pass on a constant stream of press releases, culinary and restaurant news, and gossip. To preserve anonymity he does not meet with restaurant publicists or attend food events in the Chicago area, but his editors do and they report their experiences. Wheaton also listens to friends and reads local and national culinary and restaurant publications constantly. Trends come to his attention much faster than they would to someone who was not pursuing restaurant information so vigorously. This is typical of all major reviewers I interviewed: information may arrive somewhat by chance but it is being assimilated by searching, prepared, and well-informed minds.

Restaurant choice can be driven by categories of food or dining rather than individual restaurants. There have been reviews of restaurant music (e.g., Miller 1993; Wine 1993:196). Reviewers sometimes review categories of restaurants like romantic restaurants (Miller 1986) or Eve Zibart's (1996) tripe roundup, which must have been a memorable circulation boost for the *Washington Post*. More mundanely, reviewers work with categories of restaurants like, "Best Italian restaurants," or "Best places to eat Dim Sum." Gael Greene of *New York Magazine* uses creative categories. She once recommended restaurants that fit a category titled, "I want to impress a Waspy blonde beauty from Madison, Wisconsin who makes me—a 40-year-old born New Yorker—feel uncharacteristically intimidated" (Greene 1987: 23).

## EATING AT THE RESTAURANT

In the early 1960s the *New York Times* Food Editor Craig Claiborne began writing weekly restaurant reviews.[7] He transformed restaurant reviews in the United States and defined modern restaurant reviews by applying journalistic ethical standards for the first time. Among the reasons why reviews are powerful, ethics cannot be overemphasized. Claiborne had unassailable credentials as a graduate of the *Ecole Hoteliere*, the professional school of the Swiss Hotelkeepers Association, and he was well known as a skilled cook. More important, Claiborne brought a sense of integrity and consumer advocacy to restaurant reviews. Restaurateurs and chefs could argue with his judgments, but he could not be ignored or dismissed.

The ethical issues of reviews are different from those of reporting. Audience trust is more important because the audience is being asked to lay out money and time: only a credible review can persuade. Credibility, then, is directly related to the ethical standards that connoisseurial reviewers follow. Claiborne illustrates the importance of ethics because the innovations that created the role of restaurant reviewer were primarily ethical. For a restaurant critic there are three ethical issues: conflict of interest over payment, multiple visits, and anonymity.

### Who Pays for the Product? Conflict of Interest

Reviewers must use a product to evaluate it, but who pays for the product? If the product maker donates the product to reviewers, there is a potential conflict of interest. When favors are accepted as a matter of routine, it is hard to know when courtesy or gratitude turns into bribery. Readers cannot easily determine if the reviewer's evaluation was influenced by the favor. Prior to Claiborne, meals paid for by the restaurant were a standard perk of being restaurant critic.[8] So were other gifts, some food-related, like cases of wine or alcohol. The result was significant conflict of interest. Claiborne's unwillingness to accept any tokens of appreciation from the people he wrote about was so noteworthy that it is remembered decades later (Ephron 1968; Jacobs 1990:138). Payment for meals by the publication removes one major conflict of interest. Today, the *New York Times* pays for its support of ethical restaurant criticism with a six-figure budget; other major publications provide similar support, adjusted for Manhattan prices.

Restaurant reviewers uniformly agree that accepting free meals and other gifts is unethical. But it is not entirely clear how common Claiborne's ethical standards have become. *Pittsburgh Post-Gazette* critic, "The Traveling Gourmet" Mike Kalina, committed suicide in 1992 when he learned that the

U.S. Attorney's Office was investigating him for allegedly taking payoffs in return for favorable reviews (Steigerwald 1992). At least two restaurant critics have been fired for accepting free meals: the critic of the *Dallas Times-Herald*, and *Los Angeles* magazine critic George Christy (Shaw 1984:271). Jacobs (1990) relates his experiences in the 1970s with restaurateurs who routinely expected to pay for favorable reviews. In Jolson and Bushman's (1978) study, 29.5 percent of restaurateurs and 22.8 percent of critics reported they had offered or been offered some kind of payoff or bribe. The worst of the suspicion focuses on suburban and community newspapers with small expense budgets. Chicago and New York restaurant reviewers report that some suburban newspapers routinely demand free meals in exchange for reviews.

## Multiple Visits and Food Knowledge

To be a food editor for a newspaper like the *New York Times* in the early 1960s required reporting and writing skills, but it did not require knowledge of sophisticated food, particularly since many editors made it a point to discuss what they ate with the chef after the meal. This not only required less effort by the reviewer, but it required only a single meal. Claiborne had classic French training; he could discuss the fine points of sauces with any chef.[9] Although he talked to chefs, he did not talk to the chefs he was reviewing. So he needed multiple visits to adequately sample a restaurant. Here too he set a new standard.

Today, restaurant critics for major publications agree that at least three meals is the minimum needed to adequately sample the range of food and service in a restaurant. They try to bring other people along to widen the amount of food they can sample. With one other person, counting appetizers, entrées, and desserts, a review would be based on sampling at least eighteen dishes. Wheaton talks of several restaurants where he dined with parties of five for three visits, meaning that he sampled as many as forty-five entrées. Since many restaurants don't have even fifteen different entrées, he could check consistency by sampling dishes more than once. In restaurants where the food and service are inconsistent or in important restaurants, Wheaton reports making as many as seven visits before writing a review.[10]

Although multiple visits are universally conceded to be the ideal, many smaller or less prestigious publications are unwilling to spend so much money on their restaurant reviews. There is some data on how widespread the ideal is in practice. The critics responding to Schroeder's (1985) study visited an average of 2.6 times. The number of visits is not determined by reviewers, but by their publication. Reviewers have fought attempts to reduce the number of visits. Lyn Farmer resigned from the *Miami Herald* over a new policy requiring critics to write reviews based on a single visit with one guest (Hert-neky 1995). When new management at the *Minneapolis Star and Tribune* asked critic Joan Siegel to cut back the number of meals she sampled, she re-duced the frequency of her reviews from weekly to twice a month (Ryan 1984:172).

Multiple visits not only help critics taste a wider range of dishes; they also help appraise consistency. The natural raw materials of restaurant food do not arrive in standardized sizes with the same flavor and texture. One of the great-est challenges chefs face is to handle the constant diversity of raw food so that the diner always receives a consistent, high-quality dish. In a real sense, each meal is a separate performance. In addition, when the chef takes the night off the underlings who take over are responsible for serving food that looks and tastes the same. Consistency is a major criterion for connoisseurial reviews of performances; lack of consistency is a frequent criticism.

## Anonymity

Anonymity has become the single most important and controversial ethical issue for restaurant reviewers since Claiborne began reviewing restaurants in-cognito. Anonymity is based on the suspicion that if a restaurant knows that a critic is dining it may provide better service, better food, and more food. The experience of the reviewer no longer reflects the experience of a "typi-cal" diner in that restaurant; the resulting review is biased and it will mislead potential diners.

There is a public controversy over whether a restaurant can change its ser-vice and food. Some argue that it cannot. Jay Jacobs, *Gourmet Magazine's* New York dining critic during the 1970s and 1980s, makes the argument par-ticularly eloquently.

> A third-rate chef can't be transformed into a latter-day Escoffier at the bidding of an owner or maître d' who has recognized the fat lady in the big hat, and Es-coffier himself couldn't have rejuvenated a shipment of rank fish because a known food writer happened to order a portion. Service can be more attentive, to be sure, but that usually entails the obvious neglect of other patrons and works counterproductively to the management's purposes. (1990:136–37)

Jacobs's procedure was to dine incognito and, when he had decided that a restaurant deserved a review, to identify himself to the staff and to interview the chef and the owner. Even he complains that his job became much more difficult after he became known (e.g., 1990:141–43).[11]

From the audience perspective, Jacobs's rhetorical hyperbole about "rank fish" does not speak to the point. A sophisticated, professional restaurant does not have bad food in the kitchen. The real problem with lack of anonymity is more subtle. The restaurant may be able to deliver somewhat better food, considerably more food, and better service. At the margin this may make a significant difference. At least some restaurants respond to reviewers in a way that fulfills the worst misgivings of those who fear biased reviews. Ruth Reichl reported a remarkable instance in her 1993 review of Le Cirque and the details reveal so much about how a skillful restaurant can manage the dining experience that it is worth quoting at length.

> Over the course of five months I ate five meals at the restaurant; it was not until the fourth that the owner, Sirio Maccioni, figured out who I was. When I was discovered, the change was startling. Everything improved: We had already reached dessert, but our little plate of petit fours was whisked away to be replaced by a larger, more ostentatious one. An avalanche of sweets descended upon the table, and I was fascinated to note that the raspberries on the new desserts were three times the size of those on the old ones.

Not only is the food better but the service changes too. When dining as an unknown, Reichl arrives on time with reservations and is sent to wait at the bar for a half-hour. "Finally we are led to a table in the smoking section, where we had specifically requested not be seated." On her final visit, after her identity was known, she arrived twenty minutes ahead of her reserved time.

> "The King of Spain is waiting in the bar, but your table is ready," says Mr. Maccioni, sweeping us majestically past the waiting masses. Behind us a bejeweled older woman whines, "We've been waiting a half-hour," but nobody pays her any mind.

Reichl concludes:

> Food is important, and [chef Sylvain] Portay is exceptionally talented. But nobody goes to Le Cirque just to eat. People go for the experience of being in a great restaurant. Sometimes they get it; sometimes they don't. It all depends on who they are.[12]

Cynthia Wine (1993:295) addresses the audience concerns directly: it is "difficult [to know] whether the food has been doctored," and she adds, "anonymity ensures that none of this happens and I hold that a critic is best served by it." Most reviewers concede the point to the extent that they say in the review when they have been recognized (e.g., Reichl 1995a; Reichl 1995b; Vettel 1996a). Ruth Reichl has written an entire book about her experiences in disguise (Reichl 2005).

The uniform experience of the critics I interviewed is that only some, highly sophisticated restaurants can take advantage of identifying a critic. Being identified in a less mature restaurant often causes service to deteriorate. Interestingly, chefs agree. When a reviewer is present, they say their biggest problem is calming down their staff and reminding them that they know how to do their jobs. For the restaurant, the problem goes further than the service flaws Jacobs mentions; anxiety created by a critic extends into the kitchen where flustered or agitated staff may be unable to cook or plate the dishes well. One chef described another chef staring for several minutes at two visually identical pieces of fish, unable to decide which to cook for the critic. This is why chefs, wanting to show off the restaurant at its best, emphasize soothing the staff.

Anonymity is a sensitive issue among reviewers I interviewed. Critics go to considerable lengths to avoid being recognized. Wheaton has no office at *Chicago* magazine and never goes to the magazine; he meets with his editors only outside the magazine. His phone number is unlisted and he has no email address. Of course, he never goes to food or restaurant events. When he was nominated for a James Beard award for magazine criticism, he didn't go to the awards dinner; his editors went in his place. As far as he is aware, after seventeen years he remains generally anonymous throughout the Chicago restaurant community. Phil Vettel of the *Chicago Tribune*, in the apparent hope that restaurateurs believe everything they read in the "World's Greatest Newspaper," describes himself as "part Maori, right down to the facial tattoos" (Vettel 1989:4). Standard efforts include wearing hats, wigs, glasses, dark glasses, pretending to be pregnant, making reservations under other names, having several credit cards in different names, and asking guests to pay using their credit card (Wine 1993:293–94; Kapner and Mack 1996).[13] One of the structural problems of being a restaurant critic is remembering the name that you reserved under. Several critics told of trying to read the scribbled names on the list of reservations upside down while stalling the maître d' until they remember the name they used that night. Race can create problems: Wheaton and I could not have been more conspicuous when we were the only white people dining in a crowded soul food restaurant. Generally critics avoid calling attention to themselves; they report eating bad food that they would have sent back to the kitchen were they dining as ordinary patrons. If someone is making a scene in a restaurant it probably isn't a critic.

These three ethical issues underline the importance of the reviewer in the connoisseurial review process. Although the reviewer is not the only source of credibility, if the reviewer is compromised then the whole review becomes worthless. In the integrity of the reviewer, a connoisseurial review has a single point of failure. In this sense, the credibility of a connoisseurial review rests unmitigated, directly on the shoulders of the reviewer.

## Remembering What You Ate

Although James Beard claimed that he could remember every meal he had eaten in his eight decades of gourmandizing, no reviewer claims such a prodigious memory. When they make multiple visits, they rely on notes. The problem is, how can reviewers remain anonymous if they constantly take notes? Claiborne wrote furtive notes on a small card when he thought no one was looking (Manville 1968), but anyone taking notes at dinner is conspicuous. It's easier at lunch since many lunches are business-related. Common solutions involve making notes in a car after the meal or speaking into a tape recorder after leaving the restaurant. The best solution I encountered is Wheaton's: he is wired; he has a hidden tape recorder with a microphone under his tie. He can describe the meal, tastes, service, and decor in ordinary conversation during the meal and transcribe it later. This is completely unobtrusive, improves accuracy of recall, and makes writing the review much easier (although it can be difficult in a noisy restaurant).

## Designated Eaters

Most critics take other people along to increase the number of entrées they sample. Cynthia Wine (1993:296–97) calls these people "Designated Eaters." If you ever eat a meal with a working critic you won't pay for the meal, but it is no free lunch. There are Rules. The critic is there to sample a range of dishes, so your meal is what the critic wants you to eat.

> Many Designated Eaters find that the glow comes off when they are assigned to try the creamed okra at the new Ethiopian Grill down the road, rather than the free frites at the spiffy new bistro. I am a fascist about what they order. They may have been dreaming for months about the carpaccio, but if minestrone is what I need to know about, minestrone is what they eat. Yes, in the line of duty, I have even forced spinach on children. (Wine 1993:296–97)

Arrive hungry: a major reason you are there is to help handle the overload of food so you will eat something of everything. Sampling the food means *all* the food and you will probably eat at least four courses: appetizer, salad, entrée, and dessert; in Italian restaurants add a pasta course. Being full is not an option. To help the critic sample everything, you will trade plates or at least share everything on every plate. You will ask probing questions of the waiter to help preserve the critic's anonymity. You can do nothing that calls attention to your table. Although you can discuss the food, you cannot discuss restaurant critics or reviews. Finally, like the gods of some religions whose name must never be spoken, never call the critic by name. This is the hardest Rule for me to follow; the name can slip out so easily in conversation. It's often easiest to give the critic a new name for the evening; I prefer "Bert" or "Skippy."

## WRITING THE REVIEW

Even though critics eat at a restaurant, they may not write a review. Restaurants with no redeeming qualities are visited once and written off as a loss. The consensus among reviewers I interviewed was that they published reviews of only about 60–70 percent of the restaurants they visited. If the restaurant is obscure, few reviewers publish a negative review. Why, they ask, tell people not to go to a restaurant when they don't know that it exists in the first place?

What makes a restaurant unreviewable? In most cases the answer is simple: bad food kills reviews. There are other reasons: in a Chicago case, a reviewer knew of a good restaurant in a crime-ridden part of town but did not publish a review because the publication did not want readers to be mugged or have their cars broken into while eating at its recommendation. In another case, a restaurant review was never published because the restaurant served food that was good by its standards, but the food was heavily salted and contained large amounts of fat. Such dinners would have been acceptable, even praiseworthy twenty-five years ago but they are now seen as unhealthy and they no longer merit a recommendation.

### Criteria

This invites the question, what criteria do critics use for evaluating a restaurant? This is a difficult issue. The key problem for a sociologist-researcher is that, although reviewers seem to know their criteria, they are rarely asked to articulate them and they seem not to think about them systematically. Some identify major categories, like Phyllis Richman's (1996) concise list: "food, food, food, service, and environment." This is valuable, but it begs the question: how do critics evaluate food, service, and environment? My interviews suggest some answers. Since typical categories are based on the tripartite distinction of food, service, and décor, that's what we'll use. Because food is the most complex, and most important, we'll leave it for last.

Decor, ambiance, or environment includes items like quality of the cutlery, china, and glassware, lighting, temperature, flowers, interior design and decoration, comfort of the chairs and tables, and napery, among others. The judgments here are expressed in terms of fairly conventional characteristics of quality. At issue is how well décor contributes to the overall dining experience. If it is a romantic restaurant, do the music, tables, and lighting all fit the goal? Noteworthy décor elements are often mentioned in reviews.[14]

Service refers to diners' interactions with the restaurant staff. It includes everything from initial contact with the restaurant to leave-taking: how reservations are handled, valet parking, coat check, how quickly diners are seated, the knowledge of waiters about the ingredients of each dish and possible paired wines, the intrusiveness of the service, the pacing of the meal, and how efficiently the check is handled. Little things count, like whether the water glasses are kept filled. Good waiters cater to each table's needs individually. This is enormously difficult because attentive service at one table would be suffocating at another.

Food is by far the most important and complex item that reviewers evaluate. Reviewers struggle to find ways of evaluating food. The first problem is that the criteria differ from cuisine to cuisine. Some differences are well known; for example, the difference between Japanese and Chinese rice. Other differences are less obvious and reviewers can make subtle mistakes that readers notice. For example, Reichl (1996) discussed a reviewer who criticized the jellyfish in a Chinese restaurant as too "bland." But, "Chinese do not judge jellyfish on flavor but on texture," she notes. His gaffe told knowledgeable readers that this reviewer was a poor judge of Chinese food. Restaurant reviewers today are expected to be able to judge major cuisines: French, Italian, Chinese, and others. This places enormous demands on a reviewer. What reviewer knows good Nepalese or Ethiopian food? Claiborne himself says (quoted in Rohr 1993:137):

> When I was reviewing, I went to restaurants with menus of classic French and maybe Italian; the menus were more stable and standardized. Now that they're inventing more dishes—with Asian ingredients like lemon grass, for example—you've got to simply go and pray that you're correct.

Possibly the best-known foreign haute cuisine is French. French cuisine is unusual because the classical French standard of excellence was systematized in well-known texts, notably in Auguste Escoffier's *Guide Culinaire* (1981 [1907]).[15] Critics, like Claiborne, who are familiar with these sources, can judge dishes based on a fairly clear, external standard that restricts the personal discretion of the reviewer. Bill St. John of the *Rocky Mountain News* provides an example (Sanson et al. 1990:105) of how this works in practice.

> French onion soup should be arrestingly sweet, with croutons that don't resemble manhole covers. That is not my opinion, that's according to a classic recipe in [Montagne's] *Larousse Gastronomique*. So, if you're going to put French

onion soup on your menu, that's the way it should be made, or call it something else. If your French onion soup doesn't comply with the classic recipe, I have no problem criticizing it.

French cuisine is complex in its combinations of sauces and ingredients; flavors count but so do textures and colors. Even more complex is that reviewers must judge not just individual items but the balance and harmony of flavor, texture, and color on each plate.[16] Of course, the balance and harmony of all components of a meal are important in many cuisines, Japanese in particular. The requirements of judging texture, color, and harmony of presentation make additional demands on reviewers.

Reviewers respond to such requirements and demands in a variety of ways. Some seem to punt and focus on hamburgers and all-you-can-eat buffets. In their defense they argue that that's what their readers want (Alva 1992). Other critics have a background as reporters and they tend to approach restaurant reviews like a typical news assignment. They tend to stress the information aspect of reviews, not the evaluation. Other critics face the problem directly by doing serious research before sampling a cuisine. At minimum this includes library research on unusual foods; most critics build up a personal library of cookbooks. Wheaton took along skilled Chinese cooks when he ate at Lettuce Entertain You's newly opened Ben Pao; they were not impressed; the food, they said, tasted like it was cooked by someone "who doesn't understand the cuisine." He follows this practice with other cuisines as well. Claiborne was indulging in a little rhetorical hype in the sentences quoted above because he often reviewed restaurants accompanied by Pierre Franey, executive chef at La Pavillon, then widely considered the best French restaurant in North America (Franey 1994). Reichl and Wheaton have called foreign consulates asking for a Designated Eater who knows the cuisine.

A natural experiment offers one opportunity to clarify the criteria used by reviewers. Jean Joho is the executive chef at two Chicago restaurants: a haute cuisine restaurant, Everest, and a traditional bistro-style restaurant, Brasserie Jo.[17] Everest has long been considered one of the finest restaurants in Chicago, receiving four stars from every Chicago restaurant critic. It is a small restaurant, perhaps 45 seats, serving Alsatian-inspired French food. Meal prices range around $120–$160 per person. Brasserie Jo is also a very good restaurant, receiving one and a half to three stars from Chicago restaurant critics. It serves Alsatian food and seats 220 people. Meal prices are much less, about $30–$50 per person. I asked three Chicago critics, Pat Bruno of the *Sun-Times*, Phil Vettel of the *Chicago Tribune*, and Dennis Ray Wheaton of *Chicago* magazine, to characterize and compare the food in these restaurants. A summary of their response: Everest uses the finest ingredients and spares no effort to produce the best food it can, with a superlative presentation. Although individual dishes may be either traditional or innovative, they share common characteristics. The long, intense food preparation mingles the flavors of the ingredients producing complex sauces and a subtle balancing of flavors. Of course, it is not food that can be eaten everyday, both because it is too expensive and too rich. The food at Brasserie Jo replicates traditional Alsatian brasserie cooking: relatively simple, solid, everyday cooking requiring much less time and work. A home cook with a cookbook could duplicate most of it. The flavors are more straightforward, the presentation is simpler, the ingredients are fewer, and the service is less personal. Of course, Brasserie Jo probably serves ten times as many diners on any given evening.

There is, I think, a concise way to summarize the difference between these two restaurants and, in doing so, we see one of the core criteria for excellent food. The key difference is that the food at Everest is, in both flavor and presentation, more complex and subtle. Complexity of flavor means that the different yet balanced flavors of the individual ingredients can be distinguished as you eat each dish. Similarly, the unique textures of the different ingredients should be apparent with each bite. The presentation should be pleasing to the eye. Knowing when they have been served such food is the most difficult task reviewers face.

In addition to the trio of food, service, and décor, reviewers also pay attention to value; defined as what you get for what you pay. In a sense value is at the core of restaurant reviewing; if price were the only thing that was important then reviewers would be superfluous. But price is not a very good indicator of quality of food, service, or decor. Diners can pay high prices for bad food and find good food at low prices. Food from some ethnic groups is often priced uniformly well below (or above) other ethnic groups' food of the same quality. Thai food is often very inexpensive and high quality. French food is notoriously expensive. In the trio of food, service, and decor, high quality of one does not imply that the others are of equal quality. Except in the very best restaurants, they often seem almost independent of each other. It is virtually impossible for diners to find out about these issues without spending a lot of money and enduring bad meals. Reviewers spend money to give diners this information in advance. Reviewers owe much of their existence to these facts.

Few critics articulate their criteria in a way that makes explicit the different genres of restaurants and that the genres require somewhat different judgments. Ruth Reichl is an exception, and her criteria tie together much of the preceding discussion. She says she bases her reviews on three issues: what the restaurant is, who its clientele are, and what the restaurant is trying to do. The first two issues correspond to sociological concepts of genre and audience.

Genre is important because it determines a standard of comparison. It enters at the point where a reviewer asks, what is this restaurant? Is it Mexican? French? Fusion? Pan-Asian? The criteria of good cooking differ for each cuisine, and reviewers try to take that into account.

Audiences enter at the point where a reviewer asks, what kinds of food does this audience expect and understand? Diners who do not understand the food they are being served will most likely not like it and not return, a problem explored in Stanley Tucci's 1996 film *Big Night* about the failing Italian restaurant Paradise. Commercially successful chefs adjust their cooking to their customers' comprehension and to locally available ingredients, even in some cases by modifying parts of national cuisines (Lu and Fine 1995). The standards of service, decor, and food for a successful restaurant for teenagers (featuring hamburgers and wait staff dressed in 1950s styles) is very different from, say, a restaurant for romantic couples (featuring dim lighting and strolling guitarists) or a restaurant where you would take your mother-in-law for Sunday dinner (a formal, conservative dining room).[18]

Finally, there is the question, what is a restaurant trying to accomplish? This is an omnibus issue that encompasses the previous two. How are the food, service, and decor supposed to combine to produce a dining experience? Many restaurants are not trying to do fine dining but are still excellent restaurants. Chicago examples include Army and Lou's, which serves updated soul food in a comfortable setting, or Brother Jimmy's BBQ, which is decorated as a tobacco warehouse and serves American southern food in a raucous setting. Other restaurants aspire to fine dining but they are not really excellent (e.g., Ben Pao, in the judgment of Chicago critics). Further, some restaurants focus on one element of the food, service, and decor trio. Food may dominate, but people eat at restaurants for many reasons, including speed of service, comfort, location, and others.

In a sense, this last item—the restaurant's goals—ties all the others together. What are the restaurant's standards? "Each restaurant is different. I do not judge a restaurant on my standards but on the restaurant's standards," Reichl says (Quoted in Rohr 1993:148). For a critic, the most important question is: based on its own standards, is this a good restaurant? Will the diners who want this kind of restaurant like it? Do the food, service, and decor combine in an experience that leaves diners feeling satisfied?

## Why Write Negative Reviews?

When would a reviewer publish a negative review? Since reviewers do not write about every restaurant they visit, an obscure restaurant that turns out to be inadequate is never mentioned in print. Reviewers are likely to publish negative reviews under several circumstances. Critics publish negative reviews of major, not minor restaurants. *Major* refers to prominent restaurants, restaurants readers are likely to have heard about because the owners or chef is well known, or the restaurants have a large advertising budget; in short, restaurants that are visible. When readers are likely to hear about a restaurant, negative reviews warn them that they may not have a good experience. Thus, Phil Vettel says, "It is my sworn duty to tell everybody if [a major Chicago restaurateur] opens a crummy place" (Alva 1992).

One special circumstance that often occasions a negative review occurs when a good, well-known restaurant hires a new chef, and food or service deteriorates. Changes in the kitchen can lead to a significant difference in food, but they are not easy for diners to discover. In these circumstances, a negative review warns readers about a change for the worse.

The phrase *negative review* lumps the entire review together and this is an oversimplification. Many reviewers warn readers about bad service (e.g., slow, clumsy, or uninformed). Mentioning that the decor is formica-topped tables says to readers that it is a different kind of restaurant than if it had white linen tablecloths. Specific dishes may be condemned in a review. Nonetheless, many reviewers seem to strive for an overall upbeat tone in their reviews.

## EDITING AND PRODUCTION

Once written, reviews pass through the editing process. Depending on the publication, there may be more or less attention devoted to editing. Most magazines do what is called fact checking. Staff members phone the restaurant and confirm every ingredient of every dish mentioned in the review. If the restaurant does not confirm the ingredient, then the review is changed. This is a major effort; to an outsider it sometimes seems obsessive. Newspaper reviewers do not have as much clerical support. They also don't do the same checking. The newspaper reviewers I talked with said that no such checking was necessary, and only one of them thought that they might be making very many mistakes. Another newspaper reviewer suggested that detailed fact checking was counterproductive, saying that restaurants would not necessarily tell the truth if falsehood would help them avoid criticism (e.g., Schroeder 1985:62). Newspapers check hours, phone numbers, and similar details; usually this is the critic's responsibility. Interestingly, newspapers do detailed fact-checking for restaurant reviews that appear outside of the normal review pages, such as in the travel section. Interviewees said that the reason for more careful checking of reviews in, for example, the travel section is

that these reviews are often written by outside freelance writers. Fact checking is a quality control device to reassure the editor about a writer who is distant and not a known quantity.


## READING THE REVIEW

There are several relevant audiences for reviews. Below I discuss restaurateurs and ordinary subscribers (whom I call *readers*).

### Restaurateur Response

> Shortly after midnight on what would prove to be the most important day of
> Henry Adaniya's career, he drove to the Chicago Tribune's River West printing
> plant. Inside, presses were rolling out the April 12, 1996 edition, containing the
> first review of his beloved restaurant [Trio] since his star chef and pastry chef
> left several months earlier.
>
> A negative review would have been devastating; he couldn't sleep without
> knowing the verdict. So he drove to the plant, supplied with beverage options:
> a pinot noir and Jack Daniel's to mourn a bad review, Veuve Clicquot to toast a
> good one. Outside in the parking lot, he watched and waited . . .
>
> The first delivery driver roared past Adaniya, ignoring his frantic waves. When
> the next truck approached, Adaniya flashed a twenty (he was, after all, a former
> maître d'), and got a paper. "We opened the page," he recalls. "Bingo!" He put
> the wine and sippin' whiskey away and uncorked the Veuve. . . .
>
> "It was one of the most gratifying times in my life," Adaniya says. "And to read
> it brought tears." (Allen 1996:93, 94, see Vettel 1996b for the review)

Anxiety, lots of anxiety, is often the dominant emotion that restaurateurs feel
when they think about reviews. Anxiety sometimes leads to hostility: critics
have been flailed with menus (Ross 1981), received death threats, and had a
load of manure dumped on their lawn (Shaw 1984:287). Several years ago in
Turkey, after receiving a negative review, a chef shot and killed the critic
(Barberian and Kingsmill 1992).

Although restaurateurs have a variety of responses to a negative review,
one response is particularly interesting from a sociological point of view.
The review can provide valuable information for restaurateurs. Restaurateurs, like other businesspeople, often have difficulty seeing their business
through the eyes of customers. Because they are intensely involved in their
restaurant, they often do not have the emotional or intellectual distance to

see its faults. A restaurant consultant told me "Reviewers usually tell the truth. Chefs and owners may not be happy to hear it, but their restaurants will be better if they listen." I was told of several instances where the manager of a restaurant called the reviewer after a review that demoted the restaurant. The manager wanted more details and he and the critic talked. Several months later the reviewer received a letter saying that the restaurant had made significant changes and inviting the critic to return for another review. The critic returned and restored the restaurant to its previous ranking. A chef told me that once he stopped being angry at the sarcasm "that many critics think is a requirement," he found reviews to be a valuable learning tool. He said that he had found even the most negative reviews helpful. This is exactly why Lettuce Entertain You has an in-house secret diner program: to provide managers with a detailed independent assessment that reflects the viewpoint of diners (Cox 2000). This independent perspective is one of the great strengths of the detailed discussions of food and service in connoisseurial reviews.

Bad reviews can be devastating; paradoxically, a good review can also kill a restaurant. After a good review a restaurant can become overcrowded, cooking can deteriorate, reservations systems can be overloaded, regulars can't get in, and when crowds leave there may be too few regulars left to sustain the restaurant. After a four-star review from Reichl, Lespinasse was so crowded that the backlog of dinner reservations reached three months. The crowds make good reviews stressful for restaurants. When the restaurant is filled night after night, the kitchen and wait staff are under more pressure. They never have a slow night; they require much larger volumes of food. This exacerbates conflicts or inefficiencies, and tempers can become frayed; it can be a very difficult time. *Chicago* magazine warns restaurants that a review is coming so they can prepare for the rush of people.

## Restaurateur Manipulation

The strong response of readers to a printed review tempts restaurateurs to try to manipulate the review system. Cases of this usually do not break into public view. One example became public in the late 1980s when the Knife and Fork Club's annual list of "America's Top 10 Steakhouses" was used in the advertising of several restaurants. This ended when a steakhouse that didn't make the list claimed the club was bogus, run by a Houston publicist named Tom Horan under an alias. Several restaurants on the list were paying the publicist (Chicago Tribune 1994). This can be more deliberately manipulative, as when Sony Pictures was caught printing made-up quotes from nonexistent reviewers in print advertisements for movies (Waxman 2001).

This sort of manipulation works best when anonymity and distance give protection. It would probably not work in a city where there were other reviewers or with repeat customers. One reviewer told me, "That kind of manipulation would be a great story. If I ever learned about it I would write about it and that would end it. . . . The restaurant would be embarrassed and the publicist would probably lose his job." It works best with out-of-town visitors. The restaurants themselves implicitly recognized this: Knife and Fork Club advertised solely in in-flight magazines.

## Reader Response

Restaurateurs report that a favorable review not only brings in more people; it also brings in a new and different group of diners. These diners are more demanding, more likely to complain, have more special requests and special orders, and they have a shorter temper. Generally, they are hard to handle. This too adds to the stress in a restaurant.

More elegantly, and bearing in mind his self-interest as the *Gourmet Magazine* restaurant critic, Jacobs (1990:20) describes what happens when *Gourmet* subscribers read a review.

> The consensus among New York restaurateurs was that coverage in *Gourmet* was the ultimate journalistic desideratum; that the magazine's imprimatur would yield sustained patronage by a well-heeled, cosmopolitan readership prepared to indulge itself unstintingly.

By contrast, he claims, reviews in the *New York Times* or *New York* magazine didn't attract the same quality of diners. He quotes the owner of a classic French restaurant telling what happened after the *New York Times* awarded his restaurant three stars.

> Who *needed* that bitch's three goddamn stars. The phone hasn't stopped ringing since her review appeared, and all we're getting is polyester from the outer boroughs and New Jersey. They come in, order the cheapest dishes on the menu, drink Coca-Cola with their meals, drive our regular customers away, and never show up again!

Readers often come in waving a copy of the review and, without looking at a menu, point to the review to order exactly what the reviewer liked. This can cause problems if there are limited supplies, as of wines. A reviewer points out another problem: "Most contemporary American cuisine is seasonal so the dishes I mention disappear from the menu at the end of the season." This disappoints some diners.

How many people, then, actually read restaurant reviews? Two studies have asked this question. 87.3 percent of Jolson and Bushman's (1978:69) respondents and 65.1 percent of Barrows et al.'s (1989:86) respondents read restaurant reviews. Since these are both convenience samples—see appendix B for details—the difference in the percentages is meaningless. We can conclude that a significant proportion of the population, probably over half, reads restaurant reviews.[19] Anecdotally, I can report that during my search for focus group participants among mostly upper-middle-class professionals, almost everyone I called read restaurant reviews.

Reading a review does not directly address the important question: what is the influence of restaurant reviews? A series of surveys conducted for *Restaurants and Institutions* magazine, a trade magazine for the restaurant industry, asked a national probability sample about the influence of reviews. These data are unique. The surveys from 1980 to 1983 are the only national sample that has asked about the influence of reviews on dining decisions. The results indicate that somewhere between one-quarter and one-half of all diners are influenced by reviews when they decide to try a new restaurant.[20] Certainly this provides evidence of the significant economic effect of reviews.

An alternative way to study the influence of reviews is to compare them to other ways of learning about a restaurant. Table 3.2 contains data about the relative importance of six different sources of information. There are several messages in the table. First, "friend's suggestion" is by far the most influential source. The two-step flow of communication lives (Katz and Lazarsfeld 1955). Second, in the "Entire Sample" column, reputation is second in importance; the other four items are about equal, within 2 percent of each other. Reviews are important but no more so than ads, promotions, or being taken to a new restaurant by a friend.

The rightmost column of table 3.2 examines a group called "Very Heavy Spenders," defined as households spending over ninety-five dollars per week in restaurants—the average household in the survey spends fifty-three dollars per week.[21] Very Heavy Spenders comprise 11.4 percent of the sample. Among Very Heavy Spenders, "friend's suggestion" retains the most influence, but the second most influential source is "newspaper reviews." Reputation drops to third. Ads and promotions, the only mediums that are completely under the control of restaurateurs, are the least effective way to reach these people. This tends to support the argument that people pay more attention to independent sources of information. Especially among those restaurant patrons who spend the most money, reviews are an important source of information.

Table 3.2 asks about the influence of reviews from the perspective of the question, if you ate in a new restaurant, did you read a review beforehand? We can also study the influence of reviews from the opposite perspective by

**Table 3.2.    Influences on the Selection of a New Restaurant**

|                            | *Entire Sample* | *Very Heavy Spenders* |
|----------------------------|-----------------|------------------------|
| Friend's suggestion        | 66.1%           | 67.2%                  |
| Restaurant reputation      | 34.7            | 39.1                   |
| Advertising                | 28.3            | 21.9                   |
| Newspaper review           | 27.7            | 45.3                   |
| Taken there by someone     | 27.2            | 28.1                   |
| Special promotion/discount | 26.4            | 23.4                   |

Source: Liesse (1981:112); see appendix B.

asking, if you are the sort of person who reads reviews, how are you differ-ent from people who do not? Barrows et al.'s (1989) data indicates that there are important differences between readers and nonreaders. Diners who read reviews dine out 20 percent more often and they spend 42 percent more money on each meal.

This confirms the importance of reviews from both perspectives: compared to people who do not read reviews, review-readers spend more money in restaurants. People who tend to spend more money in restaurants are also more likely to read reviews.

We've been writing in general terms about the influence of reviews on readers. Now I want to become more specific; I want to look at a puzzle. Why people respond to a positive review is not particularly surprising, but why do diners respond to a *negative* review? There is debate over the impact of neg-ative reviews and I begin by talking about the power of negative reviews in general. In one situation everyone agrees a negative review can have the most impact. One critic summarized: "My influence peaks when I'm reviewing a new restaurant that everyone has heard about but no one has visited. People are curious and my review is the best information they have."

With established restaurants, the impact of bad reviews is more diffuse. Their crucial strength is that established restaurants have regular diners who like their food. Regulars are not usually swayed by a negative review. Some established restaurants have their own following and they seem to be critic-proof. Restaurants like Antoine's in New Orleans, Hogate's in Washington, D.C., Bookbinder's in Philadelphia, Trader Vic's in San Francisco, or Bob Chin's Crab House outside of Chicago have at best a mediocre reputation among critics, but they continue to flourish. The people who go there don't care about reviewer's opinions.

Yet there are also cases when a negative review has a major impact. Jacobs (1990:132) reports such a case of apparently insecure regulars after the Coach House, a Greenwich Village institution, was downgraded by Marian Burros, then the *New York Times* restaurant reviewer.

The ink was hardly dry on the page before table reservations were canceled in carload lots, in many cases by regular customers who had dined happily at the restaurant for years. Business fell off by some 80 percent before the operation recovered its equilibrium.

If you like a restaurant, why should someone else's opinion matter? I suspect that the response has to do with the image of the restaurant. No one wants to be associated with a "bad" restaurant, especially when—as in Greenwich Village—there are many alternatives nearby. This is the modern concern with self-conscious construction of identity and personal image. If Brillat-Savarin could write in 1825, "Tell me what you eat and I shall tell you what you are," in today's culture he would have written, "Tell me *where* you eat." The language used to describe diners is rich with identity signals: "cosmopolitan," "well-heeled," "polyester," "drink Coca-Cola."

## Reader Manipulation

Diners sometimes try to get reservations, free meals, or better service by impersonating reviewers. All reviewers report this happening many times. Until a recent remake of its restaurant listings, *Chicago* magazine carried a notice warning: "Critics dine anonymously. Restaurateurs are told to treat as frauds all persons who identify themselves as *Chicago* magazine restaurant critics." Still, several times a year a restaurant calls the magazine saying that someone who said he was Dennis Ray Wheaton was there and wanted a free meal. Pat Bruno of the *Chicago Sun-Times* tells of visiting a recently opened restaurant and talking with the waiter about how the restaurant was doing. The waiter thought the restaurant was attracting favorable attention and then illustrated his opinion by surreptitiously indicating a man seated nearby. "See that man over there?" he whispered. "He's Pat Bruno and he's eating here tonight for a review."[22]

Although a source of amusing stories, impersonation is not benign. Restaurateurs tell of people bringing five friends, eating expensive food and drinking the best wines, but refusing to pay because they are doing a review. Some have been known to do this repeatedly. The expense (not to mention lack of a review) makes owners feel exploited and very angry. Lack of anonymity, as Claiborne says, "gives the whole business a bad reputation" (Kramer 1989:25). Some of the tension between reviewers and restaurateurs can be attributed to this problem. This is another reason why all parties are better served by reviewer anonymity.

Reviewers have a saying about bad restaurants and poor service: "Don't get mad, get published." One California diner tried to take advantage of the idea behind this aphorism. Before she began writing restaurant reviews, Ruth

Reichl was part owner of a restaurant called The Swallow in Berkeley, California. One busy evening she was back helping out when she heard that a customer was unhappy.

> It had been the policy of the collectively owned restaurant that any of the owners would respond to a customer's complaint. So when Reichl got wind in the kitchen that there was an unhappy woman in the dining room, she went out and tried to help. Her efforts didn't work. In a huff, the diner turned to Reichl and said, "Well, I'm Ruth Reichl, and I'm going to make you pay for this!" (Rohr 1993:154)

Readers are so knowledgeable about the form and processes of reviews that they use them to personal advantage to impersonate reviewers. Connoisseurial restaurant reviews are clearly a well-understood cultural form. Backed by a publication that supplies regular access to audiences, the central figure in connoisseurial reviews is a well-trained, ethical, experienced, well-informed reviewer.

## NOTES

1. This paragraph is based on the only scholarly history of restaurants (Spang 2000).

2. People ate meals outside of homes prior to the development of restaurants, especially travelers eating in taverns and inns. Typically these would serve a communal *table d'hôte*, where diners would have been given a simple fixed meal, served family style at a single large table. The closest modern equivalent would be boarding house meals. Cafés served primarily coffee, but they also supplied light meals.

After the French Revolution the abolition of guild privileges made it easier to open a restaurant. Cooks and servants of nobility who had fled formed the staff of many early restaurants. Their diners were often provincials or businessmen who were drawn to Paris during the Directory, but who had no family or home in the city. The chance to meet friends while enjoying food hitherto available only to aristocrats in private homes created a convivial atmosphere. By eating at a restaurant you could be well fed, participate in a democratic institution, meet business contacts, and have fun with friends all at the same time. This contributed to the establishment of restaurants as a permanent institution. The invention of restaurants created a new competitive environment that shifted the evolution of gastronomy from the private homes of the aristocracy to a public institution.

3. Exceptions are reviewers working for national magazines like *Gourmet* or *Food and Wine*.

4. The only prior academic work on restaurant reviews has been published in hospitality and marketing journals. There are three studies. Barrows et al. (1989) studied the effects of restaurant reviews using a convenience sample of college faculty and staff. Jolson and Bushman (1978) studied the attitudes of diners, restaurateurs, and

critics toward the restaurant critic system. Schroeder (1985) studied restaurant critics. The findings of these studies are discussed below; their methodology is described in appendix B.

5. The importance of chefs explains why, for example, Wolfgang Puck's various *Spago* restaurants or Jean Georges Vongerichten's *Vong* restaurants are not considered chains. A chain is not just a group of restaurants with the same menu.

6. Examples in Chicago include Gale Gand and Rick Tramonto leaving Trio and opening Brasserie T, or Jean Joho opening Brasserie Jo in addition to his work at Everest.

7. Although Claiborne had written several reviews in the six years since he became food editor in 1957, he began writing regular weekly reviews on May 24, 1963 (Claiborne 1963).

8. Claiborne was following *New York Times* policy, which prohibited reporters from accepting gifts from the people and organizations they covered. This is standard policy at all large publications.

9. He continued to develop his skills with weekly visits, beginning in 1959, to watch the cooking in Le Pavillon, probably the finest French restaurant in New York at the time (Franey 1994; Prial 1996).

10. For comments on multiple visits by critics, see Alva 1992; Kramer 1989; Ryan 1984:172.

11. Since Jacobs was working for a national monthly magazine, he became known slowly. What worked for him may not work as well for a reviewer writing a weekly column that is focused on a single city and is more important to the restaurateurs of that city. Jacobs's circumstances may have shielded him from some consequences of these ethical conflicts.

12. Reichl summarized her evaluation of Le Cirque by awarding three stars, one less than her predecessor. This was a major decline for a restaurant that had been regarded as one of the finest French restaurants in the country. A 1997 review raised it back to four stars (Reichl 1997b).

13. For a time, Wheaton used the name "Max Weber" on his credit card. One evening a waiter noticed the name and said, "I'm glad to meet you Mr. Weber; I liked your book on ethical Protestants." Wheaton said, "Thank you."

14. There are restaurants to which people go mostly for the ambiance; for example, the Rainforest Café chain, or Rex-Il Ristorante and Maxwell's Plum in Los Angeles, but they are exceptions (Reichl 1981; Vettel 1996c). These restaurants use their atmosphere to amuse their patrons rather than on focussing on gastronomical pleasures. Rather than "décor," perhaps a more accurate description is "entertainment." For real foodies, food itself is entertainment.

15. Escoffier had the good fortune to be chef d' cuisine at César Ritz's Grand Hotel in Monte Carlo at the moment when modern forms of travel, vacations, and tourism were being created by the wealthy and titled. As the head chef of the Ritz Development Company, he was also chef of the Ritz hotel at the Place Vendôme in Paris, and he spent twenty years at the Carlton in London. The social, financial, and cultural success of these ventures gave him a commanding presence. From these positions of visibility, through his kitchen apprenticeship training programs and his writing, Escoffier had a

major role in defining what we now think of as "classical" French cooking, service, and presentation. Along with César Ritz he also had a significant influence on restaurant decor (Herbodeau and Thalamas 1955).

16. Pierre Franey (1994:4) says, "All good cooking from peasant to haute cuisine must never lose sight of the need for complementary textures."

17. Other Chicago restaurant pairs could be used: Rick Bayless's Topolobampo and Fontera Grill, or Carlos and Deborah Nieto's restaurants Carlos and Café Central.

18. Chicago examples of restaurants catering to these three audiences are, respectively, Ed Debevic's, Geja's Café, and the Ritz-Carlton dining room.

19. In a surprising oversight, neither of these studies report collecting income or education data so they can't tell us how reading reviews varies by those key variables.

20. See appendix B for details on the surveys. The data are from 1980: Ashton (1980:84); 1981: Liesse (1981:110); 1982 and 1983: Ryan (1984:184).

21. The data are in 2002 dollars. The original 1981 household expenditures on restaurant dining were: Average $27.79 per week, Very Heavy Spenders $50 per week. Inflation adjustments are from *The Economic Report of the President,* table B-61, column "Food Away from Home" (Council of Economic Advisors 2002:396). The ratio of price indices is (2002 index)/(1981 index) or 173.0/90.9 1.903, which was used to calculate 2002 dollars.

22. Mimi Sheraton tells a similar story about someone pretending to be her (Sheraton 1990).

# Chapter Four

# Procedural Reviews: Statistical Software

In the early days I didn't know much about marketing and I couldn't afford to hire someone who did. [Our competitors] were bigger and better financed, but we got better reviews. They were a big sales boost and a morale boost, but it was more than that; people who read the reviews got excited about [the product]. They called me up to ask for a job. [Other publications] took notice and published reviews. I can't overstate how important those independent reviews were. They made the company.

—From an interview with a software executive.

Unlike the impact of restaurants reviews, no one has died, committed suicide, or had manure dumped on them as a result of a software review. Reviews certainly have caused anguish and turmoil. They have favored some products and weakened others. Reputations, identity, and status are always in play. In these aspects, procedural reviews are similar to connoisseurial reviews. In other aspects they differ. Since a single person writes connoisseurial reviews, the review process is mostly an invisible black box. Because procedural reviews involve multiple people, the review process has multiple stages and contingencies. Procedural reviews are more diverse textually, and the central ethical problems are more complicated.

This chapter follows the arc of a procedural software review, from conception, to testing the software, through writing the review, ending with reception. To help readers keep the major players in mind, table 4.1 summarizes the major software publications and reviewers.

**Table 4.1.　Software Publications and People**

*American Statistician*: An official journal of the American Statistical Association. It publishes regular software reviews and has a software reviews editor.

*eWeek*: A weekly controlled circulation magazine covering the computer industry. Primarily written for corporate IT professionals. Named *PC Week* until 1999. Published by Ziff-Davis Media.

*InfoWorld*: A weekly controlled-circulation magazine covering the computer industry. Primarily written for corporate IT professionals. Published by IDG.

*PC Magazine*: A personal computer magazine primarily written for business. Known for extensive performance testing of hardware and software in comparative reviews. Published twenty-two times per year by Ziff-Davis Media.

Raskin, Robin: Editor of *PC Magazine* during its 1993 review of statistical software. A consultant for the 1987 *PC Magazine* statistical software review. Publisher of *FamilyPC* magazine 1997–2001. A key informant on publications, software, and hardware reviews.

Stevenson, Ted: Senior editor (software) for *PC Magazine*, 1992–1996. Editor in charge of the 1993 *PC Magazine* review of statistical software. A key informant for information on publications, software, and hardware reviews.

## CHOOSING SOFTWARE

Choosing the products to review is the crucial first step. In contrast to connoisseurial reviews, procedural reviews explicitly compare products. The 1993 *PC Magazine* statistical software reviews examined thirteen major products, which were chosen because they provided "heavy-duty data analysis and a wide breadth of statistical functions" (Canter 1993:228). Who makes these decisions? The editor. For popular product categories like word processing or spreadsheets, editors use their personal experience. They also depend on the history of reviews. "We keep records—good records—and we depend on them to select the vendors for the next review," said an editor. For technical categories like statistical software, they depend on the advice of consultants. All magazines receive a continuous stream of information in press releases from product makers, and they receive reader mail. Editors attend software trade shows and often receive private product briefings from vendors. Like connoisseurial reviewers, software editors are at the center of a network of information. One editor said bluntly, "We tend to gather the most review-worthy products and that involves a lot of arbitrary judgment that we don't try to rationalize beyond giving our readers at least the criteria that we use."[1]

What makes a product "review-worthy"? For many publications, popularity is primary. They review market-leading products or products from market-leading companies. Some, like *PC Magazine*, try to be comprehensive and review every product in a category. More often magazines just want to review the top few products. One way to limit the number of products is by defining the category in very precise ways. One magazine reviewed "comprehensive statistics packages costing more than \$500," a restriction that simplified their task by neatly removing two products with a list price of \$495. While most commercial magazines review entire products, the editor at the *American Statistician* designs comparative reviews along functional categories, for example, as in the mixed models ANOVA review (Schwarz 1993), which reviewed BMDP8V, the SAS GLM and VARCOMP procedures, and SPSS MANOVA, or a review of weighting in different products. Once the products are chosen, the software is assembled and evaluated.

## EVALUATING THE PRODUCT

*PC Magazine* is probably the world's most successful computing magazine, with a 2003 circulation of over 1.2 million readers and a readership of over 6 million. A major element of its success is extensive procedural reviews.[2] Since pages are directly related to costs, the way pages are allocated reveals priorities. In a typical issue of *PC Magazine*, published on May 11, 1993, over 48 percent of the issue was devoted to major comparative reviews and another 11 percent to other reviews.[3] This issue was chosen because it contains a major procedural review of statistical software; it is otherwise typical of issues published during the last fifteen years. According to *PC Magazine* editors, focus groups and reader surveys say that the most important reason for reading the magazine is the comparative reviews. Because of the reader response to *PC Magazine* reviews, this chapter pays considerable attention to the characteristics of *PC Magazine*'s reviewing process, although there are frequent references to other publications.[4]

### Division of Labor

*PC Magazine* reviews are the product of a team of collaborators with a well-defined division of labor. Each team has at least five roles; some roles may be occupied by more than one person. Editorial researchers handle routine administration: asking product makers to send the products, checking facts with product makers (a big job), and compiling the features table. Support technicians set up and manage performance testing, especially in computer hardware reviews. They also oversee and assist in the suitability-to-task testing. Staff editors edit the review copy and coordinate editorial activities with production. Project leaders create the performance testing script and the suitability-to-task script. They oversee testing, and scrutinize and interpret the results. They write explanations of the methodology and the findings.

The person responsible for the entire project is an associate editor. Editors determine which products will be included in the review. They create the reviewer's guidelines, design the features table, and collaborate on setting the suitability-to-task tests. They determine every story element in the review. They assign stories, picking reviewers and the author of the review overview. They are responsible for making everything work when copy begins to flow in. They write sundry other story elements. Finally, in consultation with the reviewers and other staff, they select the Editors' Choice product(s) and usually write the Editors' Choice sidebar.

Reviews requiring special technical expertise—like statistical software—have two additional roles. Contributing editors are usually freelance writers who are called in because of their expertise on the subject matter. They help edit the reviews and often write the introductory overview. Finally, reviewers follow the test script and write the reviews based on their experiences testing the product. Reviewers are usually temporary, contract employees.

*PC Magazine* publishes twenty-two issues per year and most issues include one to three comparative reviews, each discussing, typically, five to thirty products. Hardware reviews may include sixty or more products like, for example, a review of laptops (Howard 1997). The complex division of labor evolved because of the need to produce reviews of a large number of products in a short time. Since time is short, labor has to be divided so that various tasks can be accomplished simultaneously. An associate editor may be working on as many as four comparative reviews at a time. An editor said, "*PC Magazine* must have multiple reviewers in order to be timely."[5]

Here we see several striking contrasts to the single-product reviews characteristic of the connoisseurial process; reviewing multiple products in a short time has consequences: it creates the need for a complex division of labor and for multiple reviewers. These, in turn, influence other characteristics of the procedural review process. The presence of multiple reviewers influences the way that the evaluations are conducted. Consistency among reviewers becomes a problem. The next sections discuss these issues.

## Evaluation and Testing

*PC Magazine*, like other procedural review organizations, attempts to produce an objective foundation for an evaluation. Objective in this sense means reproducible by someone else following the same methodology; and *PC Magazine* staff thinks of its work explicitly using the word *methodology.*" The review methodology calls for profiles of each product from three perspectives: features, performance, and suitability-to-task. There are various components to each of these profiles. Briefly, *features* are the capabilities of a product. In a review of statistical software, examples include: can the software do multiple regression? Multidimensional scaling? Power analysis? Features are discussed in several parts of the review, including a large table, called the features table, discussed below.

"Performance," said one editor, "is where *PC Magazine* comes from; the magazine built its reputation on performance reviews." *Performance* means the speed with which the software can perform different tasks.[6] Software performance testing is not common because it is difficult and time consuming for many kinds of software. Further, it is often unclear what sort of performance is critical to large numbers of readers. For example, what speed issues would concern a word processing user? The answer is that, in recent years, it is hard to find any that matter. There is software where standard performance issues are well understood. A good example is databases; every database has had to perform standard tasks for several decades.[7] Performance testing is an extremely important part of hardware reviews.

The third perspective, *suitability-to-task*, is a more recent addition. An editor explains:

> It arose out of the realization that software is about performing tasks. To do a fair analysis of the product you have to be able to decide which tasks the product is really designed for and you have to measure how good the product is at doing the tasks.

Both parts of this twofold analysis—tasks and measurement—cause a great deal of discussion and disagreement. There are always some users, possibly many users, for whom the key tasks are different than the ones chosen. This is particularly true for products with diverse groups of users, like statistical software. The results do not always seem worth the effort. An editor said, "The tasks are sometimes kind of innocuous. When we did the [1993] stats story we talked at great length and we finally came up with 'basic statistics' and 'advanced statistics.'"[8] A recent review of personal databases compares "ease" and "power" (Dreier 2003).

Suitability-to-task evaluations are based primarily on test scripts. Test scripts are formal written documents sent to reviewers that specify a series of steps the reviewers are to follow as they test a product. Consultants and the associate editor in charge of the story usually write test scripts. For the 1993 statistical software reviews, the test script was twenty pages long. It was accompanied by several datasets and it asked reviewers to take the software through three scenarios: data management, statistical, and reporting problems. The scenarios were specific and detailed, telling exactly how transformations were to be performed, what files were to be combined, how variables were to be labeled, what procedures were to be run, and what output was to be examined. The statistical scenario included descriptive statistics, cross-tabs, regression, reliability analysis, and robust regression, plus graphical analyses. If the software was capable of performing all the data management, statistical, and reporting steps and was not unusually badly designed, I estimate that a reviewer who was not familiar with it could have completed the test script scenarios in perhaps eight to twelve hours.

In addition to providing a basis for suitability-to-task tests, test scripts also provide a firm personal experience to serve as a foundation upon which reviewers can base their reviews. How this works is best illustrated by my experience during the 1993 *PC Magazine* review. In that review the test script problems revealed several weaknesses in the product I was reviewing.[9] As I tried to complete the test script I spent, not eight to twelve hours, but three days struggling to work around the weaknesses; even then the software could not complete significant portions of the test script. Adding to my frustration was the fact that I was being paid a flat fee regardless of how much time I needed to write the review. Plus, I knew several other statistical software products where I could have completed the test script in much less time with much less need to work around flaws in the product. As a result, I considered these problems major flaws.

During the review, I had extended conversations with the president of the company. In these conversations he made strenuous, repeated attempts to convince me that he had a great product. Nonetheless, I was frustrated by the time I had spent and by the inability of the product to complete even the relatively straightforward tests in the test script.[10] My personal experience outweighed all the talk. The test scripts implicitly say to reviewers that the items being tested are important issues worth close attention. If the product cannot easily complete portions of the tests or is unable to complete them at all, then this is a clear indication of significant weakness. My feeling was that it was a reasonable test script and the product hadn't done so well; that's what the review reported.

My experience was echoed by editors. There is extensive, continuous contact between editors and product makers, regardless of whether a review is in progress. An editor says,

> They bombard us constantly with press releases and product literature. They come to our office to demo new versions.

How much influence does this have on the review?

> This conversation is very important for us and for [the magazine]. It keeps us up to date on the products, the industry, and the evolution of the market. . . . But it

doesn't have much influence on our reviews. Test scripts and test results are much more important. We hear from vendors all the time, and they tell us all kinds of things about their products. But the testing tells the real story. We pay attention to the test results in the reviews.

The testing is decisive in vendor attempts to influence the review.

Vendors sometimes call us during a review. I check out any possible problems with the reviewer. . . . If he or she can quote test results that pretty much settles it for me.

Test scripts, and testing in general, help solve one of the crucial problems in a comparative multi-product review: ensuring that multiple reviewers use consistent criteria.

## Consistency

Consistency is the extent to which the identical criteria are used in reviews of several products. Consistency is important because, if different reviewers were to apply different criteria to evaluate products, then the evaluations would not be comparable. One editor says, "All products and reviewers have to have uniform criteria and testing procedures so that results are consistent." If the proponents and vendors of the low-rated products could point to inconsistent criteria, they could convincingly complain that the review was unfair and biased against them. This damage can easily spread to spoil the credibility of every evaluation in the review.

The editors tend to be very sensitive to these problems. If anyone, often a product maker, doesn't like the review, then the editors will bear the brunt of the phone calls and the meetings to decide what to do. Reviewers, typically freelance, usually won't be involved, except they would be asked to justify what they have written. Second, editors are responsible for editing the text so all the reviews have a single, common voice. If the reviewers don't write using the same criteria, then the editor's task will become more difficult and time-consuming. Since editors are typically extremely pressed for time, this is a significant consideration. Third, since everyone knows that the game is to produce evaluative reviews that allow some products to be declared the best—the winners—if the reviews flow into the publication based on inconsistent criteria, this tends to cast doubt on the professional abilities of the editors. Repeated problems like this do not look good at performance- and salary-review time.

Written test scripts are part of the solution. Test scripts ensure that all reviewers have common experiences upon which to base their evaluations.

Written procedures produce highly reproducible results. Presumably any competent person following the same test script would obtain the same results. Test scripts are an attempt to make reviewers more standardized and interchangeable. But as one editor said, "It's important that the testing procedures be uniform so that results can be objectively compared. But I can tell you from that experience that, while it helps, it doesn't ensure consistency or uniformity. Ultimately you're dealing with the mind and personality of the reviewer." Here the editor plays a role.

The other important link in *PC Magazine*'s quest for consistency is the associate editor in charge of the review. Editors see all of the text and they are responsible for assuring that the reviews do in fact reflect consistent application of the same criteria. They have the authority to change the entire review. Moving paragraphs, adding clarifying material, removing redundancies, and improving grammar and sentence construction are all typical changes. There are cases where editors, in the interest of consistency, completely rewrite the review, although the reviewer's byline remains. In technical software, like statistics, editors usually change text only after consultation with the reviewer or with a technical consultant. For less technical software like word processors, personal finance, or antivirus software, editors are typically less hesitant. As far as determining the final published text, editors are often more important than reviewers.[11]

## Ethics

Credibility and ethics are as central for procedural reviews as they are for connoisseurial. Conflict of interest continues to be the foremost concern. Since restaurant meals are performances, anonymity and strong rules against taking gifts suffice to limit potential conflicts. Because of the technical requirements of procedural reviews, reviewers often have a background in the industry they review.[12] This creates various possibilities for contact between reviewers and product makers; consequently, ethical issues are more complex in procedural reviews.

### Independence and Conflict of Interest

*Independence* refers to the extent to which reviewers have some interest in the outcome that conflicts with their interest in a fair and accurate review. As in connoisseurial reviews, typical sources of conflict of interest include a history of paid work for the product maker or accepting gifts from the product maker. These cause conflicts because they may bias the reviewer to judge the product more favorably, and the resulting review reflects the product maker's self-interest in selling the product. I use the terms *independence* and *conflict of interest* interchangeably. Software reviews and reviewers are a good site to study independence because the peculiar characteristics of software and the characteristics of the software industry illuminate the complexities of the issue more clearly than do, say, consumer appliances or restaurants.

Some review organizations maintain their independence by never allowing the vendor to know that the product is being reviewed. Famously, Consumers Union buys every product that it reviews on the retail market like any other consumer. By not obtaining a free review copy directly from the manufacturer, Consumers Union avoids the suspicion that the manufacturer gave it special attention, producing a defect-free copy or a copy specially tuned to the requirements of the review. In other words, a free review copy may be a product that had been altered in some important ways that made it unlike the product available to an ordinary consumer.[13]

Statistical software, like most products, is used by several different audiences; for example, the statistics needed for sample surveys are largely different from the statistics used to analyze designed experiments. These are only two of ten or more audiences whose statistical needs are largely separate.[14] Since no product serves all needs, knowing which audiences it is intended to serve is critical to an accurate assessment of its capabilities. While documentation may talk about some audiences, in most cases the only way a reviewer can learn the intended audiences is to talk to the product maker directly. *PC Magazine*'s Reviewers' Guide for the 1993 statistical software reviews specifically instructs reviewers to contact product makers:

> Get some background on each product's genesis, the vendor's view of its position and role in the marketplace, and, yes, the vendor's perspective on their competition. Ask them what their product's most important features are. More important, probe gently for the vendor's view of where their product fits into the overall stat picture.

> You should feel free to contact the vendor at any time; these reviews are not conducted in secrecy. However, never send your evaluation to the vendor, and never discuss the specifics of benchmark, performance, or suitability-to-task tests or whether you're going to recommend the product as an Editors' Choice. (*PC Magazine* 1993a:3)

Notice, first, that uncertainties about the product maker's position in the market are a measure of the fluidity of certain software markets, where product categories are not well defined and where products may shift categories from year to year. Second, the instructions imply that the competing products change as product features shift from release to release. This describes how upgrades can change the competition. Third, which features are important may also change from version to version and as the market changes. Fourth, although some products have broad capabilities, they are perceived by their product makers as particularly strong in one area (e.g., quality control); they try to sell to that audience, and they want to be evaluated on their strengths.

Although software reviewers could buy software and review it in total anonymity, in many cases they are able to write a more useful review if they are not anonymous. Comparisons to other products will be more accurate, and important features will be more clearly identified and evaluated. The software that can be reviewed, like typical *Consumer Reports* reviews of cars and consumer durable products, has characteristics implied above: the companies remain stable, the audiences for the software are stable, product features change relatively slowly, and the other products in a category are stable. By the late 1990s, some major software categories had matured to the point where upgrades added only minor enhancements and their audience was unchanging; examples include tax preparation software and word processors.[15] For less mature software, audiences and competition are not always obvious. Statistical software could be effectively reviewed anonymously, but only if reviewers focus on the market-leading products like SAS, SPSS, or Systat, and common procedures like frequency tables or regression.

Statistical software is complex and technical; the knowledge required to write an accurate evaluation is not widespread. Potential reviewers have day jobs, often with links to the product makers they might review. For example, potential reviewers may be beta testers, or they may have written articles for a company or user group newsletter, may have written an academic paper that was used by a product maker, or may have written similar software.[16] This sort of experience can improve a review because an experienced reviewer can write a much more sophisticated assessment, but it creates the possibility that a reviewer's independence may be compromised. A typical solution to this problem is to restrict reviewers to reviewing products where they have neither been paid by the product maker for work on the product nor have otherwise participated in the design of the product. This takes advantage of their experience while it eliminates the most significant sources of potential bias.[17]

From the reviewer's point of view, this is a good solution. It resolves ethical and credibility problems, and it resolves another conflict of interest: between reviewers and product makers. For example: I have been a consultant for SPSS and I could write very good reviews of several SPSS products; I know their strengths and weaknesses well. I could write a concise, informative, balanced summary and assessment, better than most reviews I've read. I do not want to write this review. The problem is if I wrote a critical review my criticisms could irritate people at SPSS. It's not worth damaging professional and personal relationships over a review. If I wrote a favorable review it would be too easy to dismiss it with the thought, "He's just writing nice things because they paid him." There's no point to writing anything that can be rejected so easily. I have in fact declined invitations to review SPSS products.

Whatever the state of ethics of large magazines, smaller publications often have lower standards. With small circulations, low pay for contributors, and the difficulty of finding publishable contributions, they are often happy to print anything they can get. Some small publications have been known to print reviews originally written by product maker marketing staff, but rewritten by another author whose byline is on the printed article.[18] As far as I know this practice is unusual even in small publications, but it brings us to the complicated subject of relations between reviewers and product makers.

## Relationships with Product Makers

Since statistical software reviews are not anonymous, product makers and reviewers often spend considerable amounts of time talking. On a personal level, product makers recognize the power of reviewers and they usually treat reviewers with deference, respect, and attention. For important reviews, product makers sometimes go to extraordinary lengths to assist reviewers. A product maker described one difficult review:

> [The reviewer] had a slow, old computer and an ancient printer. It was a marginal setup for [our software]. He wasn't technically proficient enough to handle the problems he had on his own and our technical support wasn't very helpful because we had no real information on a computer that old. . . . He began to be irritated and started to blame us. Our marketing department went out and bought a used machine exactly like his. . . . They duplicated his entire setup so they could tell him exactly how to make something work. Then marketing formed a task force that met almost every morning during the review to discuss how they could keep him going with the least trouble. We may have had the equivalent of two full time people working constantly on that review for weeks.

This exceptional effort was rewarded with a favorable review in an influential publication. The marketing people look back with satisfaction on a successful project.

"Failure" is the view of the editor and the reviewer on this project. The editor said that the review had not arrived in good shape. He rewrote most of it although the reviewer's byline remained. In retrospect, the editor said bluntly that the reviewer was incompetent and should never have been chosen. I asked the reviewer, a well-known social scientist, for his reaction. He had no complaints about the product maker, but he felt he had been misled by the publication about the timing and difficulty of the review.[19] He was very angry and swore that he would never write for the publication again.

Experienced product makers usually prepare a reviewer's guide. This is a standard marketing document that points out the best features of the product so the reviewer will take them into account in the review. A marketing manager says that reviewer's guides have a simple goal: "These guides are designed to produce favorable reviews. When I write one, I explain what we are trying to do with the new version and I highlight five or six new features that I am absolutely positive work like they should." The guides do not mention any features that are prone to malfunction. "I try to keep reviewers' attention away from all the features that are shaky and could crash the program." The reviewer's guide is sent with every review copy and it is often available on corporate web sites.

Sophisticated product makers realize that their products will be discussed in many reviews. The same reviewer will often review each new version. Repeated reviews mean that many product makers keep files on publications and reviewers. They learn to know the idiosyncrasies of each reviewer, their strengths and weaknesses. They try to manage the relationship to their benefit. They deal with a sophisticated reviewer very differently than a weak one. A skilled reviewer will often find out product weaknesses and often knows competing products so that he can judge where a product lags behind the competition. It is good policy for the maker to admit these problems and turn the conversation to design tradeoffs or how the flaws will be fixed in the next version. A marketing person commented on one strong reviewer, "We listen to his comments and we always tell him when we implemented one of his suggestions in the current version." A weak reviewer will be guided more directly. The same marketing person named several reviewers whom he considered marginal and said,

> We tell them what to write about and how [our product] compares to [other products] on those features. They often take our suggestions. . . . I am surprised how often I see one of my sentences printed in a review without quotation marks.

Editors clearly see this problem. It is a major reason why skilled reviewers are desirable. This creates the ethical dilemma discussed above, since skilled reviewers are likely to have ties to product makers. These ethical issues are only the prelude to the part of the review that is visible to everyone, the written text.

## WRITING A PROCEDURAL REVIEW

In general, reviews consist of a summary and an evaluation. In procedural reviews, both the summary and the evaluation have multiple, explicit subcomponents. *PC Magazine* and *InfoWorld* are typical, although we describe other publications where useful.

### Components of Procedural Reviews

Procedural reviews of software are a complex collection of articles, ratings, and sidebars. Table 4.2 summarizes two typical reviews. Each has the same set of articles: an introduction, a methods article, a summary of winners, a performance summary, a features table, and several sidebars.[20] It is sufficiently complex that readers need guidance; to help them, the first page of the introduction to the review has a table of contents. These are not unusually complex efforts. On November 13, 1995, *InfoWorld* published its comparative review of 32-bit operating systems: OS/2 Warp Connect version 3, Windows 95, and Windows NT Workstation 3.51. The review included nineteen separate articles, stretching over fourteen tabloid-size pages, and the testing and writing team had nine people (Petreley 1995a).

Summaries are unknown in connoisseurial reviews, but table 4.2 shows that procedural reviews summarize products from several points of view.

### Summaries

Many publications print 750-word reviews of products that install over 100 megabytes of files and contain over 1,000 pages of documentation (if it were printed instead of on CD-ROM). Since reviews are already extremely condensed, one might think that further condensation was unnecessary. One would be wrong. Extensive effort goes into writing additional, even shorter summaries—features tables, numerical summaries, and textual summaries—and, often, giving awards to noteworthy products. Each summary offers a different perspective.

### *Features Tables*

Almost every comparative review includes a large summary table of product features. An example from *InfoWorld* (Fridlund 1990a) is in figure 4.1. Features tables list the products under review in alphabetical order across the top and the features down the side. A black box in a cell indicates that the product has the feature, an open box or a gray box means it does not. In short, features tables are checklists.

**Table 4.2.  Components of Comparative Reviews**

| | Typical Article Titles in Reviews of Statistical Software | |
|---|---|---|
| Type of Article | PC Magazine | InfoWorld |
| Introduction to the review | Stat of the art | Number-crunching statistics software |
| How products were tested | Suitability-to-task: Statistics software | Crunching the number crunchers: a complex task |
| Summary of outcome | Editors' choice | Executive summary |
| Summary of product performance on tests | Suitability-to-task (box included in each review) | Report card |
| Features table | Summary of features | Features |
| Other products described in sidebars[21] | SAS Institute Windows product; S-Plus for Windows | Other software programs for statistics data management (descriptions of 6 "narrowly focused" products) |
| Total number of articles (not including reviews) | 6 | 5 |
| Total number of reviews | 13 | 4 |
| Total number of pages | 25 | 10 (tabloid-size) |
| Sources: | Canter (1993) | Fridlund (1990a) |

Why do features tables exist? The extreme condensation of the text means that most features can't be discussed. Yet, different audiences often have very specific requirements. Recognizing this, publications print a list of as many specific features as space allows. They hope that as many audiences as possible will be able to find what they need. Thus, features tables exist because they solve one of the problems created by a short review of a big product. They summarize the breadth of the products under review.

The editors in consultation with in-house experts or consultants decide which features to list in the table. For statistical software reviews, outside consultants are most important. A key role for the editor is editing the final table down to manageable size to fit the available page space. A research associate usually compiles the features table. The reviewer would be called only in the event of a conflict with the product maker. The characteristic of most features in the tables is that their presence or absence can be determined relatively unambiguously: a product can read comma-delimited files or it cannot, it can produce frequency tables or it can't. An error in a features table is embarrassing and casts doubt on the more subtle parts of a review. Thus, the

**FEATURES**     **INFO WORLD**

## Statistical Software

| | Minitab Version 7.1 | SPSS/PC+ Version 3.1 | Statgraphics Version 4.0 | Systat/Sygraph Version 4.1 |
|---|---|---|---|---|
| **Analysis of variance (Anova)** | | | | |
| Analysis of covariance (Ancova) | ■ | ■ | ■ | ■ |
| Latin-Square design | ■ | opt. | □ | ■ |
| Multiway factorial | ■ | ■ | ■ | ■ |
| Nested designs | ■ | ■ | ■ | ■ |
| Planned comparisons | □ | ■ | □ | ■ |
| Post-hoc comparisons | □ | ■ | ■ | ■ |
| Repeated measures | ■ | opt. | L | ■ |
| Split-plot designs | ■ | opt. | L | ■ |
| Unbalanced designs | ■ | ■ | ■ | ■ |
| **Batch/Command files** | ■ | ■ | ■ | ■ |
| **Cluster analysis** | □ | opt. | ■ | ■ |
| **Contingency tables** | | | | |
| Chi-square tests | ■ | ■ | ■ | ■ |
| Multiway tables | ■ | ■ | L | ■ |
| Other tests | □ | ■ | ■ | ■ |
| **Correlation** | | | | |
| Fisher's r-to-z transform | □ | □ | □ | ■ |
| Partial correlations | L | ■ | ■ | ■ |
| Pearson correlations | ■ | ■ | ■ | ■ |
| Spearman rank-order | L | ■ | ■ | ■ |
| **Custom programmable menus** | □ | L;opt. | ■ | ■ |
| **Data handling** | | | | |
| Conditional case selection | ■ | ■ | ■ | ■ |
| Computed variables | ■ | ■ | ■ | ■ |
| Flexible file input formats | ■ | ■ | ■ | ■ |
| Joins data files | ■ | ■ | ■ | ■ |
| Merges data files | ■ | ■ | ■ | ■ |
| Missing values | ■ | ■ | ■ | ■ |
| Reads/writes ASCII files | ■ | ■ | ■ | ■ |
| Reads/writes Lotus/Dbase files | L | ■ | ■ | ■ |
| Searches for cases | ■ | ■ | ■ | ■ |
| Sorts cases/variables | ■ | ■ | ■ | ■ |
| Split data files | ■ | ■ | ■ | ■ |
| Spreadsheet data editor | ■ | opt. | ■ | ■ |
| Transformations | ■ | ■ | ■ | ■ |
| Transpose data | ■ | ■ | ■ | ■ |
| Variable labels | ■ | ■ | ■ | ■ |
| **Format** | | | | |
| Can use math coprocessor | ■ | ■ | ■ | ■ |
| Works on floppy-based PC | □[1] | L,opt. | ■ | ■ |
| **Graphics** | | | | |
| Graph types | | | | |
| Axonometric plots | L | □ | L | ■ |
| Box-and-Whisker plots | ■ | ■ | ■ | ■ |
| Casement plots | □ | □ | ■ | ■ |
| Chernoff faces | □ | □ | □ | ■ |
| Contour (density) plots | ■ | ■ | ■ | ■ |
| Histograms/frequencies | ■ | ■ | ■ | ■ |
| 3D histograms | □ | opt. | ■ | ■ |
| Line graphs | ■ | ■ | ■ | ■ |
| Logarithmic/semi-log plots | ■ | opt. | ■ | ■ |
| Pie charts | □ | ■ | ■ | ■ |
| Probability/cumul. prob. plots | □ | ■ | ■ | ■ |
| Scatter plots | ■ | ■ | ■ | ■ |
| Stem-and-Leaf plots | ■ | ■ | ■ | ■ |
| X-Y-Z plots | □ | □ | ■ | ■ |
| Stat. process/quality control | ■ | □ | ■ | □ |

SOURCE: PRODUCT EVALUATION/SOFTWARE MANUFACTURERS
■ = Feature exists; L = Feature present in basic package, but with limited capacity; □ = Feature does not exist; opt. = Feature available optionally.
[1] The previous version of Minitab, Release 6.1, is still being sold and does work on a floppy-based system.

---

**FEATURES**     **INFO WORLD**

## Statistical Software

| | Minitab Version 7.1 | SPSS/PC+ Version 3.1 | Statgraphics Version 4.0 | Systat/Sygraph Version 4.1 |
|---|---|---|---|---|
| (Graphics continued) Graph Features | | | | |
| Color graphics support | ■ | ■ | ■ | ■ |
| EGA/VGA support | ■ | ■ | ■ | ■ |
| Error bars | □ | opt. | ■ | ■ |
| Flexible chart sizing | ■ | opt. | L | ■ |
| Free-form text pos./orient. | □ | opt. | ■ | ■ |
| Mouse support | □ | opt. | ■ | ■ |
| Multiple text fonts/sizes | □ | opt. | L | ■ |
| Overlaid plots | □ | opt. | ■ | ■ |
| Plotter support | ■ | opt. | ■ | ■ |
| **Linear prog./Simplex algorithm** | □ | □ | ■ | □ |
| **Log-Linear models** | □ | ■ | ■ | ■ |
| **Macintosh versions avail.** | ■ | ■ | □ | ■ |
| **Mainframe/workstat. (Unix) versions avail.** | ■ | ■ | □ | ■ |
| **Multidimensional scaling** | □ | ■ | □ | ■ |
| **Multivariate analysis** | | | | |
| Analysis of covariance (Mancova) | □ | opt. | □ | ■ |
| Analysis of variance (Manova) | L | opt. | □ | ■ |
| Axis rotations | □ | opt. | ■ | L |
| Canonical correlation | □ | opt. | ■ | ■ |
| Discriminant analysis | ■ | opt. | ■ | ■ |
| Factor analysis | □ | opt. | ■ | ■ |
| Factorial Manovas | □ | opt. | □ | ■ |
| Hoteling's T-Squared | □ | ■ | □ | ■ |
| LISREL | □ | □ | □ | □ |
| Multivariate classification | □ | opt. | ■ | ■ |
| Planned multivariate comparisons | □ | opt. | □ | ■ |
| Post-hoc multivariate comparisons | □ | opt. | □ | ■ |
| Principal-component analysis | ■ | opt. | ■ | ■ |
| Repeated-measures Manovas | □ | opt. | □ | ■ |
| **Nonparametric tests** | | | | |
| Chi-square | ■ | ■ | ■ | ■ |
| Fisher's exact test | □ | ■ | ■ | ■ |
| Friedman Anova-by-ranks | ■ | ■ | ■ | ■ |
| Kendall's Tau | □ | ■ | ■ | ■ |
| Kruskal-Wallis | ■ | ■ | ■ | ■ |
| Mann-Whitney U | ■ | ■ | ■ | ■ |
| Wilcoxon | ■ | ■ | ■ | ■ |
| **On-line help** | ■ | ■ | ■ | ■ |
| **Path/latent variable analysis** | □ | □ | □ | opt. |
| **Regression** | | | | |
| Logistic | □ | ■ | □ | opt. |
| Nonlinear | □ | ■ | L | ■ |
| Residuals analysis | ■ | ■ | ■ | ■ |
| Simultaneous ridge | □ | □ | ■ | ■ |
| Standard multiple | ■ | ■ | ■ | ■ |
| Stepwise | ■ | ■ | ■ | ■ |
| **Reliability/Test item analysis** | □ | opt. | ■ | opt. |
| **Session log file** | ■ | ■ | L | ■ |
| **Survival analysis** | □ | □ | □ | opt. |
| **T-Tests** | | | | |
| Independent | ■ | ■ | ■ | ■ |
| Matched pairs | ■ | ■ | ■ | ■ |
| **Time-series analysis** | | | | |
| Autocorrelation | ■ | opt. | ■ | ■ |
| Auto spectral analysis | □ | opt. | L | □ |
| Box-Jenkins ARIMA models | ■ | opt. | ■ | ■ |
| Cross correlation | ■ | opt. | ■ | ■ |
| Cross spectral analysis | □ | opt. | □ | ■ |
| Data tapering/smoothing | □ | opt. | ■ | ■ |
| Fast Fourier transformation | □ | opt. | ■ | ■ |
| Partial autocorrelation | □ | opt. | ■ | ■ |

SOURCE: PRODUCT EVALUATION/SOFTWARE MANUFACTURERS
■ = Feature exists; L = Feature present in basic package, but with limited capacity; □ = Feature does not exist; opt. = Feature available optionally.

**Figure 4.1. Features Table**
Source: Fridlund 1990a:61

features table is one part that product makers may be asked to verify before publication.

Features tables are only one of several summaries. They focus on the characteristics of the product. Other summaries are more closely linked to the experience of the reviewers. In many reviews, reviewers are responsible for providing numerical scores on various criteria.

## Numerical Ratings

Numerical ratings are a major component of most procedural software reviews. They allow the different aspects of a product to be explicitly weighted and summed into an overall rating. This makes the criteria on which the evaluation is based more transparent to readers. *PC Magazine* (1993a:4) explains that ratings "provide objective, quantified evaluations of what a product is good at." There are many different procedures for generating and displaying numerical ratings. We discuss typical examples.

An enormous amount of work goes into creating the numerical ratings. Being explicit about criteria is difficult, as is creating criteria that can be numerically scored, and the assignment of weights is another potential source of problems. If these problems can be overcome, the additional clarity may be extremely valuable. Stewart Alsop (1994a), editor in chief of *InfoWorld*, makes the case for the value of numerical scores:

> We believe that scoring products in our reviews and product comparisons is a key value for readers. Scoring products is incredibly difficult to do, as evidenced by the decision of one of our competitors to discontinue the practice earlier this year. But our readers tell us over and over that our product scores are one of the few independent sources they have for making product decisions and that it demonstrates our willingness to stand up and say what we believe.

The difficulties involved in creating explicit criteria and assigning weights are resolved in several ways. Until a recent remake, *InfoWorld* conducted opinion surveys of its readers and used readers' priorities brought to light in the surveys as the basis for its weights and the criteria. "Weightings represent average relative importance to *InfoWorld* readers involved in purchasing and using that product category" (*InfoWorld* 1995). *PC Magazine* and *eWeek* use in-house expertise, or if necessary outside consultants, to establish criteria. Product makers have no role here. I know of no instances where any product maker participated in creation of the criteria.

Items used for numerical scores do not refer to individual features; instead, they cover the broader ability of a product to perform a task. Because they cover broad capabilities, they ask questions that cannot be answered with a simple *Yes* or *No*. *InfoWorld* scores products on a six-category scale: excellent, very good, good, satisfactory, poor, and unacceptable or not applicable. The reviewers attempt to map the capabilities of products to the scoring as clearly as possible. In some cases, the criteria are precise to the point where the testing results leave no room for reviewer discretion. The rating consists of simply measuring performance and reporting the result. No statistical software review reaches this point; however, other software reviews do. Typically, the most precise testing is done on more measurable characteristics of a product, such as speed and capacity. For example, here is *InfoWorld*'s (1995:114) explanation of speed ratings for its review of 32-bit operating systems:

> We logged the speed of six tasks—modem download, floppy copy, word processing, database, File Transfer Protocol (FTP) download, and spreadsheet—running one at a time on each 32-bit OS, and compared them to the speed running on Windows for Workgroups 3.11. . . .

> To receive a score of satisfactory, a product had to run three out of six applications faster than Windows for Workgroups 3.11 by an average of at least 20 percent. If a product ran six out of six applications faster than Windows for Workgroups 3.11 by at least 30 percent, it received an excellent. Products that could run four or five applications at least 20 percent faster than Windows for Workgroups 3.11 earned scores of good and very good, respectively. Products that could only run two applications 20 percent faster than Windows for Workgroups 3.11 earned a score of poor. We gave a score of unacceptable if a product was incapable of running at least two applications faster.

In its evaluation of "security levels" *InfoWorld* even created a Guttman scale (without using that name) to determine how to score different products.

The key to assigning numerical scores is the procedure used to derive the scores. The result is a strong emphasis on methodology. Every review describes methodology in a "How we tested" article. The point is to be clear to readers how the results—and the evaluations—were obtained. The argument is that in principle anyone using the identical procedure would obtain identical results. Readers are to conclude that they don't have to test because the reviewer has done it for them. Bill Machrone (1993) loves his job:

> Staying at the forefront of technology is great fun, but it burns off the days and hours as if they were nothing. Believe me, you don't want any of your employees to spend their time this way. The whole point of folks like me bleeding all over the cutting edge is so you won't have to.

The extensive methodology is designed to produce results that are reproducible. If the test results are reproducible, then reviewers also achieve other goals. Notably the criteria used to evaluate all the products in the review will be consistent. In fact, reviewers can apply the same criteria to reviews published months apart and directly compare the results. *InfoWorld* has used the same test plan for its statistical software reviews since 1994 (Fridlund 1994).

As a result of all this emphasis on methodology and measurable scores, the numbers may sometimes seem more important than the actual text. But one text is key: the text summary.

## Text Summaries

Most procedural reviews summarize their conclusions in text, discussing the products in order from best to worst. The description highlights comparisons between the other products, emphasizing why certain products won and others lost; for an example, see figure 4.2.

### Executive Summary

Each of the four statistical packages reviewed here is competent in its own right. Use our evaluation in the context of your needs and existing resources. For example, issues such as existing site licenses or which package is already on your company's mainframe may affect your buying decision.

Systat 4.1/Sygraph 1.1 is still unparalleled in both number crunching and graphics for the PC. Its wise combination of documentation, speed, customizability, analytic breadth, and utterly mind-boggling graphs set it completely apart. Furthermore, at the price, it's a steal. However, this sophistication comes at the cost of a steeper learning curve than you'll encounter with menu packages, and the graphics take time to produce. Ideal for pros, a little tougher for novices.

SPSS/PC+ is getting better and better. Its menu-based command-insertion facility bypasses the program's finicky commands, and the speed and smoothness of operation of the whole SPSS/PC+ system belie its massive size. New add-ons do analyses uniquely available within SPSS, and expanded memory support makes more analyses possible. Also, the documentation is the best in the business. Still, SPSS graphics are not as versatile as Sygraph's, and the cost of obtaining analytic capabilities that equal those of Systat can run many times what Systat costs.

With its increased data work space and a new macro facility, Statgraphics 4.0 has become a serious statistical package supporting a wide range of analyses and dazzling graphics. However, it is comparatively sluggish, and next to Systat or SPSS/PC+ its data capacity is still paltry. It doesn't have SPSS/PC+'s or Systat's data management skills or analytic depth, and it lacks Sygraph's graphical versatility. But of the four packages we reviewed, it's by far the easiest to learn, and ideal for the occasional user. Considering its quality control and forecasting procedures — and if your data sets are small — it may be the perfect all-around business stats package. It's a very good buy as well.

Though Minitab has its roots in education, it also has a broad user base in business and government. Version 7.1 is a solid command-oriented package with fine data management, but with comparatively limited statistical and graphics capabilities and a data capacity akin to Statgraphics'. The range of its quality control procedures stand out, and are almost as complete as Statgraphics'. Given the close pricing of the more competent Statgraphics 4.0 and Systat 4.1/Sygraph 1.1, we're reluctant to recommend this package over them, except to Minitab converts.

**Figure 4.2.   Text Summary of a Comparative Review**
Source: Fridlund 1990a:60

What is the point of all these summaries when the reviews themselves are only 750 words? Editors say that the text summaries are the single most-read part of a review. Readers, especially those who are not heavy users, skim the summary just to read about the products, the criteria, and the rankings, and to keep in touch with the current state of the category. *PC Magazine* software editor Ted Stevenson says:

> I think that a large part of why we have these . . . quick thought boxes is that the publishing industry is convinced that people don't want to read and so they talk about something they call "skim-ability." Regardless of the demerits of the word, that's responsible for a lot of the way stuff is presented. . . . If it's done superbly it's very valuable, but it's extremely hard to do it superbly well. We have to devote an inordinate amount of time and energy to it, which usually isn't good because it's not an appropriate use of resources.

The editor in charge of the review often writes the summary, with input from reviewers, testers, and other staff. Summaries may demand a great deal of discussion in order to reach consensus. Text summaries must, of course, be consistent with the numerical scores.

Closely related to text summaries are awards that publications give to the top-ranked products in a review.

## Awards

Since procedural reviews compare many products they often draw special attention to particularly noteworthy products. These products receive awards, like *PC Magazine*'s "Editors' Choice" or *Consumer Reports* "Best Buy." Most publications do not recognize bad products with a special designation, but for a time *eWeek* gave a poor quality product the "Caution" award. The criteria for high quality recognize technically superior products, but they are also explicitly comparative. *InfoWorld* (1995:111) says concisely, "To receive the Test Center Hot Pick seal, a product or solution has to offer what *InfoWorld* deems to be a standout technology or set of capabilities that are unusually valuable or revolutionary compared to the competitors." The *PC Magazine* Editors' Choice sidebar names the leading product(s) in the review and explains why they are they are best. If no products qualify for Editors' Choice—say, a review of speech recognition software (Rash 1994)—the sidebar explains why there are no suitable candidates.

These awards serve many purposes. In the first place, they indicate the best available product. There may be many products in the review, and the results can be confusing without a summary. An award is the simplest form of summary. The product given the award can be recommended with confidence to a broad audience.

Second, the awards serve valuable symbiotic marketing purposes for the publication and product maker alike. Most publications award a logo to products that receive an award. Product makers are allowed to use the award logos in ads and product literature.[22] This puts the name of the publication in front of readers at someone else's expense. *PC Magazine* has been by far the most successful with this; for many people, describing a product as an "Editors' Choice" implies *PC Magazine*. The award logo always includes the name of the publication.

Usually, the editor in charge of the review decides what product gets these awards. Reviewers and testers have input. They may suggest candidates and argue in favor or against certain choices, but the editor makes the final decision.

## Review Text

The summaries we've been describing beg several important questions. With all these summaries and supplementary textual material, why print a review? Don't the summaries give all the information that any reader could want? What do the reviews of individual products add to a procedural review?

Reviews provide an opportunity for the reviewer to talk about the actual experience of using the product from the point of view of a user. Reviews can describe the overall look and feel of the product, its design and usability characteristics. These are important components of a product that can't easily be quantified; yet they are of vital importance to potential users. A good design makes software easy to use and easy to learn; a bad design can make it hard. For example, since statistical processing is complicated, each procedure often requires that users navigate multiple dialog boxes. Thus dialog box design is important. How commands are placed on the dialogs, how users make choices, which choices are made by users and which are made by the software, how easily the default choices can be changed, and the order in which the choices are presented are significant issues that can be described in the review text but not elsewhere. For repetitive processing like regular weekly, monthly, or quarterly reports, ability to easily write and run command files without using menus is vital. How easily users can do this can be described in the text. Simple ways to find unusual data points or outliers can be an important plus. The product may come with indexed manuals, but how good is the index? These are only a few of many usability, design, and interface issues that may be covered in the text but not elsewhere.

Further, software product categories are not tightly defined, and apparently similar products may be targeted at different groups of users. Since the comparative summary articles in the review tend to be oriented toward characteristics that are common to all the products under review, they may not reveal these differences. The review text provides an opportunity to describe subtle differences.

The text gives reviewers an opportunity to write about their impressions of a product, and this is especially important when other elements in the review may not highlight important parts of users' experience. *PC Magazine* (1993a:4) instructs reviewers:

> The review is our opportunity to clear up any ambiguities that the "objective" measures may create and generally stress for readers what you feel are the most important issues in relation to the product and the category.

The text is a dense summary of the experience and impressions of the reviewer. As they write, reviewers are constrained by the requirement for brevity. A dominant fact of reviews is that in 750 words there isn't room for complex explanations. There is a lot to cover and most issues cannot be discussed in more than a few sentences. If readers won't understand a short explanation, there is strong pressure to drop the whole point. Reviews place a premium on simple descriptions and simple explanations because there is no room for anything that requires a long or complicated explanation. This biases review texts toward the simple.

Before we leave the topic of comparative procedural reviews, it may be useful to summarize how the components work together. The introduction describes the significance and scope of the product category being reviewed. At least one article describes the testing methodology. Several elements sum up the review. Features tables summarize the breadth and depth of a product. Testing and numerical summaries attempt to provide objective, quantified evaluations of a product's strengths and weaknesses. Text summaries describe how the products ranked in the review. Awards call attention to particularly noteworthy products. The individual product reviews give overall impressions, describe target audiences, and discuss design and usability issues. Of course, not every procedural review has as many discrete components. But even simple reviews have to perform the same tasks, although the different tasks are often not differentiated into separate articles. What is constant is the collection of tasks that reviews must perform in order to be credible and useful to their audiences.

Once the review is written, it goes into the hands of the editor and the production process. These also have significant influence on the final outcome.

## EDITING AND PRODUCTION

Although editors are important in all reviews, they are particularly central when there are multiple reviewers. We're not talking copy editing here; although, of course, every review is copy edited. In comparative reviews with multiple reviewers, editors are responsible for assuring that the reviews have a single voice. As emphasized in the discussion of consistency, above, because of their authority and mandate, editors are at least as important as reviewers in determining the actual words that appear on the final published page. Since they see the review last, they may be more important.

Some editors feel that many software reviewers (especially statistical software reviewers) have a fairly technical orientation that is reflected in their text. Technical details tend to make text stiff, constrained, and uninteresting. While it is necessary to be technically accurate, most editors do not believe this conflicts with good writing. One editor describes what he saw as one of his major tasks:

> I try to generalize from technical mentalities, which are often a little bit stilted, and make them flow in a more literary way. I use wit and irony whenever possible and just turn the review into a more conversational kind of a read. I do that in part because I enjoy doing it, but I do it in part because I think it's more palatable. In a magazine of the kind that I work for there's no obligation on the part of the reader to read anything and I've always wanted to draw them in. . . . I think it's part of an excellent review.

Editing often takes place under intense pressure from a deadline. Many deadlines in the review process are nominal; the real deadline is the date when the entire review, including screen shots, photographs, artwork, and everything else, has to be in the hands of the production process. This is governed by the need to ship the publication to subscribers and by the open slot allocated to the publication at the press. The time required for production varies with the publication. At most magazines this date is no less than two months before the magazine is mailed to subscribers, and more often it is ten weeks. This is the absolute bare minimum for a review. Any kind of problems will cause such a tight schedule to slip. The production issues are similar to those encountered in connoisseurial reviews, so we do not discuss them further.

## READING THE REVIEW

There are several relevant readerships for reviews. Below I discuss product makers and ordinary subscribers (whom I call "readers").

## Product Maker Responses

Previous pages describe product makers' efforts to influence reviews before and during the review process. In this section we examine how product makers respond after they see the final review. We consider how reviews help product makers compete by giving them independent information about the effectiveness of their product. Product makers use reviews in many ways. One software executive described how reviews are used both outside and inside the company:

> When we can put a reviewer's stamp of approval on our product, that gives us a valuable marketing tool. We quote the reviewer in our ads. If we won an award we put that in our ads too. It helps us persuade undecided customers. . . . A strong review gives the whole company a morale boost. We make sure that everyone knows about it by putting something in [our company newsletter] and we do special recognition for the team that produced [the product].

On an institutional level, product makers make strategic moves; that is, through their actions they attempt to alter the relative costs and benefits of different kinds of behavior of other institutions, thereby making the review process more favorable. When product makers feel mistreated they may write letters to editors, threaten to withdraw advertising, talk to the publisher, or complain to editors. Although publications regularly print letters from product makers, all things considered, they receive relatively little feedback from product makers. One editor said,

> We don't get much. We get complaints if they feel we don't cover them fairly or they don't feel that we printed all the propaganda that they put out there for us to reproduce. There's not a whole lot of response.

This can be a policy. A software executive explained the logic and tradeoffs:

> We think about what we can do every time we don't like a review. We keep coming back to the same decision each time. Unless we are on very firm ground we don't gain anything by complaining. Our influence is strongest when reviewers think of us as cooperative and helpful. It encourages them to listen to our point of view. . . . We think a reputation for complaining or for going over a reviewer's head to editors or the publisher would cause more damage than we could possibly gain. . . . Our policy is simple: we don't respond to reviews.

Companies may phone or write the editors about reviews they don't like. Given the central importance of the editor in the division of labor of procedural reviews, complaining to the editor is not a complaint about someone else's work; it is a complaint about the editor's work. An editor explained,

"When they [complain], I listen. But I edited the text and I know the reviewers. My staff checks the facts. These complaints rarely have substance."

Most product makers have a broad enough vision so that they understand many of their product's strengths and weaknesses. They plan to fix the weaknesses in later versions. There is a problem, however, when product makers do not understand how they compare to other products. This leads them to underestimate other products' strengths and to overestimate the positive things that independent reviewers will say about them. It is easy for product makers to become insulated, to talk too much to their own users, staff, and supporters. Since the company pays staff members and users bought the product, we would expect their criticism to be muted. Muted criticism makes this a warm, fuzzy, comfortable trap. While a product may serve existing users the trap is that there is no channel providing information about the needs of users who did not buy the product or those who were dissatisfied and abandoned the product for another. Companies find it difficult to get an independent assessment of how their products compare to other products on the market.[23]

Independent reviews provide a solution to this critical problem. Independent reviews explain where products fit in the hierarchy of a market and describe their relative strengths and weaknesses. This is particularly important in the fluid markets of computer software. It is even more important given the insular nature of statistical software. Most companies are small and run by people whose primary experience tends to be academic, not business. Reviews can provide valuable market intelligence. Many product makers realize this and actively seek out reviewers and editors. One software editor said,

> Vendors are always asking questions about what other people are doing. That is one of the roles that I think the reviews should play. It is on my part an active role. Vendors can call me up and talk. It is more typical to have casual conversations, over lunch or dinner. It is quite normal that vendors ask me to dinner.[24]

A part of a review that compels product maker attention is the features table. Product makers want to see a check mark beside their product in every line. I have attended staff meetings where company officials have given a photocopy of a features table to a programmer and asked for time and cost estimates to add every capability that wasn't checked. Not having features becomes a mark of a weak product. Ted Stevenson of *PC Magazine* described the dilemma at the 1994 Social Science Computing Association conference:

> The features are clearly important. Everybody wants them, everybody thinks they're important. I'm not sure who uses them [laughter], but from the vendors' point of view, it's "build-em or die." In the hard-core commercial software world, you can't afford not to provide features that your competitors are pro-

viding and this gives rise to better products and to a certain amount of distortion. This is one of the difficulties that we deal with.

There is what I call a checklist or cumulative check [syndrome]; the product that has more X's in the features table tends to be viewed by readers as the stronger product. This is not necessarily true. There is the problem of make-or-break features, which may or may not be useful. We reviewed fax software over a year ago. Optical character recognition was a brand new feature in fax software. Now every fax software package has optical character recognition capabilities. Most vendors seem to feel that nobody's using it. But there it is. Competition forced them to build it into the product; we had to review it. [laughter]

*Question*: Do you feel that there are too many features? Like word processing, my faculty users say they don't want all those features?

Yes, we do hear that. . . . Most people spend most of their time using only between 10 and 20 percent of the features of a product. It's an ongoing problem. You can't rewrite reality. If the vendors don't put the features in then people aren't going to buy their product. If we don't report on them then we're not giving them a fair representation in a review.

Some product makers take preemptive actions to prevent negative reviews. The licenses under the shrink-wrap of several products, including some Sybase, Oracle, and Microsoft products, prohibit their use for the purpose of reporting benchmark scores without the company's permission. Oracle has threatened to sue reviewers, including *InfoWorld* (Petreley 1995b).[25] Timothy Dyck (2002a:58), *eWeek* database editor, reports that he had not published comparative benchmark tests of databases from 1993 to 2002 "due directly to legal threats by database vendors."

But this issue is more complex than just negative reviews. Product makers are reasonably concerned with the accuracy of the tests and their generalizability to other environments. This is a problem that Ziff-Davis faces since it distributes benchmark tests like PC Bench and WinBench to anyone who asks. Robin Raskin, former editor of *PC Magazine* and publisher of *FamilyPC*, explains the problem and the Ziff-Davis solution.

How would we know that vendors were accurately portraying test results? Our license permits anyone who used our benchmark test to print the results as long as they fully disclose the testing environment. This ensures that the results can be repeated and validated.

The final sentence is the key. If the results can be repeated then they can be validated. The requirement for public disclosure tends to encourage a more generalizable environment. Anyone suspicious of the results will check to see if the environment is similar to real world problems. If it is not, then the whole testing program is open to immediate question and possible invalidation. No one wants to make it too easy for their opponents or too hard for their friends.

## Reader Responses

Why do people read statistical software reviews? People care about statistical software mostly when they are going to buy the product. Since they don't buy a new statistical software product very often, they won't read reviews very often. This is true of software in general. *PC Magazine* editors report that most readers scan the Editors' Choice box and glance at a review or two but they don't read the reviews. They keep the magazine for two to three years, and refer to it when they need information. They also often pass it along to friends to help them make decisions. Even a negative review can have a positive effect on readers. A marketing executive:

> I've learned that a bad review matters less than you would think. We get inquiries for [our products] from customers who say they read about them in a review that we know was very critical. We've asked about this in our focus groups. We found that many people save computer magazines, sometimes for years, and use them as references when they are looking for a [product].
>
> *Question*: So they don't look at whether or not the product received a positive review?
>
> When we first got this result it seemed so counterintuitive to me that I insisted we add the question to several more focus groups. The results were consistent. People do pay attention to the overall rating, but just being in the review is a strong positive.

Ordinary readers are likely to be interested in reviews only when they need to buy. Ranked products in a procedural review make the buying decision simple. Said one *PC Magazine* reader:

> The best thing about the [comparative ratings] is that they make my life simpler. More than once I had to buy software that I didn't want to learn much about. I didn't have the time or energy to find out all the details of different products. But I can read a table of ratings and I know what being rated Editors' Choice means. I don't really need to know anything else.

Once the decision has been made and the product is purchased, most readers feel no further interest. Since most current products are being updated on a regular schedule they will continue to serve the needs of their users into the future. Users can buy updates without looking at another review.

There are audiences who closely identify with their software, even software as technical as statistics. One interviewee told me, "I use the best software I can . . . and I'm proud of that." Like many identity arguments these debates boil down to a simple argument: using their preferred product was evidence that they were better people. For readers whose identity is tied to particular software, their identity will be confirmed or disconfirmed by the results of the review. Reviews explain which product is on top and if it's the product they like, this is powerful, independent confirmation of their professional knowledge and judgment. When products become identity symbols, reviews invoke these symbols by the language they use.

Even for readers who don't identify closely with their statistical software product, reading a review can help justify a utilitarian choice to a boss or an employee. It can give them language to express why a product is best. Part of this is the ability of a review to cue readers to the important issues, to the considerations that are more significant in the choice of a product. In this way it provides a language to express differences among products.

For most people, however, the ability to talk knowledgeably about statistical software is not something that will contribute to their self-image or their colleagues' view of them as a sophisticated, cultured, well-rounded individual. These people form the obvious audience whose members need to buy a statistical software product and want advice. They read statistical software reviews looking for information and direction. They want to see comparisons and guidance so that they can match their needs with the capabilities of different products. Their goal is to find the best product for them. In addition to the initial purchase decision, some of these readers want to learn about upgrades. What does the upgrade offer? Is it worth paying the money? Should they upgrade? These questions can be answered by reviews. Major review publications explicitly construct this kind of reader. For example, the *PC Magazine* reviewer's guide (1993a:5) explains the goal of the review:

> Our combined job in this review is to make a purchase recommendation. If you don't think anyone should seriously consider this package, explain why. If you do recommend it, please include a clear assessment of what type or types of analysis it is best suited for and any significant limitations. Please be concrete and provide details.

It is easy for an observer to see technical reasons for reading statistical software reviews. If you need to know what is good statistical software, then reviews are the place to go. They tell readers what product is best. They explain why.

In addition to individuals, corporate and higher-education readers are important beneficiaries of these arguments. One of the common uses of a review is to copy it. Many corporations and educational institutions do their own internal reviews before they approve software or hardware. Certain parts of published reviews figure heavily in these reviews. Features tables are particularly influential. Corporations and colleges may use features tables to screen products. One corporate IT professional told me,

> When we evaluate new products we usually start from the features tables in *PC Magazine*. . . . From the features tables we construct our own list of must-have features and we actually evaluate only the products that make it through the filter.

The IT organizations of many large corporations and colleges employ people whose job includes testing and recommending hardware and software products. They pay serious attention to the tests, evaluations, and recommended products of procedural reviews. One tester told me, "We use [published] reviews as a starting point when we go to work. . . . If we can limit our work to the top products our jobs are faster and easier." Sometimes they use reviews more directly. A corporate tester confessed that he plagiarized published reviews:

> When we get into a real time crunch, we have taken reviews that we trust, rewritten them in our words, and retyped the tables of tests. We added a cover memo and, presto, we had our report. We didn't like it, but . . . they've been fairly successful.
>
> *Question*: I suppose that would also make it easier to get away for that long weekend?
>
> [laughter] That too.

Their careers depend on accurate, informed recommendations, and so they pay close attention to major reviews. Even when they know the best product, the tests are important. Comparative test results are the way that they convince the rest of the company.

> An even more important reason is that we have to justify our recommendations. . . . We always get calls from department managers asking if they can buy their favorite product *du jour*. We need to be able to explain why their favorite didn't make the approved list. If we had only our opinions . . . [and] we didn't have test results we would be much less persuasive. The conversation could degenerate into some corporate version of he-said/she-said. To make a strong case we

want to say the approved product is better because it outperformed their candidate on tests A, B, and C. The only way to do that is to have actual comparative test results.

If everyone agrees that tests A, B, and C are important, then this is a convincing argument. The value of procedural reviews is that the information they yield can be a convincing tool to settle arguments. They create a transparent hierarchy, a hierarchy visible to everyone. It is technical—meaning it is politically neutral—but it still points toward the best products. It is a way of settling arguments where everyone can say they are winners. This has enormous appeal in organizations where people need to agree on a collective decision. We return to this issue in later chapters.

## NOTES

1. Until recently *InfoWorld* selected products using a formal procedure. It sent surveys almost every week about specific product categories to about 1,000 subscribers. Respondents were chosen because they indicated that they recommended, bought, specified, or approved the purchase of products in the category. *InfoWorld* is a controlled-circulation publication, so this information is available from the subscriber information that *InfoWorld* requires to determine if potential readers qualify to receive the magazine. The surveys asked readers about their opinions and experience with specific products. "This allows us to choose the products you are most interested in and test them in the ways you want them tested" (Darling 1994:104). The surveys were a key part of the review process in several ways. The products that respondents say they most want to see reviewed are included in the review, for example whether to test a Mac or Windows version of a product. The characteristics of the machines readers used—for example, processor speed, amount of memory, or type of video adapter—were the basis for the testing platforms *InfoWorld* used. The surveys were used to help build features tables and decide on relative weightings of various features. For example, the survey of low-cost desktop publishing packages showed that most use was occasional; thus the review gave a heavy weight to ease of use incorporated into features like templates and wizards (Darling 1994:107). *Consumer Reports* uses input from its Annual Survey (Karpatkin 1999a).
2. Another advantage of analyzing *PC Magazine* reviews is that it separates the different components of a review into different named parts of an article. This facilitates analysis and explanation. In other well-known review organizations, like *Consumer Reports*, the staff think about the same issues but the components are not always so structurally clear in the articles.
3. The issue, volume 12, number 9, contained a total of 458 pages. There were 165.5 pages of editorial material, so 292.5 pages or 63.9 percent were advertising. The editorial page counts were measured with a ruler.

4. Several potential problems result from a focus on the *PC Magazine* process during those years. Written description tends to freeze a dynamic process that changes over time. It also seems to ignore other publications, which have their own processes. There are two answers to these objections. First, the substantive aspects of *PC Magazine* reviews were standardized years before its first comparative statistical software review in 1989. While the reviews have changed some since then, the differences tend to be stylistic remakes, such as changes in titles, page allocations, or locations where certain information is presented. These changes are cosmetic, not substantive. For procedural reviews, the major substantive elements in the process have remained similar from the mid-1980s to 2003. Second, the process in other publications is described when it illuminates a point. However, to anticipate a conclusion, one of the lessons of this study is that the central elements of procedural reviews remain similar no matter where published. Where these elements differ, I point them out and discuss them.

5. This is an important point: Nothing *inherent* in a procedural review requires a complex division of labor. A single person could do an effective procedural review of multiple products. It would just take a long time. The complex division of labor is a result of the need for speed.

6. Speed was not tested in either of the *PC Magazine* statistical software reviews and it is not part of most recent *PC Magazine* software reviews. Several statistical software reviews included performance testing (Parker 1986; Software Digest 1991). The results of these tests showed some large speed differences. Software Digest reviewed BMDP PC-90, Minitab, SAS, SPSS/PC+, Statgraphics, and Systat. It reported, "the programs' execution speeds vary significantly, frequently exceeding an order of magnitude. In one test, a program requires 45 times longer than another" (p. 32). Despite these results, I know of no other statistical software reviews that include performance tests. The time required to devise and run tests is too great.

7. A 2002 review of five SQL databases (Dyck 2002b) compared performance on three measures of transaction performance. For example, one test measured throughput (number of pages served per second) as the number of virtual users increased. The results, displayed graphically, showed peak performance varied from 209 to 629 pages per second.

8. When I checked I found that the 1993 suitability-to-task also included a rating for "data management," but the way the editor said it makes a better story. In 1993 suitability-to-task was a separate sidebar; now it is usually a graphic displayed as part of the review.

9. Some problems were two separate, partially integrated file managers, weak character variable support, a weak batch language, poor documentation, problems with analysis of categorical data, and the requirement that users often refer to variables by their ordinal position in the dataset (i.e., by variable number rather than name), among others.

10. For example, one of the first tasks in the script requested elementary statistical output: a table of frequencies and percentages. I was disappointed to discover that I needed a workaround to do the frequency table interactively and the command language couldn't produce it at all. Every other product in the review would have been able to produce the table easily.

11. The importance of the editors is partially concealed by the way *PC Magazine* presents reviews. While the editor and other people involved are usually credited in a sidebar, the only byline attached to the review is the reviewer's. To my knowledge, the division of labor in the review process, the extent of the standardization of review criteria, and the final role of the editor have never before been described in print. Consequently, many readers, who have not thought about the difficulties of producing a large number of consistent, credible reviews in a short time, believe that a *PC Magazine* reviewer is like a book reviewer, giving a personal opinion about the software. This can lead to confusion and misunderstandings. This is discussed below in the section on product maker reception of the review.

12. Restaurant reviews also have a technical skill component. However, restaurant reviewing is a full-time job. Software reviews in technical subjects like statistics are written by freelance reviewers. These reviewers' day jobs often involve statistical software.

13. It is questionable whether this is true. Rick Popely, editor of *Consumer Guide Auto*, describes repeated, major defects in cars he had received for review directly from manufacturers (Popely 1997). Further, many of the overall characteristics of the car—things like the interior room, trunk capacity, fuel economy, stability, smoothness of the ride, engine performance, and the price—cannot easily be changed. This is true of many other products like refrigerators, software, or printers. Since these are major components of an evaluation there is a question about the value of anonymous purchases. However, anonymous buying avoids a certain opportunity that the manufacturer might use to manipulate the review. Consumers Union argues that its reputation for independence is its most important asset. Given this, anonymous purchases may be a minor price to pay to avoid the suspicion that a review was manipulated.

14. The major audiences include survival analysis, time series forecasting, designed experiments, survey analysis, reduction of dimensionality, and quality control, among others. There are numerous smaller niches: test item analysis, kinetic modeling, meta-analysis, and multilevel analysis, among others. Overlaid on top of these categories are the audiences that every product has to decide how to handle: novices versus experienced users.

15. This statement is too simple for word processors. The ubiquity of Microsoft Office and Word has reduced the variety, but there are still low-end products like Yeah Write for Windows as well as products for specialized audiences, like Tex or VEDIT.

16. Even *Consumer Reports* is not immune to the issues of shared professional interests. In interviews, *Consumer Reports* engineers told me of instances where they met product maker engineers at conferences and informally shared design, performance, and testing information. Similar interests are a strong bond.

17. For a discussion of this problem and its resolution, see the controversy surrounding *InfoWorld*'s review of OS/2 Warp (Alsop 1994b; *InfoWorld* 1994; Kennedy 1994).

18. After being told I could not identify the company or the publication, I was shown a manuscript of such a review. When I asked how common this practice was, I was told, "We do this every few years for . . ." and four small publications were named. I checked the publication and the text was printed largely as written, with the

byline of one of the magazine's editors. The product maker connection was not disclosed in the published article.

19. The reviewer is a senior social science professor whose name would be recognized by many readers. He talked to me only under the condition that his name not appear anywhere in this text. It is one of several names omitted from the list of interviewees in the appendix.

20. Sidebars are typical of recent *PC Magazine* reviews: review the high end products and cover the less sophisticated products in a sidebar. *PC Magazine* has long since given up its goal of comprehensively covering all software and hardware. A compromise is to review only the more complex, expensive, sophisticated products that are market leaders. The editors believe these products are most interesting to readers. Sidebars discuss less complex products.

21. The criteria used to include in the review often require exclusion of important or interesting products. These may be covered in sidebars, which may contain more text than any actual review. SAS and S-Plus, in the *PC Magazine* column of table 4.2, were in prerelease "beta testing" and ineligible for that reason. Some products weren't important enough to be fully reviewed, thus the *InfoWorld* sidebar briefly describes six additional products that "offer very specialized capabilities" (Fridlund 1990a:59). Sometimes sidebars contain actual reviews of products that are in a related product category of interest to readers, like the review "Choosing the Right Statistic with Statistical Navigator," an expert system that helps users select appropriate statistics (Blank 1989c). Another typical sidebar would be a glossary of technical terms, for example, a review of graphics software included "A Guide to Graphics Lingo" (*PC Magazine* 1997a). A final kind of sidebar contains reviews of "Entry-Level Desktop Publishing Tools" (Levine 1997) as part of a review of major desktop publishing software. Sidebars provide readers with additional useful information without requiring that the publication commit the resources and time needed for a full-scale review. Sidebars provide a flexible way to expand the scope of the review without increasing the number of products actually reviewed.

22. *Consumer Reports* is notable in that it refuses to allow its ratings to be used by product makers. It feels that this could be interpreted to be a possible tie between Consumers Union and the product maker. Such ties could compromise its reputation for independence and damage the credibility of its reviews.

23. This paragraph is based on my experience as a consultant to software companies. Some software companies explicitly attempt to survey nonusers or users who don't upgrade. In my experience, this is unusual.

24. This editor is very conscious of not compromising his independence; "I always pay for my own dinner, absolutely."

25. For other instances see Raskin (1994), Foster (2002a, 2002b), and Miller (2002). In 2003 a New York court ruled that Network Associates may not require prior permission (Richtel 2003). If this ruling stands up under appeal, it may settle the issue.

*Chapter Five*

# The Production of Reviews

Can any product be reviewed using either connoisseurial or procedural methods? Is the rating system forced by characteristics of the product or is it a choice? Connoisseurial reviews of statistical software are easy to find; for example, Peter Coffee's review of JMP in *eWeek* (Coffee 2002) or Hollander's review of Forecast Pro in *InfoWorld* (Hollander 2000). Publications that print procedural reviews, like *eWeek* and *InfoWorld*, also print connoisseurial reviews of the same products. The speed, low cost, and organizational simplicity of connoisseurial reviews are major advantages and, as a result, connoisseurial reviews are common. Any product can be reviewed by a connoisseurial expert. Are procedural reviews different? The central characteristic of a procedural review is that it relies on explicit procedures to mass-produce a review of multiple products. Their more complex organization and higher costs are disincentives. But these are technical problems; the real question is: can any product—at least in principle—be reviewed using procedural methods? To answer this question, we turn to another case study: Zagat's restaurant reviews.

## THE ZAGAT CHALLENGE

The prevailing Claiborne paradigm of connoisseurial restaurant reviews is one restaurant, one reviewer, and one review. In 1983 Tim and Nina Zagat pioneered an alternative model embodied in a pocket-size red book of New York restaurant reviews. Now published in forty-five North American cities plus Paris, London, and Tokyo, this has been a spectacularly successful cultural innovation.[1] Each little red book reviews a large number of restaurants, but their real uniqueness lies in the way they rate the restaurants. Zagat's relies on diners who fill out a questionnaire, ranking restaurants on a scale from zero to three on food, decor, and service. Diners are also asked to estimate the price of a single meal, including one drink and tip, and to rank their top five favorite restaurants. In addition, Zagat's requests comments, asking respondents to "be descriptive, pithy and witty." The scores of respondents are averaged and multiplied by ten to create a ranking in each category on a zero to thirty scale (see the example page in figure 5.1). The reviewer's role is limited to filling out a questionnaire and sending it in for tabulation. Tim Zagat has designed a series of checks during tabulation to assure that the criteria are consistently applied, that restaurateurs do not stuff the ballot box, and that restaurants are fairly rated. The editor of each volume assembles the quotes into a readable paragraph that reflects the overall evaluation of the restaurant. As in other procedural reviews the editor, not the reviewer, is the key person. It would be hard to imagine any system more different from connoisseurial reviews.

Zagat's has grown explosively from a single New York City guide in 1983 to forty-five cities in 2003. One measure of its popularity is that for months after a new edition is released Zagat's sits near the top of local New York, Washington, D.C., and Los Angeles nonfiction best-seller lists. A clue to its popularity is in the fact that Zagat's never appears on the local Chicago best-seller lists; it has had much less influence in Chicago than in New York or Los Angeles. Critics knowledgeable about the three cities suggest that the difference is due to *Chicago* magazine and the *Chicago Tribune*. Alone among major city magazines, every issue of *Chicago* magazine prints a listing of recommended restaurants. The September 2003 issue listed 154 restaurants with star ratings and a short 100-word review (*Chicago* magazine 2003).[2] Unlike any other major metropolitan newspaper, the *Chicago Tribune* also prints restaurant listings every Friday.[3] One important attraction of Zagat's, perhaps the preeminent use, is as a reference when people try to decide where to eat. If you just want a list of good restaurants, Zagat's works. A Chicago diner said, "Zagat's? I bought a copy of the New York edition last time I was there but I don't use it in Chicago. . . . I already subscribe to *Chicago* magazine and it lists all the important restaurants." Where there are alternative lists of good restaurants, Zagat's has not been as attractive.[4]

Zagat's review-by-public-opinion-survey is a striking innovation. To what extent does it challenge the classic one-reviewer, one-restaurant, one-review approach? One advantage is that Zagat's can list far more restaurants. The 2003 Chicago Zagat's reviews 1,061 restaurants in Chicago and suburbs (van Housen 2003). The wealth of space allows it to include many smaller neighborhood places that would never be included in the more limited list in

**Figure 5.1.  Survey Review: Zagat's Restaurant Reviews**
Source: Zagat and Zagat (1996:94–95).

*Chicago* magazine or the *Chicago Tribune*. Zagat's includes moderately priced chains like Outback Steakhouse and Rainforest Café that, because they are chains, would usually not be on the other dining lists. As with *Chicago* magazine, Zagat's cross-lists restaurants by cuisine, by location, and by various special features. Zagat's also has a convenient format—8½ by 3¾ inches—that fits easily in a coat pocket or purse. It's easier to carry around than *Chicago* magazine or the *Tribune*. It is very user friendly.

The ability of Zagat's to publish frequent, complete revisions is a significant plus. Keeping up with the food at the 154 restaurants listed in *Chicago* magazine stretches several reviewers full-time; more restaurants would be increasingly difficult. Zagat's model makes the work much easier on the stomach and waistline of his editors. They just pass out questionnaires and summarize the results. Tim Zagat points out that guidebooks compiled by individual critics are limited in scope and frequently out of date because there are only so many places an individual can go and only so much one can eat. He argues that his pool of sophisticated palates provides a much broader and more timely portrait of a city's dining scene than other books (Rice 1990). Tim and Nina Zagat have invented a way to mass-produce reviews on a scale that no one else can match. Their application of public opinion survey technology and statistical computer processing to restaurant reviews is a real innovation. The production aspect of Zagat's is its most innovative feature.

While Zagat's can produce updated information more easily than other guidebooks, it suffers when compared to newspapers and magazines. *Chicago* magazine and the *Chicago Tribune* can respond to restaurant changes much more quickly than Zagat. If a restaurant changes significantly after the survey is complete, Zagat's ratings will be based on out-of-date information. This situation occurred in the 1997 Chicago Zagat's. Gordon, a contemporary American restaurant, installed a new chef, Don Yamauchi, about a month before Zagat went to press in late 1996. The 1997 Zagat mentions in its text that Yamauchi is new but it can't do anything about the fact that the deadline for turning in questionnaires was months before he arrived. Worse, in January 1997, Yamauchi decided to revamp the entire menu.[5] So, for the rest of the year, Zagat's ratings are based on a chef who is no longer there and food that is no longer served. Compared to Zagat's, readers of *Chicago* magazine or the *Chicago Tribune* receive fewer reviews but a more accurate picture.

Tim Zagat argues that a survey is more objective—by which he means not subject to the taste eccentricities of an individual—and more comprehensive—because it is not limited by the number of restaurants an individual can evaluate in a year. The data collection effort certainly impresses with its scale. The 2003 New York Zagat's, for example, is based on almost 26,000 questionnaires. The 2003 Chicago Zagat's is based on nearly 2,400 respondents. These enormous numbers, Zagat argues, create results "as close to scientific as you can get" (Scherer 1995). Yet the ratings have problems that stem from Zagat's use of volunteer respondents (see also P. Richman 1986 and Shaw 2000). The key question: who are the respondents?

Suppose an old and a new restaurant are being rated. Returning patrons make up most of the diners at older restaurants. Since diners return because they like the restaurant, such places will receive a favorable rating. New restaurants have a disproportionate number of first-time diners. If some first-timers don't like what they eat, they will give the restaurant a lower rating. Even if this happens in only a few cases the average rating will decline. In the language of sample surveys, two different populations are patronizing these two restaurants and to some extent their ratings reflect the population differences rather than the quality of food or service.

Consider another case: an inexpensive restaurant and an expensive restaurant. Suppose some people dining at the inexpensive restaurant think of restaurant chains like the Olive Garden or Red Lobster as excellent restaurants, and rank the inexpensive restaurant accordingly. Suppose some of the people dining at the expensive restaurant think of Charlie Trotter's as an excellent restaurant and rank accordingly. If even a small group thinks like this they will influence average ratings; the inexpensive restaurant will be ranked higher and the expensive restaurant lower than the food or service would dictate. Again, the result is that the ratings differ because of differences in the populations rating the restaurants.

Both problems have the same origin—the self-selection of Zagat's volunteer respondents—and the same consequences—biased survey results. The technical name for these problems is *sample selection bias*. For this kind of bias there is no safety in numbers. If the respondents are selected in a way that produces bias, then the results will be biased no matter how many people fill out the survey. This is why a survey can be less accurate than a single expert reviewer who applies the same criteria consistently across all restaurants.

Some significant strengths and weaknesses of Zagat's can be seen by a comparison with the *Chicago* magazine listings. Table 5.1 contains typical text and ratings from both publications. They describe one of the most popular Chicago restaurants of 2003, Blackbird. The special formatting and the special symbols like credit cards or hours of operation have been removed; what remains are the text and ratings, and even a casual reader will notice sharp differences. Notice, first, the ratings. In the upper left corner, *Chicago* magazine awards an overall three-star rating (four stars are the maximum). Zagat's prints three ratings, the numbers on the upper right, based on a possible maximum of thirty, and they grade Blackbird as twenty-five (food), nineteen (decor), twenty-three (service), and forty-eight dollars (estimated average cost of a meal including one drink and tip). Second, the texts are different length. The *Chicago* magazine text is 110 words, while Zagat's is 66 words. These lengths are somewhat atypical. *Chicago* magazine listing reviews tend to be nearer 100 words, while Zagat's tends to be nearer 55 words; Zagat's New York restaurant reviews are shorter, typically about 30–40 words (see table 5.1).

**Table 5.1.  Comparison of Reviews of Blackbird**

| Chicago *Magazine* | Zagat's |
| --- | --- |
| **Blackbird**<br>Contemporary American. Chef Paul Kahan's balanced seasonal dishes are as stylish as the minimalist setting and the hip throngs it attracts. Your first clue might be an appetizer of sautéed diver scallops on wild mushroom broth, served with chanterelles, baby leeks, and sea beans (aromatic marine greens). Roasted breast of bobwhite quail and confit legs with prosciutto di Parma hits robust high notes, as does wood-grilled pork tenderloin with pancetta, oyster mushrooms, and vinegar sauce set off with cavoli neri (dark Italian greens). Finish with fine cheeses or a terrific dessert by pastry chef Elissa Narow, perhaps banana and walnut cream tart with vanilla malt ice cream. Many boutique wines. | **Blackbird**                25 19 23 $48<br>"Wear black" within the "white surroundings" of this "see-and-be-scene" West Loop New American where "brilliant" chef Paul Kahan employs French influences to take you on "a wonderful journey of amazing flavors" and "knowledgeable" servers "match the food" with "great wine selections"; "go with people you like," though, "because you'll be squeezed in tight" in a "minimalist" room that strikes some as "elegantly stark," others as "antiseptic." |

Sources: *Chicago* magazine (2003:223)          van Housen (2003:33)

Third, Zagat's uses quotes from diners instead of being entirely written by a reviewer. To the extent that readers identify with food-loving Zagat's readers, this has instant credibility. If they are suspicious that the reviewer's criteria may not be theirs—perhaps he or she is too sophisticated—then Zagat's quotes have a kind of proletarian, homespun appeal. There is independent evidence that this appeals strongly to readers. Jolson and Bushman (1978:76) asked respondents to rank alternative methods of guiding consumer restaurant choices. Diners ranked "A large panel of consumers who dine out often" as their first choice. This is a good description of Zagat's method.

The most important difference is in the content of the texts. In its 110 words, the *Chicago* magazine text packs a great deal of food information and evaluative advice, listing recommended appetizers, entrées, and a dessert, plus evaluative comments on the food and dessert. It also mentions the "minimalist setting and the hip throngs it attracts." Zagat's text focuses on the decor described as "white surroundings" and "minimalist," and the atmosphere of the room, "squeezed tight." In 66 words, food is mentioned only in general terms, "wonderful journey of amazing flavors," and there is no mention of specific entrées, appetizers, or desserts whatsoever. Zagat's questionnaire asks for "pithy, witty" comments and respondents may find it hard to turn a witty phrase while recommending the quail.[6] The language is mostly descriptive; evaluation appears in only a few phrases: "knowledgeable," "great," and "brilliant." The text has no evaluation of the food. The evaluations are carried entirely by the numerical ratings for food, decor, and service. A lot of weight rests on three numbers. To people who enjoy food and dining, Zagat's numbers, although meaningful, seem thin compared to the evaluations in *Chicago* magazine. Zagat's text, on the other hand, gives a better sense of the nonfood experience of the restaurant; particularly, a feel for the tone and intensity of the environment, although this is not omitted from the *Chicago* magazine review.

In the final analysis, what have Tim and Nina Zagat done? They have developed an innovative review method that combines several new ideas: index numbers constructed from restaurant diner questionnaires, and person-in-the-street diners quoted in the reviews, all combined in a convenient, inexpensive format that covers a large number of restaurants and can be easily revised. While many of these ideas have been used elsewhere, they haven't been combined or pushed as hard.[7] It's a remarkable concatenation of ideas. What is innovative about Zagat's is the application of social science survey technology to the production of reviews. By one measure the brilliance of Zagat's approach is that they implemented a consumer panel that offers so much useful information that it is economically self-supporting. The three numbers measuring food, service, and décor contain the evaluation in Zagat's reviews and the text is dominated by descriptions of atmosphere. This clearly fills a niche; the three averages seem to be all that many diners require. Comparison of the impact of Zagat's in Chicago to New York and Los Angeles suggests that the niche, however, may be based mostly on convenience. Zagat's probably serves a different audience than the traditional Claiborne-style review. Zagat's formula is here to stay but it can easily co-exist with existing reviews in newspapers and magazines. Traditional connoisseurial reviews will not be supplanted by it, nor are they likely to be much influenced by it.

The remainder of this chapter describes production issues in connoisseurial and procedural reviews, while the following chapter emphasizes credibility, which involves both production and reception. Zagat's innovation raises two questions: First, the core of reviews is their evaluation of the product. Do connoisseurial and procedural reviews produce different evaluations? Second, Zagat's evaluations are based on impersonal procedures and this fits the definition of a procedural review. However, Zagat's does not test anything in the same sense that *PC Magazine* tests computer hardware or *Consumer Reports* tests cars and appliances. Zagat's is a different kind of procedural review. Are there other kinds? These questions are discussed in the next three sections. The final two sections compare connoisseurial and procedural reviews, ending with differences in the audiences that each construct.


## DO CONNOISSEURIAL AND PROCEDURAL REVIEWS
## PRODUCE THE SAME EVALUATION?

The question of whether connoisseurial and procedural rating systems produce the same evaluation is not easy to answer. A simple way to see one problem is to consider the following example. If we think of a single continuum of restaurant quality stretching from very bad to very good, then an evaluation assigns individual restaurants to locations on this continuum according to how good they are.[8] The problem stems from the fact that there will always be disagreement about the appropriate ordinal position of any restaurant. Even two people who share the same standards are unlikely to rank hundreds of restaurants in exactly the same order. Given this fact, the problem is, what exactly does "agreement" mean?

A second problem is that in order to compare connoisseurial and procedural reviews, we need examples where both evaluate the same product. Such data are not readily available. It is particularly difficult to find connoisseurial reviews using a consistent set of standards on a sufficient number of products to warrant using statistical procedures.[9] A unique characteristic of the *Chicago* magazine restaurant listings allows comparison of connoisseurial reviews to Zagat's procedural reviews. In addition to short paragraphs, *Chicago* rates each restaurant on a scale from one to four stars. To my knowledge, no other major city magazine in the country prints restaurant listings along with ratings.[10] *Chicago* magazine's stars are based largely on food quality and are comparable to Zagat's food ratings. Although the food ratings are based on a zero to thirty point-scale, the lowest twelve points never occur and there are no restaurants ranked twenty-nine or thirty, so the scale sorts restaurants into a range from twelve to twenty-eight, seventeen ordinal categories. Since *Chicago* magazine's scale of one to four stars includes half-stars, the restaurants are sorted into a total of seven ordinal categories. The distribution of ratings for the two publications is shown in figure 5.2. The horizontal scale in each graph is the Restaurant Rating category: number of stars for *Chicago* magazine, food ratings for Zagat's. The vertical scale is the Number of Restaurants in the category. To enhance comparability both graphics in figure 5.2 have been drawn with identical vertical scales, ranging from zero to ninety.

The visually obvious point about figure 5.2 is that the distributions are very different. Zagat's food ratings are generally symmetric around a mode of

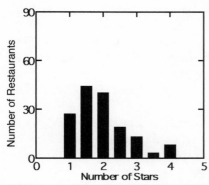

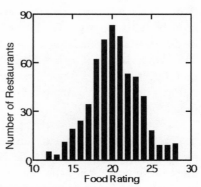

**Figure 5.2.**   *Chicago* **Magazine Stars and Zagat's Food Rating**
Source: Tabulated from *Chicago* magazine (2003) and van Housen (2003).

twenty. (There is a slight right-skew: about 40 percent of the cases are below twenty while 46 percent are above twenty.) *Chicago* magazine stars are extremely left-skewed. *Chicago* magazine staff members were not surprised when I showed them figure 5.2. *Chicago* believes it lists the best restaurants in the city. These are the restaurants on the right side of Zagat's distribution. Producing high-quality food day after day is very hard, so as quality goes up, *Chicago* expect to find fewer and fewer restaurants. Further, they suggest that Zagat's rates every restaurant that catches the attention of its editors. Some attract attention not because of their food but because they are brew pubs, or because of their location, or some other special quality. This is why there are restaurants in Zagat's with food quality scores as low as twelve. The restaurants reviewed by *Chicago* have a median Zagat's food rating of twenty-three compared to twenty for the restaurants not included in *Chicago* magazine. In general, we conclude that *Chicago* magazine tends to review restaurants that have above-average Zagat's food ratings.

If we look at individual restaurants, there are exceptions. Two well-known restaurants were strangely omitted from Zagat's: Ed Debevic's and Home Run Inn. These may be errors. Two other discrepant cases tell interesting stories about Zagat's. Le Francais has a stellar Zagat's food rating of twenty-eight but no listing in *Chicago*. For decades it was one of the best restaurants in Chicago. In recent years it has been up and down as it has gone through several new chefs and it closed repeatedly. Now, in Wheaton's opinion, it is living off its reputation. Former *New York Times* restaurant critic Mimi Sheraton (2004:193) agrees. Zagat's diners remember it like it was, not like it is now. This instance shows that history and reputation matter even when a survey explicitly asks diners to rate food they have eaten in the past year. The other restaurant with a twenty-eight food rating—but no *Chicago* listing—is David's Bistro. This restaurant has the "low response/less reliable" symbol and that probably tells the story. The rating is being inflated by the tastes of a small set of diners whose standards are not high. A similar case occurred in the 2003 New York Zagat's (Grimes 2003). David's Bistro is probably a good restaurant, but it isn't a twenty-eight. Zagat's appears to agree because, despite its stellar rating, David's Bistro is not listed among the "Top 40 Food" restaurants (van Housen 2003:10).

These discrepancies show that connoisseurial and procedural reviews do not produce identical results; in this sense, they do not agree. Yet, there remains the question asked at the beginning of this section: what is "agreement"? We would not expect any two people to agree on the rank ordering of hundreds of Chicago restaurants. We wouldn't expect two different procedures to agree, either. Analysis of individual ranks is very low-level work. This much detail shows hypervariation—every restaurant becomes a special case—and it cripples our ability to see patterns. The question of agreement is a question about the overall distribution of the data, not the location of individual restaurants. We need to look at a figure that would show us the overall pattern of the relationship between *Chicago* magazine's connoisseurial reviews and Zagat's procedural reviews. We have been looking at the trees. We need to look at the forest.

Figure 5.3 displays a visual picture of the forest, a plot of the relationship between *Chicago* magazine connoisseurial reviews and Zagat's procedural reviews. The horizontal axis is the *Chicago* magazine star rating. For every star category the figure displays a visual picture of the distribution of Zagat's food ratings for restaurants in that category. The boxes are drawn to enclose the middle 50 percent of all cases.[11] In other words, the ends of the boxes are drawn at the twenty-fifth and seventy-fifth percentiles. The line in the middle of each box marks the median or fiftieth percentile.

This figure shows a strong positive relationship. The easiest way to see it is to compare the boxes of each *Chicago* magazine rating. Adjacent boxes often overlap, but boxes that are separated by another box (like the boxes for three stars and four stars) tend not to overlap. This indicates overall strong agreement between the two rating systems. Further, the agreement stretches across all the star categories; that is, they agree on the top-ranked restaurants as well as on the one-star restaurants.[12] If you feel comfortable with a statistical description of data like these, the Goodman-Kruskal Gamma coefficient for the relationship is 0.647. Since these data are the complete population, not a sample, statistical significance has no meaning. We conclude that despite their dramatically different evaluation procedures, *Chicago* magazine and Za-

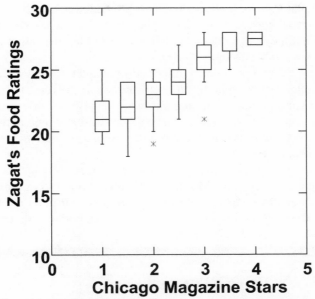

**Figure 5.3.** Box Plots Comparing Zagat's and *Chicago* Magazine
Source: Tabulated from *Chicago* magazine (2003) and van Housen (2003).

gat's ratings exhibit strikingly high agreement. In this case at least, connoisseurial and procedural reviews produce identical results.[13]

There are reasons to expect this kind of result in many settings. People interested in fine dining tend to read the same magazines—*Chicago*, *Gourmet*, *GQ*, *Food and Wine*, *Wine Spectator*, and so on—and visit the same restaurants. If you read restaurant reviews in these publications, there appears to be a broad consensus about the appropriate criteria and their application. All over the world, reviewers and diners generally agree on the characteristics of excellent food. Fine dining is a community of people engaged in a continuous conversation about food and restaurants. While no one should expect agreement on every restaurant or every dish, on average there is a great deal of harmony. The results in figure 5.3 reflect this agreement. We expect similar results in any field where a broad consensus exists.[14]

## TYPES OF PROCEDURAL REVIEWS

The performance testing that *PC Magazine* performs on computer hardware cannot be done on products like restaurant meals, mutual funds, music, or movies.[15] Zagat's example shows that there are additional kinds of procedural reviews: in fact, there are four kinds. They share a common dependence on procedures but they differ by methodology. Describing the full range of procedural reviews indicates their range and flexibility.

First, there are the procedures described in chapter 4: conduct a series of performance tests on a group of products and report the results. This is typical of most computer software and hardware reviews as well as *Consumer Reports* appliance and car reviews. Since the tests usually require that a group of products be brought into a laboratory or testing area, here these are called *laboratory reviews* (see figure 5.4).

Reviews may be based not on actual performance tests but on historical records of past performance. Morningstar Mutual Fund reports are an example. Other examples include credit ratings and stock or bond ratings. These are called *historical performance reviews*. Unlike laboratory reviews, the re-

---

**BENCHMARK TESTS**

# Value Notebooks

Secondary cache speed is more important than cache size: The fastest processor was the Celeron, whose full-processor-speed 128K cache beat out a Pentium II half-speed system that had four times the L2 cache.

The **ZD Business Winstone 99** score shows differences in overall system performance. Notebook hard disks and graphics chip sets are not as fast as their desktop counterparts, contributing to lower Winstone scores. Some notebooks still use EDO DRAM instead of faster SDRAM, which also results in notebooks performing more slowly than desktops with the same processors.

Among the tested group, systems using processors based on the Intel Pentium II core, either Celeron or Pentium II, performed extremely closely. There was only a 7 percent difference between the top-scoring Celeron/300-based Compaq Armada 1500c and the Pentium II/233–based Gateway Solo 2500SE that we used for comparison. The WinBook XL 300 TFT unit using the AMD K6-2/300 fell behind the leaders by about 15 percent, edging out only the Pentium MMX/233–based WinBook XL 233 DSTN system. Our **CPUmark32** test shows the differences among processor

scores, their cache and speed. The Celeron-based systems come with 128K of integrated L2 cache running at full processor speed. That's enough to make them equal to the Pentium II/233–based Gateway system we used for comparison, which has 512K of off-die L2 cache running at half the processor speed. While the K6-2/300–based WinBook has the most L1 cache, 64K compared with 32K for the Celeron and Pentium II, the system came with 256K of off-die L2 cache that runs at the 66-MHz system speed. The slower cache made the difference for the AMD K6-2/300 unit, placing it behind the two 300-MHz Celeron-based systems.

For road warriors, the **ZD BatteryMark 2.0** gives a good measure of useful battery life. Lithium ion still has the highest electrochemical potential among notebook batteries, and the two Gateway notebooks prove that point. The Celeron-based Gateway unit came with a nickel hydride battery, while the Pentium II comparison system came with a lithium ion model. Because lithium ion is lighter and denser than nickel hydride, the battery in the Pentium II system has a higher capacity, leading to a battery life more than double that of the test unit.

## How We Tested
We tested all notebooks with Windows 98 and 32MB of RAM. Before testing, we prepared each system following a standard procedure to create a common testing state for all notebooks. We stripped each system's start-up configuration of all processes or tasks except for Systray, Explorer, and graphics card control panels. We set the display to the system's maximum internal resolution, 800-by-600 or 1,024-by-768 with 65,536 colors and small fonts. We also disabled power management features. We defragmented hard disks before each test and let Windows 98 manage virtual memory settings. We used the vendor's provided graphics driver for all systems. For our ZD Battery-Mark 2.0 test we used standard power-management settings during testing: 2 minutes for hard disk time-out (or the closest value available), and Auto or Fast CPU speed. BatteryMark also uses Microsoft Advanced Power Management where possible to automate procedures and provide information.

For more detailed information on these ZD benchmark tests, go to *www.pcmag.com/howwetested*.

| | ZD Business Winstone 99 | | ZD CPUMark$_{32}$ | ZD BatteryMark 2.0 (Hours: minutes) |
|---|---|---|---|---|
| *High scores are best.* | | | | |
| *Bold type denotes first place among reviewed products.* | | | | |
| **PC** *denotes Editors' Choice.* | | | | |
| Compaq Armada 1500c (Celeron/300) | 10.6 | | 606 | 2:01 |
| Dell Inspiron 3500 (Celeron/300) | 10.0 | | 619 | 3:09 |
| Gateway Solo 2500SE (Celeron/266) | 10.5 | | 563 | 2:30 |
| **PC** Winbook XL 300 TFT (AMD K6-2/300) | 9.0* | | 517 | 3:00 |
| WinBook XL 233 DSTN (Pentium MMX/233) | 8.4* | | 404 | 3:00 |
| Gateway Solo 2500SE PII 233** (Pentium II/233) | 9.9 | | 610 | 5:13 |

* With 32MB RAM. When tested with its standard 64MB, the AMD-based unit scored 11.3, and the Pentium MMX–based unit scored 10.5.    ** Reported for comparison.

BETTER ►

▲ Systems based on the mobile Celeron with 128K of full-speed L2 cache swept the field on our Winstone tests. Cache speed, not size, made the difference here (some other units had two to four times more cache). Lithium ion batteries lasted longest on our test. The Compaq unit was especially hindered: Its nickel hydride battery lasted about an hour less than the others.

**Figure 5.4.   Laboratory Review:** *PC Magazine* **Tests of Notebook Computers**
Source: Metz (1999:110)

viewing organization for historical performance reviews does not create the data on which the evaluations are based. It only assembles, summarizes, and presents it in a consistent set of standard reports. These reviews tend to be based on financial information, because that is often the only information that is collected and archived in a standard form. An unusual example of a nonfinancial historical performance review is the *Consumer Reports* automobile frequency-of-repair data. These data are unusual because they are not financial and because Consumers Union collects them solely for frequency-of-repair reports. In most cases, however, historical performance data are already public. Figure 5.5 displays a historical performance review example, Morningstar's review of the Vanguard 500 Index fund.[16]

A third way to answer the question *what is the best product?* is to find out which is most popular. Popularity offers the advantage of knowing that many other people made the same choice. Accepting other peoples' preferences is an easy way to judge quality. This is the basis of reviews like the *New York Times Book Review* best seller lists, movie box office gross data, or *Billboard Magazine*'s Top 100 Singles. We call these *popularity reviews*. Figure 5.6 contains an example of a popularity review, the *New York Times* Hardbound Best Seller list.

Popularity reviews are often presented in an extremely simplified form that highlights only the winners, such as reports on the most popular toys during Christmas season. I am tempted *not* to call these presentations a review because the evaluation is so minimal. Certainly, they shade into ordinary news articles. Yet the presentation of a single table of numbers, like the *New York Times* Best Seller list, has a clear evaluative goal. In this sense, popularity assessments are reviews, even though they are an extremely simple form.

Finally, there are reviews based on a survey of users of a particular product. These are here called *survey reviews*; Zagat's restaurant reviews are an example (see figure 5.1). Survey reviews differ from popularity reviews in that they attempt to assess the quality of a product directly, not indirectly through its popularity. Like Zagat's three categories of food, décor, and service, they typically evaluate several dimensions of quality. Survey reviews are based on votes or other reports from a relevant population. Examples include *Consumer Reports'* automobile frequency-of-repair records from auto owners' reported experience with their cars, the Academy Awards voted by members of the Academy of Motion Picture Arts and Sciences, and Zagat's restaurant reviews based on reports from frequent diners. Survey reviews are relevant to the general population to the extent that the audience being surveyed has some special attributes that make it particularly interesting and well qualified. A film buff explains his logic for seeing Academy Award winners, "The Academy is all actors . . . and movie people; they must know a good movie when they see one. It stands to reason."[17]

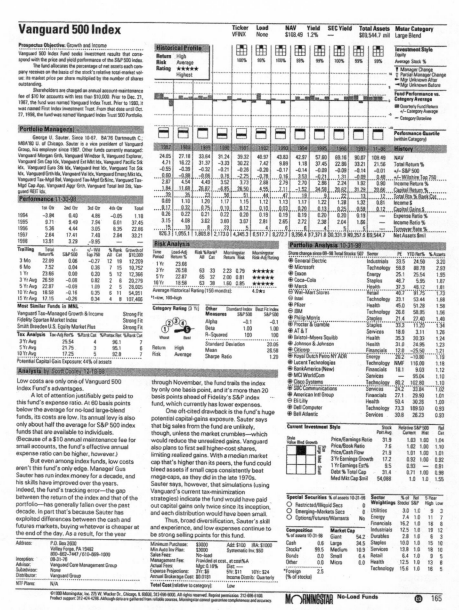

**Figure 5.5. Historical Performance Review: Morningstar Mutual Funds Review**
Source: Morningstar, Inc. 1999:165.

January 3, 1999          THE NEW YORK TIMES BOOK REVIEW

# Best Sellers

| This Week | Fiction | Last Week | Weeks On List |
|---|---|---|---|
| 1 | **A MAN IN FULL,** by Tom Wolfe. (Farrar, Straus & Giroux, $28.95.) Life in Atlanta on the cusp of the millennium, as Old South values collide with a new world. | 1 | 7 |
| 2 | **BAG OF BONES,** by Stephen King. (Scribner, $28.) A series of terrifying events besets a best-selling novelist four years after his wife's sudden death. | 2 | 13 |
| 3 | **RAINBOW SIX,** by Tom Clancy. (Putnam, $27.95.) John Clark, heading an international task force, investigates terrorist incidents in Switzerland, Germany and Spain. | 5 | 20 |
| 4 | **MIRROR IMAGE,** by Danielle Steel. (Delacorte, $26.95.) Identical twin sisters experience quite dissimilar lives in New York and France early in this century. | 4 | 7 |
| 5 | **THE SIMPLE TRUTH,** by David Baldacci. (Warner, $25.) The appeal by a man serving a life sentence for murder creates chaos in Washington's legal community. | 3 | 5 |
| 6 | **THE POISONWOOD BIBLE,** by Barbara Kingsolver. (Harper Flamingo, $26.) Five female characters, a missionary's family, narrate this novel set in the Belgian Congo during that country's fight for independence. | 6 | 10 |
| 7 | **WHEN THE WIND BLOWS,** by James Patterson. (Little, Brown, $25.) A young girl helps a widow and an F.B.I. agent uncover a deadly plot. | 7 | 8 |
| 8 | **HARRY POTTER AND THE SORCERER'S STONE,** by J. K. Rowling. (Levine/Scholastic, $16.95.) A Scottish boy, neglected by his relatives, finds his fortune attending a school of witchcraft. | 16 | 2 |
| 9 | **THE VAMPIRE ARMAND,** by Anne Rice. (Knopf, $26.95.) The progress of an eternally young man from ancient Constantinople to contemporary New Orleans. | 9 | 10 |
| 10 | **A NIGHT WITHOUT ARMOR,** by Jewel Kilcher. (HarperCollins, $15.) The singer-songwriter's poems. (†) | 14 | 14 |
| 11 | **ALL THROUGH THE NIGHT,** by Mary Higgins Clark. (Simon & Schuster, $17.) The mystery of a missing child and a missing chalice is solved in time for Christmas. | 8 | 10 |
| 12 | **CHARMING BILLY,** by Alice McDermott. (Farrar, Straus & Giroux, $22.) At a party to celebrate a man's memory, many secrets of the past come to life. | 12 | 2 |
| 13 | **MEMOIRS OF A GEISHA,** by Arthur Golden. (Knopf, $25.) The life of a young woman growing up in Kyoto who has to reinvent herself after World War II begins. | 10 | 58 |
| 14 | **TODAY I FEEL SILLY & OTHER MOODS THAT MAKE MY DAY,** by Jamie Lee Curtis. Illustrated by Laura Cornell. (Cotler/HarperCollins, $15.95.) The ever-changing moods of a young girl. | 13 | 9 |
| 15 | **THE LOCKET,** by Richard Paul Evans. (Simon & Schuster, $15.95.) A young man learns much about life, love and compassion while working in a nursing home. | 11 | 10 |

| This Week | Nonfiction | Last Week | Weeks On List |
|---|---|---|---|
| 1 | **THE GREATEST GENERATION,** by Tom Brokaw. (Random House, $24.95.) The lives of men and women who came of age during the Depression and World War II. | 1 | 3 |
| 2 | **THE CENTURY,** by Peter Jennings and Todd Brewster. (Doubleday, $60.) An account of the 20th century, complete with photographs and first-person narratives. | 2 | 5 |
| 3 | **TUESDAYS WITH MORRIE,** by Mitch Albom. (Doubleday, $19.95.) A sportswriter tells of his weekly visits to his old college mentor, who was near death's door. | 3 | 63 |
| 4 | **BLIND MAN'S BLUFF,** by Sherry Sontag and Christopher Drew with Annette Lawrence Drew. (Public Affairs, $25.) American submarine espionage. | 4 | 5 |
| 5 | **THE PROFESSOR AND THE MADMAN,** by Simon Winchester. (HarperCollins, $22.) How a murderer helped compile the Oxford English Dictionary. | 5 | 14 |
| 6 | **THE AMERICAN CENTURY,** by Harold Evans with Gail Buckland and Kevin Baker. (Knopf, $50.) A copiously illustrated political history of the 20th century. | 6 | 5 |
| 7 | **WE INTERRUPT THIS BROADCAST,** by Joe Garner. (Sourcebooks, $45.) How radio and television reported historic events over the past 60 years. | 16 | 3 |
| 8 | **FOR THE LOVE OF THE GAME,** by Michael Jordan. Edited by Mark Vancil. (Crown, $50.) The N.B.A. superstar's profusely illustrated memoir. | 8 | 8 |
| 9 | **THE ENDURANCE,** by Caroline Alexander. (Knopf, $29.95.) Ernest Shackleton's 1914 Antarctic expedition. | 7 | 3 |
| 10 | **A WALK IN THE WOODS,** by Bill Bryson. (Broadway, $25.) A journalist hikes the Appalachian Trail. | 12 | 28 |
| 11 | **LINDBERGH,** by A. Scott Berg. (Putnam, $30.) The checkered life of Charles A. Lindbergh. | 9 | 13 |
| 12 | **EVERYTHING AND A KITE,** by Ray Romano. (Bantam, $22.95.) The comedian and star of the television show "Everybody Loves Raymond" describes his life. | | 1 |
| 13 | **A PIRATE LOOKS AT FIFTY,** by Jimmy Buffett. (Random House, $24.95.) Traveling from Florida to the Amazon, the singer-songwriter reflects on his life. | 14 | 27 |
| 14* | **CONVERSATIONS WITH GOD: Book 3,** by Neale Donald Walsch. (Hampton Roads, $22.95.) More discussions of moral questions. | 13 | 7 |
| 15 | **THE TEN COMMANDMENTS,** by Laura Schlessinger and Stewart Vogel. (Cliff Street/HarperCollins, $24.) The significance of the Ten Commandments today. | 10 | 15 |
| 16* | **BEST FRIENDS,** by Sharon J. Wohlmuth and Carol Saline. (Doubleday, $24.95.) Thirty-four accounts of relationships that became more significant than family ties, illustrated with photographs. | 11 | 2 |

## Advice, How-to and Miscellaneous

| This Week | | Last Week | Weeks On List |
|---|---|---|---|
| 1 | **THE GUINNESS BOOK OF RECORDS 1999.** (Guinness, $24.95.) Updated and profusely illustrated. | 2 | 4 |
| 2 | **THE 9 STEPS TO FINANCIAL FREEDOM,** by Suze Orman. (Crown, $23.) How to manage your money. (†) | 1 | 38 |
| 3 | **SIMPLE ABUNDANCE,** by Sarah Ban Breathnach. (Warner, $21.) Advice for women. (†) | | 118 |
| 4 | **EMERIL'S TV DINNERS,** by Emeril Lagasse with Marcelle Bienvenu and Felicia Willett. (Morrow, $25.) Recipes televised by the New Orleans chef. (†) | 4 | 2 |
| 5* | **ONE DAY MY SOUL JUST OPENED UP,** by Iyanla Vanzant. (Fireside/S&S, $13.) How to raise one's morale and realize one's ambitions. (†) | | 5 |

Rankings reflect sales, for the week ending Dec. 19, at almost 4,000 bookstores plus wholesalers serving 50,000 other retailers (gift shops, department stores, newsstands, supermarkets), statistically weighted to represent all such outlets nationwide. An asterisk (*) indicates that a book's sales are barely distinguishable from those of the book above. A dagger (†) indicates that some bookstores report receiving bulk orders. Expanded rankings are available from The New York Times on the Web: www.nytimes.com/books.

**Figure 5.6.    Popularity Review:** *New York Times* **Hardbound Best Seller List**
Source: *New York Times* (1999:22).

Survey reviews may seem to be connoisseurial in the sense that they depend on opinions of individuals. However, they do not depend on the opinions of a single reviewer, a fact of major importance to their proponents. Survey reviews are procedural in the sense that the organization that assembles the results has no stake in any particular outcome. It only reports a summary such as total votes or average ratings. These reviews are procedural because they are based on purely mechanical, formal procedures. There is no human judgment involved.

## COMPARING PROCEDURAL REVIEW TYPES

The four procedural review types do not form a hierarchy. Rather, they tend to be used for different products and different audiences. Which kind of procedural review is used for a product results from a combination of the characteristics of the product, the audience, and the production process of the review. Laboratory testing can be very powerful. Chapter 4 describes how it regularly produces surprising, counterintuitive results. However, laboratory testing is expensive and only certain products can be subjected to laboratory testing. Similarly, historical performance reviews require consistent historical data and only a few products have the necessary data. These tend to be financial products like stocks, bonds, and mutual funds.[18]

Since sales data are available for most products, popularity reviews are often possible. There seems to have been a recent increase in popularity reviews. *Entertainment Weekly* assistant managing editor Mark Harris said the weekly film box-office chart is considered his magazine's most popular feature (Caro 1999:1). He describes rising audience interest in movie sales data:

> When we started [in 1990] we would print the top five movies of the week and their grosses. Now we print the top 20 movies of the week, their grosses, their studios, the number of screens they're on, their per-screen average, the number of weeks in release, their cumulative grosses, and still we get mail saying, "Couldn't you print the top 30?"

John Pierson, host of the Independent Film Channel's "Split Screen" and author of *Spike, Mike, Slackers & Dykes*, describes booksellers' use of the *New York Times* Best Seller list (Caro 1999:1):

> The single chart that can make the biggest difference in the commercial potential or prospects for your work is still the best-sellers list in The New York Times Book Review. Making the chart makes your book. That's both because stores will carry and more prominently display the book, and readers will go off that. You think readers are smarter than moviegoers, but they're more influenced by that list than any moviegoer is by the box-office chart.

A final reason for the newfound influence of popularity reviews is that product makers use them to make both inventory decisions and to promote the product.

It is theoretically possible to conduct a survey review of any product. In practice there are two barriers. Survey reviews cost significant amounts of money, and finding a funding source is not easy. Second, it is often unclear how a published survey review could connect with an audience. One solution is to incorporate a survey review into a magazine or newspaper. Then the subscribers pay for it along with the rest of the publication. This is the solution that supports *Consumer Reports* frequency-of-repair data and movie reviews. In contrast, the genius of Tim and Nina Zagat's restaurant reviews is that they found an audience that was willing to buy their reviews alone without additional magazine content. While Zagat's approach of new editions every year or so works for restaurants, it is not feasible for many other cultural products. A magazine editor said,

> We thought about asking subscribers to vote on the best theater or music productions. Our focus groups liked the idea. But we would have to allow weeks to collect data plus our publication process adds another eight weeks . . . [and] they are ephemeral [products]. By the time we could collect and publish the data . . . most productions would have closed.

The Internet has had a major impact on the time lag in some cases, but the short-lived nature of many cultural products discourages any review that can't be written and published quickly.

*FamilyPC* magazine is known for "family-tested reviews." These are survey reviews where the magazine sends copies of products to selected subscriber families along with a test script. The families run the tests, rate the product, and write a report. A *FamilyPC* editor summarizes the reports in a text review and the magazine prints the average ratings. *FamilyPC* does both family-tested survey reviews and reviews based on laboratory tests.[19]

*FamilyPC* refined its reviews for several years and its experience clarifies the relative strengths and weaknesses of survey and laboratory reviews. The largest difference emerges in the contrast between software and hardware. Survey reviews (i.e., family tests) of software are much easier to do than family-tested hardware. Comparison of different experiences is very important in software, where the central issues are the user interface and ease of use. Robin Raskin, publisher of *FamilyPC*, says, "These families don't have a lot of time. Simplicity is more important than any other issue."

For hardware, precise measurements are more important. Families are not able to do the benchmark testing that is standard for computer hardware. The key criteria for hardware are the speed, capacity, and other technical characteristics. Families do not have the equipment to do the required measurement. Benchmark tests are done in an in-house lab and families supply anecdotal information to supplement the results of expert laboratory testing.

This discussion illustrates how different kinds of procedural reviews fit different situations. Certain evaluations require specific, standardized, well-defined technical skills and survey-based procedures can't handle them. When expert technical knowledge or specific technical situations are required, laboratory procedures are best. When the reports of audience experiences are important, then survey-based procedures may be superior.

The case of *FamilyPC* indicates some of the limits of connoisseurial and procedural reviews, as well as the differences between laboratory and survey reviews. The next section looks more systematically at the question of why an organization chooses to produce connoisseurial or procedural reviews.


## WHY IS A REVIEW CONNOISSEURIAL OR PROCEDURAL?

There are connoisseurial and procedural reviews of many products. Why do some organizations construct connoisseurial reviews and others produce procedural reviews? The first answer is that almost any product can, in principle, be reviewed using either connoisseurial or procedural methods. Many products are reviewed using both. Restaurants, for example, are reviewed by connoisseurs, following in Craig Claiborne's footsteps, as well as by Zagat's procedural reviews. We can read both connoisseurial reviews in the *New York Times Book Review* or the *New York Review of Books*, and also procedural reviews like best seller lists. Computer hardware is typically reviewed procedurally, but it can be reviewed connoisseurially. For example, suppose a computer printer were to be added to the Museum of Modern Art's Industrial Design Collection, along with Kryptonite bicycle locks, helicopters, and other examples of modern design. How might the description of the rationale for the printer read? It could describe the color, line, form, and other aesthetic qualities of the printer. It would be unlikely to mention quantitative, utilitarian measures that are serious concerns of business and professional buyers: speed, cost, or the capacity of the input bins.

When certain products are consistently reviewed using only one approach, observers may conclude that they can only be reviewed in that way. This describes the situation of restaurant reviews up to the 1980s. The fact that a certain rating system has predominated in the past should not blind analysts to alternatives. Cultural entrepreneurs like Tim and Nina Zagat emerge only rarely. How a different rating system would find an audience is a difficult question, and their large audience again underlines the distinctiveness of Zagat's little red books.

Since, in principle, either connoisseurial or procedural reviews can be produced, we can conclude that the choice of a procedural or connoisseurial review is contingent. What is it contingent on? The answer to this question occupies the remainder of this section.

One answer focuses on the extent to which standardized measurements are relevant to the audience. Publications that print both hardware and software reviews are fully aware of the measurement differences between the products and how this impacts their reviews. Ted Stevenson of *PC Magazine* explains,

> We can do good hardware reviews in about 250 words. We can't review software in that space.
>
> *Question*: "Why? What is different about software?"
>
> Hardware has become so standardized that we don't need to say much about individual products. The tests do it all. Software is not so standard. The Windows interface has standardized many parts. Some of the most idiosyncratic software that we used to see has disappeared. But once you get past standard things like the File Open dialog [box], interfaces still aren't very standard. This is more apparent in the statistical software we reviewed than in, say, spreadsheets where everyone follows Excel. We have to talk about the interface and how well it works for the product.

Laboratory and historical performance reviews require standardized measurements. If that is not possible the alternatives are a connoisseurial review, a survey review, or a popularity review.

The stability of product categories influences the rating system. A *PC Magazine* editor explains:

> Including planning, our comparative reviews take at least two months, probably more. The printing and distribution process adds another eight weeks. We feel some pressure from Internet review sites so we have begun to put more emphasis on individual reviews of new products.

For connoisseurial reviews, the speed with which they can be completed and their one-reviewer-one-product-one-review nature makes them particularly suitable for new or unstable product categories, where the products are changing rapidly and the interests of the audience are not yet clear. Procedural reviews, on the other hand, are better suited to products in stable, well-established categories where the criteria for a good product are well understood.

These are some of the broad differences between connoisseurial and procedural reviews. To explore more systematically the circumstances that encourage the production of one or the other, the next pages compare the resources, reviewers, organizations, production process, and content of connoisseurial and procedural reviews. The audience is so important that it is treated alone in the following section. The three actors—publisher, reviewer, and audience—are tightly bound together by the review process. Product makers are not much influenced by whether the review uses connoisseurial or procedural methods; hence they are omitted from this analysis.

The resources needed to produce a review are the largest difference between connoisseurial and procedural reviews. Connoisseurial reviewers typically review one product at a time. The product maker often donates the product being reviewed: the book, the tickets to the performance, or a special screening of the film. They can also be completed relatively quickly. Theater or music reviewers for newspapers may have as little as forty-five minutes writing time between the end of the performance and the deadline when the finished review is due (Christiansen 1998). Because few people are involved and costs are low, connoisseurial reviews are easy to manage. Low resource costs means that they are attractive to small, resource-constrained publications like suburban newspapers, low-circulation magazines, and academic journals.

Procedural reviews tend to be more expensive. The planning, organization, and delivery of a multi-product review by a team of people with a complex division of labor requires money, technical skills, testing equipment, planning, and management skills. The tests, surveys, or historical measurements often require substantial investment in overhead, including space, expensive and specialized testing equipment, trained staff, and skilled managers. A single, large procedural review may cost over one hundred thousand dollars. The need for extensive resources explains why procedural reviews tend to be undertaken by large, well-established, wealthy organizations. Procedural reviews are out of reach for small publications.

Some of these differences in resources point to differences in the reviewers. Connoisseurial reviewers write a personal response to the product. Their primary qualification is experience and a refined sensitivity; no formal training or formal qualifications are necessarily required to become a connoisseurial reviewer, although substantive experience or formal academic training in the subject of the review are often valuable. They are experts who are called upon to deliver an expert opinion. Because they can deliver their opinion quickly, connoisseurial reviewers are particularly attractive on TV programs or in other settings where space or time are major constraints. Connoisseurial reviews are often complex constructions, but their production process is hidden. It is hidden because it takes place in the person of the reviewer who becomes a black box of production. Connoisseurial reviewers have a great deal of discretion in terms of what they write in the text of the review and what criteria they use as the basis for their judgments. The reviewer is the most important person in the review. Connoisseurial reviewers can become celebrities; examples include Claiborne, Clement Greenberg on modern art, and Pauline Kael on film.

Procedural reviewers are also skilled, but skilled in the sense of being technically trained rather than exhibiting a refined sensitivity. Their role is to follow a precise script where each product is treated exactly like the others and extraneous sources of variation are properly controlled. Restricting the discretion of the reviewers is often an explicit goal of the testing procedures and is seen by proponents as a major strength of the review. This is why procedural reviewers can be technicians; their qualifications are certain technical skills. The criteria and reasons for the judgments are detailed, often quantitative, and explicitly explained in the review. These are transparent reviews. The most important person in procedural reviews is the person who writes the test plan and manages the review, usually an editor or a manager. Procedural reviewers never become celebrities. The person writing the review is often a technical writer who may be anonymous and not particularly well paid.

Reviewers, of course, work for an organization. While organizations can be designed to produce either connoisseurial or procedural reviews, they often produce only one kind of review or the other, but not both. Some, like the Museum of Modern Art, can produce only connoisseurial reviews. Others, like Zagat's, produce only procedural reviews. Inertia also plays a role: once an organization begins doing one system, it may have great difficulty adding an additional system to its repertoire. The review organization does what it is capable of doing and ignores what it can't do. The repertoires of organizations are often limited. As a result, the capability of the review organization may often be decisive in determining the kind of reviews it produces.

There are exceptions to the point that review organizations generally produce only one kind of review. An exception is some kinds of survey reviews that are so well standardized and routinized that they can be produced by a small bureaucracy inside a connoisseurial organization. Until recently, this was the way newspapers handled the best seller lists printed among the connoisseurial book reviews in book review sections. A second exception results from the fact that the details of procedural reviews can be fully described and outsourced. Thus, in recent years the best seller lists in many newspapers are constructed from data gathered by the BookScan system, which was originally established to report sales data to publishers. A third exception stems from the systems' asymmetric requirements for organizational support. Connoisseurial reviews require little support. Organizations committed to connoisseurial reviews generally don't produce procedural reviews. Procedural reviews, on the other hand, require a great deal of organizational support. But, because connoisseurial reviews require so little, organizations that are primarily dedicated to procedural reviews also produce connoisseurial reviews. *PC Magazine* is an example. None of these exceptions contradict the point that the capabilities of the review organization are usually narrow and often determine the kind of reviews produced.

The production of a connoisseurial review is relatively straightforward and simple. An editor assigns the review to a reviewer, stating the deadline, length of the finished review, and other relevant characteristics. Although reviewers sometimes include comparisons to similar products in their review, in general, such comparisons are left to the audience. The goal of the review is a recommendation from the reviewer. The key source of knowledge is the reviewer's personal response to the product. In summary, a connoisseurial review is a craft product. It is produced one at a time and it is one of a kind; each product is unique (Woodward 1965).

Procedural reviews have a different production process. Instead of a simple division of labor, they have a complex division of labor. Procedural reviews typically cover the most important products in an entire product category in a single review. The goal of a procedural review is to help readers make sense out of the category by summarizing the important characteristics, assessing how each product performs on the criteria, and ranking all products. The key source of knowledge is the detailed, explicit, formal procedures. The actual reviewing itself involves assembling the products to be reviewed and subjecting them to the procedures in a more-or-less assembly line fashion. In contrast to their connoisseurial counterparts, procedural reviews are mass-produced.

The reviews themselves are also very different. Connoisseurial reviews usually consist almost entirely of discursive text. Although they typically focus on the particular product under review, some are broader. For example, book reviews contain a subgenre better described as reflective essays stimulated by the publication of a book rather than strictly a critical review of the book itself.

Procedural reviews are usually longer than connoisseurial reviews but since they review so many products they devote much less space to each product. The cost of page space combined with the need to review dozens or hundreds of products reduces each product to a brief summary. Editors considering procedural reviews find quantitative tests attractive. It would be impossible to satisfactorily review a large number of products using only text because the text would require too much space and too much work from readers. As everyone writing for scientific journals discovers, tables of quantitative results are very concise. The numbers also lend themselves to effective overall summaries so that all the products can be ranked. A small table to display the winning products for each audience is sufficient guidance for many readers. Only readers interested in the details need look at the larger tables containing all the test results. Some test results can even be published on web pages, with only a reference in the printed article, and so don't incur the cost of paper publication.

## CONSTRUCTION OF MULTIPLE AUDIENCES

Consider audiences: what kind of audience reads the gray text of the *New York Times Book Review* or Wheaton's restaurant reviews in *Chicago* magazine compared to the multiple tables, summaries, and sidebars in *PC Magazine* or *Consumer Reports*? Among culturally literate people, either rating system is readily understandable. However, it is clear from typography alone that these two systems of reviews construct their audiences very differently.

Connoisseurial reviews construct an audience interested in a complex, discursive analysis of products. The audience must have the facility and time to take in a long narrative. This audience is comfortable with the demands of textual reviews: comparatively long, discursive analyses. They can handle the high levels of cognitive processing that accompany this sort of text. This audience is not especially interested in a summary of the evaluation. It is an audience that likes the product (or at least the product category) and by reading invites the reviewer to teach it. These reviews are designed for an audience whose interests can only be characterized in general terms and the relationship of audience interests to the characteristics of the product has to be reestablished in every review. This is what makes connoisseurial reviews so personal and why matching the reviewer to the audience is so important.

The connoisseurial audience also reads the review in part to learn how the review was put together by the reviewer. In this sense, the review may be as interesting as the product itself, and it may be as attractive to the audience. Some reviews are read because of audience interest in the reviewer, not the product. Examples are reviews by John Kenneth Galbraith or George Bernard Shaw. A selection of George Bernard Shaw's music reviews from the 1880s and 1890s was published in 1961 (Shaw 1961) despite the fact that the performers and audience members were dead and many of the musical organizations no longer existed. The complete text of all book reviews written by Shaw for the *Pall Mall Gazette* between 1885 and 1888 was published in 1991 (Shaw 1991). This is an extreme example of how connoisseurial reviewers can become celebrities, more important and more interesting to the audience than the products they review.[20] The prominence of the reviewer in the minds of a connoisseurial audience means that it is as interested in the reviewer's perspective and reaction to the product as in the product itself. This audience likes the reviewer in addition to the product.

Procedural reviews construct a very different audience. It is an audience primarily concerned with making decisions. In this sense, procedural reviews address an audience interested in reviews as a means to an end. There are really at least two audiences. One is a large audience interested in picking the best product in a category using a fairly standard set of criteria summarized in a single table. This audience has a short attention span. It wants a simple, unambiguous answer in an easily digestible format and does not want or need to understand the details of why a product is the best. It is an audience that does not have a lot of time and so it is willing to read a quick summary to find the best product. This avoids the chore of actually reading the review.

There is also a second audience. Procedural reviews are more flexible than the preceding paragraph implies. Audiences that are seriously interested in the product category can consult the information in the introduction, in the "How we tested" sidebar, and in the extensive tables. For sheer quantity of information, procedural reviews dwarf any connoisseurial review. For example, *InfoWorld* reviewed 32-bit operating systems (OS/2, Windows 95, and Windows NT) in nineteen articles with a separate table of contents and multiple cross-references to previously published articles (Petreley 1995a). I estimate length at about twenty thousand words plus tables and graphics.

In any procedural review, the tables and the description of testing procedures are particularly flexible. They present the review in a form that can be regarded as a collection of fragments that can be easily rearranged, reweighted, and reconstructed by each reader in their own way, according to their own purposes. The review offers guidance and its own preferred interpretation of the review outcome in the summary and the "Editors' Choice" or "Best Buy" selections. This does not, however, preclude other outcomes from the same review data. One reader told me,

> I've subscribed for more than 10 years even though I've never liked *PC Magazine*'s criteria. But it prints all the data. I can read those tables and I use them to find the product that's right for me.

Some procedural reviews openly invite readers to use alternative weights to construct their own outcome. For several years, *InfoWorld* included a blank column for readers to use their own weights to recalculate the summary scores for the products in the review. The disk version of *Software Digest Ratings Report* allows users to use their own weights to recalculate scores. Ziff-Davis Media benchmark tests from the eTesting Labs allow users to customize the benchmark test results to meet their needs. Testing procedures articles often explicitly invite readers to perform the same tests on their own products. If readers don't like the tests as presented, test procedures can be modified to suit. These possibilities open up considerably more flexible ways to tailor the information in a review to address the needs of various audiences.

This is one of the sharp distinctions between procedural reviews and connoisseurial reviews. Connoisseurial reviews rarely recognize multiple perspectives. Indeed, their entire focus is on providing a single interesting perspective by an attractive connoisseur. By the same token, they almost never recognize different or multiple audiences. Even in the how-to-read-a-film-review recommendation from Roger Ebert, quoted in chapter 2, the reader still depends on the perspective of the single reviewer-connoisseur.

Procedural reviews produce a single winner and an ordinal ranking of all products in the review. The tables of performance summaries may look like they have a single perspective. However, this understates their flexibility. By allowing or encouraging readers to reweight test results or conduct their own tests, procedural reviews add an entirely different dimension to reviews. They concede a fundamental point: that the published review may not be the only appropriate way to evaluate the product. As a matter of policy, many publications print procedural reviews with the explicit recognition that there are many, many audiences for a review and that the publication cannot anticipate the needs of all its readers. Under these circumstances the goal of the publication is to provide readers with tools, not definitive answers. The publication no longer claims that its judgments are authoritative. With these possibilities, procedural reviews move the responsibility for an authoritative evaluation from the reviewer to the audience. A good procedural review, then, is a complex collection of elements that serve several different audiences. These possibilities expand considerably the scope and usefulness of procedural reviews.

This chapter compares connoisseurial and procedural reviews along many dimensions. Although our discussion mentions audiences, we have been primarily concerned with the production of reviews. The next chapter extends this comparison by asking, why are these very different rating systems credible? Although the answers are intimately linked to production, they primarily concern audience responses to reviews.

## NOTES

1. Recently, Zagat's began using the same methodology to review golf courses, hotels, movies, music CDs, and nightlife.

2. Comparisons in this chapter use 2003 Chicago Zagat's (van Housen 2003) and the September 2003 *Chicago* magazine (*Chicago* magazine 2003). Both would have gone to press at about the same time in summer 2003. This means that they evaluate restaurants at identical times. See appendix C for details.

3. These lists appear in the Friday section, but they don't appear every week. When they are printed, the list includes as many as forty recent reviews. The *Washington Post* publishes a similar but shorter list of restaurants recently reviewed by Eve Ziebart. It publishes no list of recent reviews by its restaurant critic, Tom Sietsema, perhaps because he wrote a book of restaurant reviews.

4. This comment, of course, applies largely to local restaurant-goers. Out-of-town visitors, who don't know local restaurants, find it a convenient way to find a good restaurant. Zagat's national name recognition helps sell guides to tourists.

5. Zagat's now tries to include such changes when they occur before publication, and the web edition of Zagat's also notes significant changes, but there is no fix for outdated food ratings.

6. Reading this, Wheaton laughed and said, "It's *so* hard to be witty about food. Every review I struggle to write witty descriptions. English just doesn't have enough funny words to describe dishes. Calvin Trillin can do it because he doesn't describe the food, mostly the people and their comments." Wheaton agreed that it is easier to achieve pithiness.

7. One example of similar ideas: For years *Consumer Reports* has used questionnaires to rate movies and to construct frequency-of-repair indices for automobiles. Consumers Union never added text or developed the convenient format. Another example: Gault-Millau has used numerical restaurant ratings for decades. A third example: Reichl separately evaluates several different components of the restaurant experience, such as atmosphere, service, and recommended dishes, in the summary box in the upper right corner of her reviews (see table 3.1), although the star rating reflects her simultaneous reaction to food, ambiance, and service.

8. As we see in chapter 7, there are many possible dimensions of restaurant quality and, hence, many potential continua, but for this illustration we consider just one continuum.

9. There has been a single prior study. I summarize it here to provide additional context for the results to come. Wanderer (1970) compared movie ratings by professional critics with ratings by members of Consumers Union. He frames his study by asking the question, is there a significant difference between the evaluations of professional critics and popular audiences? The most general test of this question indicates that critics' rating was the same as the popular audience 53 percent of the time, critics rated 19 percent of films more favorably, and 28 percent less favorably (1970:267, table 2, N=5,644 films). These data and other evidence, he argues, support the proposition that critics and audiences evaluate films similarly. He suggests that these results support Gans's (1957, 1999 [1974]) argument that they both come from the same upper-middle taste public.

10. I examined New York, Boston, Los Angeles, and San Francisco city magazines and newspapers. None prints lists of recently reviewed restaurants with stars or other summaries of their longer restaurant reviews. For reasons explained in chapter 3, few connoisseurial restaurant reviewers award stars. Tom Sietsema, *Washington Post*, began awarding stars in October 2003.

11. These are standard Tukey (1977) box plots. My description in the text oversimplifies slightly. It says that the ends of the boxes enclose the cases from the

twenty-fifth to the seventy-fifth percentile, or the interquartile range. Actually, the boxes enclose the hspread, which is close to but not identical to the interquartile range. The technical name for this figure is a grouped box plot. It includes all 127 restaurants rated by both *Chicago* magazine and Zagat's.

I also produced plots of *Chicago* stars against Zagat's décor and service ratings. Their overall pattern is identical to the plot for food ratings. Since star ratings are based mostly on food quality, Zagat's food ratings are the most appropriate comparison.

12. There are two outliers of note. One is the outside value in the three-star category. This is Red Light, a pan-Asian restaurant. When I asked Wheaton, he said that Red Light had shone briefly under an excellent chef and that accounted for the three-star rating. Several months after September 2003, he reevaluated it as two and a half stars, which is more consistent with Zagat's twenty-one food rating. This illustrates a monthly magazine like *Chicago* responding more quickly than Zagat's to changing quality. The second is the outside value in the two-star category. This is Adobo Grill, a Mexican restaurant. Wheaton simply said, "It's better than that." He thinks Zagat's diners are in error.

13. Analysis of 1997 and 1999 data from Zagat's and *Chicago* magazine shows identical results.

14. This is not an argument that there are in some sense objective criteria for evaluating restaurants (or any other product). These data do not contain evidence of objective criteria. They are only evidence that—on average—*Chicago* magazine's connoisseurial restaurant reviewers and Zagat's ordinary diners use the same criteria. There is no evidence here describing what the criteria are, although the restaurant reviews chapter describes such criteria. This figure only shows evidence of a consensus among reviewers and diners about a good restaurant and a good meal.

15. Restaurant meals can be tested for their nutritional content (e.g., Boger 1995; Hurley and Schmidt 1993), which is similar to *PC Magazine* tests. However, the usual material evaluated in a dining review could not easily be tested.

16. Morningstar bases its ratings on a history of price changes of investment funds. Funds are based on reviews in the sense that they attempt to buy stocks with the best performing market prices. A market price is the sum, or in effect a review, of multiple (for stocks, tens of thousands) individual reviews. Since Morningstar summarizes the review that funds and price perform, it is a review of reviews of reviews. See chapter 8 on prices and reviews. (I thank an anonymous reader for this point.)

17. Of course, politics are also involved in the Academy Awards, and this respondent recognized that. The fact that there are politics involved does not discredit his point. Also, there is always some disagreement. See the prior section for a discussion of how people differ in their rank ordering of products, and the extent to which the differences matter.

18. The question why certain data are retained and made publicly available, while other data remain confidential or are discarded, is worth serious investigation in itself. The most common public data are the financial indicators required to inform outside investors about the performance of their investment. The widespread availability of these data—for public corporations, at least—recognizes that investors need to be

able to evaluate their investment. The fact that it is legally required to be audited shows how it is related to issues of credibility and trust, see chapter 6.

19. The information in the section is based on interviews with Robin Raskin, publisher of *FamilyPC* magazine, and several of her top editors. *FamilyPC* ceased publication during the recession in 2001.

20. Of course, George Bernard Shaw was well known for many reasons, but he first made his reputation as a music and book reviewer—and he wrote novels—before he became a playwright.

*Chapter Six*

# Audiences, Credibility, and the Social Construction of Reviews

The critic doesn't have any power except what's given to him voluntarily by the guy who reads him.

—Walter Kerr, Sunday drama critic of the *New York Times*
(quoted in Cooper 1973: 96)

For over twenty years, Carla Kelson was one of the most powerful restaurant critics in Chicago. She wrote a dining column for *Chicago* magazine with her husband, Alan, from 1969 to 1989. When he left to pursue other business interests—including consulting for Chicago restaurants—she continued the column on her own. In early 1993, several restaurateurs publicly accused her of giving preference to restaurants where Alan was a consultant in the 1992 awards that the magazine gave to the top twenty-five restaurants in Chicago. She firmly denied it. "I was always open and straightforward about Allen's business" being separate from her own, she said. That probably didn't matter. Ethics are a sensitive point because they influence reader interpretations of any review ever published. One reader commented to me, "This is difficult. It raises questions about whether [*Chicago* magazine] understands conflict of interest. I don't know whether I can trust any of its reviews." Such a far-reaching impact makes ethical allegations extremely damaging. The perception alone is dangerous: on June 8, 1993, the editor fired Kelson.[1]

This example illustrates the power of ethics. Ensuring impartial production is central to credibility and to readership. Since the influence of reviews rests solely on their persuasiveness, credibility is a core issue. Strong ethical conduct is a foundation that makes this institution work.

## ETHICS

Ethical issues may change the way audiences look at reviews. For connoisseurial reviews ethical problems involve corruption of a single person; for procedural reviews they involve a whole process. Connoisseurial reviews can be protected by ensuring the integrity of the reviewer. When reviewing products this is relatively simple as long as the reviewer accepts no gifts and has no close personal involvement with the product maker. Reviews of performances are more complex because the reviewer must be present to witness the performance. If product makers know a reviewer is present, they can try to improve the quality of the performance especially for the reviewer. Ensuring distance between product maker and reviewer, including reviewer anonymity, is the ethical solution.[2] Claiborne's influence stemmed in part from his commitment to ethical standards that convinced readers that he had their interests at heart. Similar ethical independence enhanced wine critic Robert M. Parker's influence (Echikson 2004). Both critics began reviewing in a category that had no standard of independent, reader-oriented reviews. Their strong personal ethical standards and authoritative taste combined to force product makers and audiences to take them seriously.

Procedural reviews involve more people and allow more entry points for ethical issues. Distance is harder to manage; as a result, procedural review ethics are more complex. There are at least three entry points. A subtle entry point is when the test plans are being constructed. Here are echoes of a connoisseurial review: like the evaluation process in a connoisseurial review, test plans are largely hidden from readers, yet they establish the major criteria for the review. These criteria will determine which products score well and which do badly. An example showing the importance of criteria comes from a series of studies that compare the cost of ownership of Linux—which can be downloaded for no charge—to Microsoft Windows—which is definitely not free. Those studies that were funded by Microsoft have concluded unanimously that Windows is cheaper in the long run. If you pay for the study, you get to write the test plans. Another entry point is through contact with the product maker during the review. Although *Consumer Reports* does not allow these conversations, most other review publications do, and in emerging product categories they are almost required, if only to learn about the products included in the category and their capabilities. Product makers try very hard to spin the test result in their favor. A third entry occurs during internal debates about special awards like Editors' Choice. Editors have considerable discretion: one or more products can receive an award, some can be given honorable mention, occasionally no award is given. Since these are not tied to strict procedures, any biases could influence the result.

Reviewers and editors tend to be sensitive to these points, and rules for conflict of interest in procedural reviews are often written and specify in detail what is not appropriate (e.g., Alsop 1994b). Because connoisseurial reviews are written by one person, publishers often have no formal, written ethical standards. Instead they rely on reviewer's professional ethics to inform the editor of any personal contact or relationship that may constitute a conflict of interest. This is typical of, for example, book reviews in academic journals.

As a result of these differences, connoisseurial reviews may be more prone to ethical problems than procedural reviews. The process in a connoisseurial review is a black box. Readers cannot easily see how evaluations were reached. On the other hand, procedural reviews have a major ethical protection built into their testing. Their test procedures are often described in sufficient detail so that readers could—in principle—replicate the results themselves. Also, the tables of test results can be used by readers without reference to the reviewer's conclusions. Readers can reweight the results and reach their own conclusions. We return to this point when we discuss the construction of audiences near the end of this chapter.

Ethics are only one of several mechanisms that enhance credibility. In addition to ethics and the credibility mechanisms described in previous literature, reviews suggest two other new credibility-enhancing mechanisms that I will call iterative trust building and third-party validation. The remainder of this chapter describes how these credibility mechanisms influence both production and reception of connoisseurial and procedural reviews. Recent work in the sociology of knowledge focuses on the role of social organizations in constructing knowledge. We use this work to discuss differences in the credibility arguments of the two rating systems. Having discussed production and reception separately, they are combined to look at the context in which credible knowledge is produced and understood. This addresses a central issue in the sociology of scientific knowledge: how can knowledge escape the local context where it originated? The chapter ends by summarizing how credible knowledge is produced and understood in reviews.

## RECEPTION: WHEN DO AUDIENCES TRUST REVIEWS?

Prior sociological work on credibility is in the sociology of scientific knowledge, especially Shapin (1994, 1995a, 1995b) and Porter (1995). Shapin (1995a) discusses two general mechanisms of generating trust.[3] The first mechanism works in small groups, for example, small scientific research networks.[4] In these settings trust in each person's veracity and competence is the norm. The consequences of radical distrust would probably lead to the breakup of the group. Why would anyone belong to any primary group if they did not believe what other members said? This is credibility much like it existed in the primordial *Gemeinschaft* village, long before the onset of the modern division of labor. It is probably characteristic of all small groups that member's statements are assumed to be credible. Shapin (1994:14) quotes Goffman (1969:104):

> The willingness of an individual to credit another's unconditional and conditional avowals is an entirely necessary thing for the maintenance of collaborative social activity and, as such, a central and constant feature of social life.

Shapin's second mechanism relies on Porter's (1995) discussion of the role of quantification. Drawing on examples from accounting, insurance, cost-benefit analysis, and civil engineering, Porter argues that quantification is a technology used to make decisions at a distance, without direct personal knowledge. The mathematical tools of quantification are highly structured and rule-bound. They discipline users and reduce their discretion, thereby minimizing bias and self-interest. Reliance on numbers substitutes disciplined procedures for the personal trust characteristic of small groups.

There is a methodological contrast between this book and Shapin's and Porter's work; their research is primarily historical. Although part of this book uses historical research, the methodological core is interviews with people involved in all aspects of reviewing. Unlike historians, I can actually ask review readers how they make credibility judgments. This book looks in detail at audiences and their responses to reviews. In this respect, it is similar to the source credibility research (summarized in chapter 1) that suggests the character and competence of each reviewer are central to readers' judgments of credibility. To extend both Shapin and the source credibility research, we can ask, how do readers actually judge character and competence: What is the process? What evidence do they use? In the course of answering these questions, I have identified two additional credibility mechanisms that I call *iterative trust building* and *third-party validation*.

## Iterative Trust Building

Although it is possible to read a single review and make a judgment about credibility, this is not typical. Typically readers repeatedly read the same reviewers in a daily, weekly, or monthly publication. At the same time they have personal experiences with some of the products being reviewed. Over time they compare reviewer's evaluations with their experiences. During this iterative process, as readers match their experience with the descriptions of the review author, judgments about credibility often solidify. A representative example is a movie buff:

> After I moved to Chicago I started reading [the reviewers]. . . . [Roger] Ebert [of the *Chicago Sun-Times*] and [Jonathan] Rosenbaum [of the *Chicago Reader*] seemed to like the same movies that I did and the same actors too. Now I read all their reviews. After a while, I stopped reading other movie reviewers regularly.

We usually think of this buildup of trust in a positive sense. A *Washington Post Book World* reader describes his response to book critic Jonathan Yardley's Sunday book reviews:

> The first thing I knew about Yardley was that I didn't share his political opinions. I made it a principle of mine not to read his reviews. . . . One Sunday he reviewed a book that I had just ordered from Amazon.com so I read the review. It was a well-written, interesting, erudite review; I was surprised. When I read the book, I found he described it perfectly. . . . That surprised me too. . . . I read him a few more times. I guess I warmed up to him. His review in the book section . . . [is the] first thing that I read on Sunday. My wife jokes about my "Yardley fix." . . . I still don't like his politics, though.

There is also a negative sense in which credibility can accumulate. The quote from Roger Ebert in chapter 2 illustrates this perspective: a reader has learned that she isn't interested in any movie that Ebert likes.

As a result of this iterative process, readers gain confidence in their understanding of reviewers. In the minds of readers, reviewers acquire a reputation (positive or negative). Reviewers gain reputations with respect to specific issues that readers consider important. A typical example concerns a restaurant reviewer: "[He] is good on the entrées, but his comments about wine are poor. He doesn't say much and what he says is so bad that I think he must drink his wine by the glass." Experienced readers make fine-grained judgments.

The iterative credibility mechanism links both to small groups and to quantification. In small groups trust is unlikely to be granted the moment people join an established group. There is likely to be a period of building trust where the same iterative mechanism operates. In this sense the iterative process works in small groups where credibility of group members is the norm. The credibility of quantification is also not automatically granted. Readers must pick the review that uses the appropriate criteria. The example of computer hardware reviews in the previous chapter shows how quantified criteria can be weighted differently for different audiences. There are also different ways of quantifying: lab testing, a user survey, historical performance, or a measure of popularity. Readers have more confidence when they have experience with a publication that produces some form of quantification that has proven useful in the past. Here is a reader reflecting on his initial encounter with *PC Magazine* reviews.

> I hadn't heard of [*PC Magazine*] when I was looking for a new printer in the late 1980s . . . [but] someone showed me their printer review issue. I had never seen anything like it: the number of printers, the tests, and the careful work. I bought my [printer] on its recommendation. It was a great printer; [it] lasted for years. After that experience I used it to buy a computer. It was a good computer. Then I was sold on it and its reviews. . . . I never let my subscription lapse.

In this sense the iterative process is an important component of trust in quantification.[5] Thus, iterative trust building is a general mechanism; it works in small groups; it also operates in large-scale, impersonal settings.

The process works best when certain conditions hold. I have identified five conditions. *The first and minimum criterion for this process is simple: individual reviewers must have a consistent point of view.* Consistency means that should a reviewer write about, say, two similar products during a year, both evaluations will be similar. In one sense this is the definition of a good reviewer; someone with a stable perspective so that audiences can reliably contrast the reviewer to their own point of view. As audiences come to know a reviewer, they can make allowances for idiosyncrasies and biases of the reviewer. This kind of understanding allows audiences to locate a reviewer more accurately with respect to their own perspective. Consequently, the reviews become more informative and more useful. An example of how this can work comes from a reader's remark about a Chicago restaurant reviewer: "His taste seems to be off when he eats in Chinatown. He *cannot* judge Chinese food. I never read those reviews. . . . But his reviews of American food are superb." (Emphasis in the original.) A stable perspective clearly fits the conditions of connoisseurial reviews, with their emphasis on the reviewer's personal reaction to a product. Procedural reviews also have a stable point of view. For example, *PC Magazine* emphasizes computers suitable for business use.[6] These reviews emphasize networking capabilities, remote management, and overall suitability for common business tasks. In contrast, *PC Gamers* magazine reviews hardware in terms of gaming potential, which emphasizes disk and CPU speed but above all graphics performance.

*Second, product genres and publications must be stable.* This condition works in tandem with the prior condition. Stable product genres ensure there are comparable products. Stable publications ensure that reviewers are employed and that reviews are available to audiences on a regular basis. Under these conditions an established set of reviewers can review the constant stream of new products: movies, restaurants, music, art, theater, or consumer products. Book reviews are probably the most important exception to this description. Many publications that print book reviews have reviewers who regularly review books; for example, Jonathan Yardley, book critic of the *Washington Post*, writes two reviews each week. In addition, these publications pay outside reviewers whose qualifications are matched with the subject matter of each book. In this case, the same reviewer does not review a new book each week. Here, readers make judgments about credibility based on a single review.

In the case of products like books, a third condition helps readers judge credibility. *Most publications assist readers by printing a short description of the qualifications of the reviewer.* One subscriber to the *New York Times Book Review* said,

When I see a review of a book that interests me the first thing that I do—before I even read the review—is look at the credentials of the reviewer.

*Question*: What information is does that give you?

The background of the reviewer says something about what the reviewer is going to be able to say. I'm looking for his point of view. . . . What does he know? How is he likely to approach the book?

The one- or two-sentence descriptions of the background of the reviewer are necessarily superficial. Yet readers find them valuable and make at least tentative credibility judgments based on them. Thus reviewers' qualifications play an important role in credibility judgments.

*Often a fourth condition holds: readers must be able to find a reviewer whose point of view matches their prior knowledge.* The description of credibility judgments as an iterative process understates the role of readers' prior knowledge. People—at least adults—usually read reviews in the context of a set of preexisting opinions and personal judgments. People come to most reviews with judgments about products, so to an extent they can match reviewers' assessments with their prior understanding of the product genre. If these judgments are well formed, they may allow readers to short circuit some or all of the iterations. A film buff said,

I always liked [director Martin] Scorsese and I started reading Chicago film reviews about when *Cape Fear* was released. . . . I knew that Roger Ebert thought Scorsese was the best living American director, so I read his review with great concentration. When I saw the movie I had exactly the same reaction he did: I expected more of a Scorsese film. . . . That's what started me reading Ebert's reviews. I've read them ever since. It's the only reason I buy the *Sun-Times*.

*Fifth, readers judge credibility based on the publication printing the re-view, specifically, the quality and reputation of the publication.* When I pressed respondents for their reactions to example reviews, I was typically assured, "It's a good review. . . . It must be, otherwise the *Tribune* wouldn't print it." Many interviewees could not remember the names of individual reviewers and these people seem particularly likely to simply assume that anything printed in a major publication like the *Chicago Tribune* or the *New York Times* is trustworthy. For these people the default value for any review was simply to trust it. One man explained his reasoning about the *Chicago Tribune* by saying, "It's an important paper and it must check out what it prints. . . . At least I think so." From a reader's point of view, this perspective economizes scarce resources of time and energy. Not much work or thought is demanded of the review reader whose succinct credibility judgment was, "If the *Tribune* hired him, he must be good."

This assumption simplifies reading for many people, but even readers who read reviews carefully and critically usually assume that reviewers for major publications are qualified professionals. One regular restaurant review reader explained this perspective,

> Every few years a new reviewer will start writing for *Gourmet* or *Food and Wine*. I read their first column or two perhaps a little more skeptically than usual. But these are sophisticated magazines with intelligent editors. When they hire someone new, I assume they know what they're doing. I trust the reviews unless the reviewer says something really stupid.

This is a typical response: reviewers who work for credible publications are presumed correct and they generally have to prove that they are unsuitable.[7]

As the previous quote suggests, these reader assumptions are based in part on the reputation of a publication. Reputation is important because it is present before any reader examines text. For some readers, knowing that a certain publication published a review was all they needed to know. One restaurant review reader asserted, "*Gourmet* only prints reviews of restaurants that it likes. If it was reviewed in *Gourmet* I know it's good."[8] A strong reputation means the publication has influence with the public and a prestigious position in the hierarchy of publications. The managers of publications are aware of this link and they go to some lengths to safeguard their reputations. The most common mechanisms used in reviews were fact checking the text and ethics policies. Both restaurant reviews and software reviewers do extensive fact checking. Here publications tend to be extremely sensitive. An editor explained,

> We want to make it easy for a subscriber to trust us. . . . If our review says a dish is beef but the subscriber who orders it finds that it is really pork, that's embar-

rassing. . . . It is worse than embarrassing. Readers can check just a few things that we write. If one of those things turns out to be wrong—and a simple thing like an ingredient, at that—how can readers trust that we're right about all the things they can't check? Getting easy facts wrong is a serious mistake. We work hard to avoid making it.

Thus the text of the review is a locus that readers use to judge credibility. Accurate text shows readers that the review can be believed.

Ethics policies are an important source of protection for a publication's reputation. Ethics policies establish boundaries for acceptable conduct. They enforce the boundaries by disciplining or even firing reviewers who ignore the policies. Disciplinary action is often private, but two examples are more public. Ron Wynn was fired by the Memphis *Commercial Appeal* after he filed—and the paper published—a review of a band's performance even though, it turned out, the band never appeared at the concert (*Chicago Tribune* 1991). The Carla Kelson controversy has been described above. An experienced Chicago journalist explained how *Chicago* magazine's reputation suffered and it had no choice but to fire Kelson:

> The magazine was in an extremely difficult position. The reputation of *Chicago* is built on the restaurant reviews. They are the reason people save their copies. . . . Several individuals felt confident enough to make plausible, public accusations of conflict of interest. . . . [These] accusations challenged the core of the magazine. *Chicago* couldn't afford the damage. The only way to remove the perception that *Chicago* might condone that conflict was to jettison the person.

When an employee is accused of ethical violations, there are conventional responses. The publication demonstrates its fealty to proper ethics by firing the employee. This implicitly says that the publication is not at fault, the ethical violation is not a systemic failure, instead it is the work of a deviant employee (who is now gone—so you can trust us again).

In summary, audiences judge credibility in an iterative process based on the publication, the author, and the text. The weight given to each component varies. To some extent the components are interchangeable and they interact. A publication with a strong reputation can carry an unknown author. Similarly, a reputable author will be credible regardless of the publication. And, a strong text may be credible despite an unknown author.

## Third-Party Validation

A fourth mechanism for judging credibility is the extent to which the knowledge is used by a trusted third party. This is important because readers see these uses as indications of the value of the knowledge. One *PC Magazine* reader told me,

> I knew that our [corporate information technology] staff used *PC Magazine* reviews when they bought our computers. . . . When I was trying to decide on a new home computer, I thought "they're the experts. If that's what they used, it works for me." I bought my computer from a *PC Magazine* review.

We see this in reviews when product makers use the results of a review. Product makers complain about reviews but, in fact, most are ambivalent. Favorable reviews are welcomed. Product makers send copies to financial backers and board members; they can be used to help persuade banks to give loans. Product makers reprint favorable reviews in their marketing literature. Product makers use awards to improve the credibility of their advertising. Readers notice; as one reader said, "Every time I see the Editors' Choice logo in an ad, I take a second look because it is probably a quality product."

A more subtle impression is also created. When product makers republish reviews or awards, they are implicitly saying that reviews are important and credible, that readers should pay attention. In this way product makers reinforce and legitimate reviews as arbiters of quality products. A typical description of this process was:

> For a long time I never looked at reviews . . . [but] I kept seeing copies posted in restaurants. One slow evening at [my favorite restaurant] I asked the maître d' about them and what he thought of them. He said they were a big deal: a lot of people used them to find good restaurants. He particularly liked Wheaton and he suggested that I look up *Chicago* magazine. He had been part of the Chicago dining scene for years so I thought I would check it out. I bought a copy. . . . There were some intriguing restaurants. I'd never have found [some of those restaurants] without *Chicago*.

Product maker use of reviews seems to validate reviews, and it is linked to people starting to read the reviews. Reading reviews is evidence of a belief that reviews can be trusted. For example,

> I used to think that the reviews in the newspaper were, well, arrogant: one person deciding what was good or not. Then I started to notice the stars and reviews posted in restaurants and I thought, "Well, maybe not. If restaurants think it is OK then maybe it isn't so arrogant. And if [the reviewer] knows what he is talking about, maybe I should read some of the reviews." That's when I began to read restaurant reviews.

This is a general process. If you are unsure about some knowledge, then a third party visibly using the knowledge is a powerful affirmation of the credibility of the knowledge. Actually, more than credibility is involved. If a third party seems to be able to make use of the knowledge, then this suggests not only that it is credible but also that it is useful, and that means it is even more important to pay attention.

Thus, we have two additional mechanisms whereby audiences judge credibility. All four of these mechanisms operate on reviews in general. These are audience-focused mechanisms. We can gain additional understanding of credibility if we look at production. Since there are two basic production processes—connoisseurial and procedural—we examine them separately. Production processes are linked to the social bases of knowledge. Thus, it is useful to begin with recent research in the sociology of knowledge.

## PRODUCTION: SOCIAL ORGANIZATION OF REVIEWS AND CREDIBILITY

Reviews evaluate products. The evaluations attempt to create new knowledge about a product and, to the extent that they are convincing, they create credible knowledge. In its most general form the sociology of knowledge is concerned with the social bases of knowledge. Traditional sociology of knowledge, exemplified by Karl Mannheim, was concerned with the social locations of individuals and how this influenced their knowledge. It focused on formal systems of ideas, paying particular attention to the worldview of intellectuals, and it was particularly concerned with the ways that social interests bias the understanding of even the most neutral observers. While Mannheim continues to be relevant to contemporary work (e.g., Schwartz 2002), Swidler and Arditi (1994) have recently described an alternative focus: a new sociology of knowledge that "examines how kinds of social organization make whole orderings of knowledge possible."[9] Following in their spirit this section examines the relationship between the social organization of review production and the credibility of knowledge.

One larger objective of this book is an investigation into the forms and practices of credible knowledge.[10] In the case of reviews, forms and practices are tightly bound together. I found two forms of knowledge: connoisseurial and procedural. They turn out to be intimately linked with the practice of knowing. As chapter 5 describes, the forms are created by specialized production processes embedded in specialized organizations. Since any product can be reviewed using either connoisseurial or procedural methods, which method to use is a choice of the review organization. The previous chapters describe the social conditions for the production of each form of knowledge. Generally speaking, review organizations can produce one kind of knowledge but not both.[11] Organizations that produce procedural knowledge generally cannot produce connoisseurial knowledge, and vice versa. In this sense, in the case of reviews, organizational structure determines the knowledge that is produced.

The two forms also influence content. As we have seen, the actual content of procedural and connoisseurial knowledge differs: there are differences in the number of products reviewed, in the comparisons done, in the transparency of the knowledge produced, in the openness to alternative weightings of the review criteria, and other issues. The differences in content are directly traceable to the process whereby each form of knowledge is produced. Organizations produce a certain kind of review and, in consequence, they produce a certain kind of knowledge. Production strongly influences content.

Up to this section the chapter has focused on audience judgments; now we turn to the production of credibility. Knowledge never appears disconnected from people or organizations. Regardless of whether it appears written in books, magazines, or newspapers, or in conversation, or spoken on television, knowledge is carried by individual writer/speakers and the organizations that support them. In this sense, knowledge is always "embodied"; inextricably linked to particular people and organizations. So, the problem of identifying credible knowledge requires identifying trustworthy people and organizations. We begin by placing organizations on a single continuum according to how they frame their credibility arguments.

## The Credibility Continuum

Connoisseurial and procedural reviews use different frames to argue for their credibility. We can represent the extent to which different organizations are committed to connoisseurial or procedural reviews by placing them on a continuum that I call the *Credibility Continuum* (see table 6.1). The Credibility Continuum forms a space within which reviews argue for their credibility. Connoisseurial and procedural reviews hold down the endpoints of the continuum and frame the space. Notice that the actual examples on the contin-

**Table 6.1.   The Credibility Continuum**

| *Connoisseurial Reviews* | *Procedural Reviews* |
| --- | --- |
| *Chicago* magazine restaurant reviews<br>*New York Times* book reviews | Zagat's restaurant reviews<br>*New York Times* best seller list<br>Morningstar mutual fund reviews<br>*Consumer Reports* appliance reviews<br>*PC Magazine* hardware reviews |

uum are combinations of both a review and an organization. Reviews are embedded in their production process and that is reflected in the organization names included in the table.

The Credibility Continuum is based on the two different arguments invoked by reviewers to justify the credibility of a text. Whether these arguments are successful in convincing an audience is a separate issue. The degree of success or failure of the arguments is another dimension unrelated to the Credibility Continuum. In other words, the Credibility Continuum is about how reviewers justify the credibility of their statements. It is not about how audiences judge their statements. Further, there are multiple audiences and there is no reason to believe that different audiences will reach the same conclusion.[12]

Reviews tend to cluster at each end of the continuum and few reviews are located in an intermediate position. This is not accidental. This configuration is the outcome of organizational processes. As organizations initially commit to one system or the other, three pressures tend to push them toward either end of the continuum. First, each rating system has an internal logic: connoisseurial reviews strive for a personal response, procedural reviews aim to test or measure all important aspects of the product. Once they announce their approach to reviews, they raise expectations and are judged by how well they fulfill them. To the extent that they fall short, various audience members, especially product makers, may criticize them, using their failings to attack the credibility of negative reviews. This tends to push review organizations to extend their existing organizational repertoire and become more and more committed to a single approach (e.g., Alsop 1994a). Second, independent of external pressures, review organizations tend to elaborate the logic of their rating system. They develop theories of what their reviews should be like. Practices that are defined as central become privileged candidates for further development. This tends to lead to expansion of the organizational repertoire in a particular direction. Third, review organizations exist in an environment with other organizations also producing reviews. Successful review organizations provide culturally legitimated templates.[13] These models can be adapted to new settings or used in the construction of new reviews. Since most model review organizations are at the ends of the continuum, new organizations tend to move there also. As a result of these three mechanisms review organizations tend to concentrate at the ends of the continuum.

These effects are particularly apparent in procedural reviews, where each review builds on the division of labor and the standard procedures established for prior reviews. For example, in the 1990s, Consumers Union installed its own pressure tank to supply consistent water pressure during tests of washing machines and dishwashers. Eliminating dependence on vagaries of city water pressure controlled a source of possible variability in test results (Arons 1997). A portion of *Consumer Reports* history could be written in terms of increasing control over the testing environment. *PC Magazine* shows similar development. Charts and other elements are introduced and become standards thereafter. For example, the "Bang for the Buck" chart has been used in computer hardware reviews since 1991 (Machrone 1991), although it was recently retitled the "Price/Performance Index." These effects occur in connoisseurial reviews also. One of the reasons for the rapid spread of restaurant reviews in the late 1960s was the example of Claiborne's successful restaurant reviews in the *New York Times*. The *Times* national prominence meant that any successful innovation was highly visible. The result of these mechanisms is a steady incremental refinement. As organizations acquire resources of specialized expertise, standardized procedures, and an audience that expects certain content, they find it harder and harder to deviate from established paths. In this way, cultural logics and audience expectations congeal into sets of institutional practices and organizational forms.[14]

While there is a tendency for reviews to become more connoisseurial or more procedural over time, under some circumstances publications move in the opposite direction, toward the middle of the credibility continuum. The most significant issue is resource constraints. If the resources needed to produce procedural reviews are no longer available, then publications may shift away from the procedural end of the continuum. For example, following the collapse of the dot-com boom in 2000, many computer magazines experienced major declines in readership and advertising. Both *eWeek* and *InfoWorld* found extensive product testing to be too expensive. They continued to do procedural reviews, but the testing was less extensive and less expensive than before, and the connoisseurial elements became relatively more important.

## Credibility Arguments in Procedural Reviews

The Credibility Continuum summarizes the broad outlines of credibility arguments in reviews but it tends to obscure differences between types of procedural reviews. Although they all have the same general argument—reliance on procedures—each of the four procedural review types relies on a different version of the argument. Methodologically, these credibility arguments become apparent when we look at the controversies that have erupted over these reviews. The controversies tell us what people object to and why.

For laboratory reviews the key credibility issues tend to be how the testing was conducted. Does the testing represent the experiences of an ordinary user? Reviews are not credible when the product was "enhanced" in some way by the reviewer. A striking example of a "negative" enhancement occurred in 1993. The TV news magazine *Dateline NBC* argued that certain General Motors pickup truck models were unsafe because they had a tendency to catch fire after a collision, and it aired video showing a truck colliding and then catching fire. What the report did not mention was that when test trucks failed to catch fire on their own, *Dateline NBC* used incendiary devices to start the fires (Alter 1993, Brill 1993, Widder 1993). This embarrassing episode resulted in a public NBC apology; the resignation of the head of the NBC news division, Michael Gartner; and the firing of three NBC employees (Associated Press 1993).

For historical performance reviews the credibility issues tend to be accuracy. In particular, are the summaries accurate? Do they represent something that readers need to know? For example, see Barnhart (1998) for critical comments on how Morningstar assigns star ratings to its mutual funds. Also, see Morningstar changes in the procedure for assigning star ratings in July 2002 (Morningstar 2003).

The issues for popularity reviews are how the popularity data are collected; specifically, do the data actually represent the universe of sales? The lists are not credible if they can be manipulated. There have been occasional accusations of attempts to manipulate best seller lists (Stern 1995a). Charles McGrath, editor of the *New York Times Book Review*, says that the book *The Discipline of Market Leaders* by Michael Treacy and Fred Wiersema, which spent fifteen weeks on the *New York Times* Nonfiction Best Seller list, "may very well not have belonged on our list at all some weeks" (quoted in Stern 1995b). The source of the suspicion was that the names of some of the bookstores that were polled to obtain sales figures had become known, and sales could be directed to those stores. To ensure the continued credibility of the best seller list the *New York Times* changed some of its procedures to make them more resistant to manipulation by improved filtering of bulk sales and efforts to better hide the store names (*Business Week* 1995).[15]

The credibility argument for a survey is often made in self-conscious contrast to a connoisseurial review. Tim Zagat, publisher of Zagat's, says, "a survey is bound to be more objective and more accurate than any one person can ever be" (Richman 1986). This points to the central credibility issue: does the survey represent the wishes of the population? Tensions occur when it appears that some small group of the population has been able to thwart the will of the larger majority, thereby ignoring or downgrading high-quality products. Recent examples include the failure of the movie *Hoop Dreams* even to be nominated for an Academy Award (Adelson 1995; Ebert 1995), and how the internal politics and voting procedures of the National Society of Film Critics combined to deny *Saving Private Ryan* the award for the Best Picture of 1998 (Wilmington 1999). These objections can weaken the legitimacy of the awards, prompting changes; for example, the Academy documentary film nominations process was changed after the *Hoop Dreams* incident.

In three of these four examples, the central problem has been manipulation of the results of the review so that the final review does not faithfully represent what it claims to represent. The review was influenced by the self-interest of a product maker. Instead of being disinterested, it is biased. A characteristic of each example is that it became public; an audience observed the bias. An observable disconnection between claims and reality threatens the credibility of any review. The response of the publisher in some cases was to adjust the procedures; that is, to make the procedures harder to manipulate. In the case of NBC the response was to reassert the validity of its procedures: the problems were caused by rogue employees who violated its procedures. This justified firing the employees.

Connoisseurial and procedural reviews make different credibility arguments. These arguments do not exist in a vacuum. Reviews are embedded in organizations, they are produced by organizations, and they serve the purposes of the same organizations. Organizational production processes are a key to understanding the rating systems and their credibility.

## CONTEXT AND CREDIBLE REVIEWS

One major theme of much sociology of scientific knowledge research is that scientific knowledge is contextual; that is, it depends on the local, parochial context of time, place, and purpose. In the jargon of sociology of scientific knowledge, this is called "local knowledge." There is not space to do justice to this material, but a brief summary is in order. One strand has argued that there are no special, extraordinary norms of science. Instead it is sufficient to use ordinary forms of social interaction to create scientific knowledge (Latour and Woolgar 1986, Lynch 1985; Shapin 1994). A second theme has been that written descriptions of scientific work are not sufficient to allow replication. Collins's classic study (Collins and Harrison 1975) of the building of a laser shows how literally no one was able to duplicate the laser from written descriptions. The only way that knowledge of how to build a laser was successfully transferred was by researchers actually participating in construction. This points to the importance of tacit knowledge and to craftlike skills in the growth of scientific knowledge. The work has been extended to many areas (e.g., Lynch 1985, Schaffer 1999, Shapin and Schaffer 1985).

These empirical studies ask an important question. If scientific knowledge is so dependent on local context, how can it spread with such success?[16] Similar questions can be raised about reviews. What experience could be more lo-cally situated or more idiosyncratic than dinner in a restaurant? Isn't it inex-tricably linked to the mood of the other people at the table, the time of day, the quality and types of the food available that day, a particular set of servers and chefs? How can a reviewer's report on the meal be used to help others understand what they might experience in the restaurant? These are questions about audience responses. A reader who believes that knowledge is dependent on local context would never read a review. Since millions of people read and use restaurant reviews, these problems are solved in practice by every re-viewer and every reader. In the next section we combine production and re-ception as we discuss how reviews solve this problem for procedural and con-noisseurial reviews.

## How Does Procedural Knowledge Spread?

Many characteristics of science are apparent in procedural reviews. The devel-opment of standardized testing scripts, standard benchmark software, and stan-dardized procedures all contribute to the creation of standard contexts where identical knowledge can emerge repeatedly. Reviewers often test standard objects — cars, computers, or appliances — and this creates a stable environment. Much of the culture of procedural reviews is devoted to discussion of test stan-dards and to development of consistent testing across a group of objects. In this sense, major effort goes into assuring what would be called "reliability" in the language of research methods. The result is a set of standard categories that make it plausible for reviewers to supply recipes for successful purchase of a product. Different audiences have different criteria, but that doesn't change the key point, that the same criteria can be applied consistently and the results will be replicable. Like other institutionalized environments, these standards create consistency. So far this is a fairly straightforward application of standard soci-ological theory and sociology of science to procedural reviews.

The contrast between connoisseurial and procedural knowledge points to an additional item that has not been widely appreciated. The question of how a restaurant experience can be anything but local has a solution that is elegant in its simplicity: Zagat's. Zagat's reduces the entire restaurant experience to three index numbers and a price. The numbers measure categories that are very simple and very general. *PC Magazine* does something similar. Its re-views of statistical software reduced the complexity of statistical software to numerical ratings in three broad categories: basic statistics, advanced statis-tics, and data management. These simple tools allow audiences to create or-dinal rankings. Indeed, *PC Magazine's* Editors' Choice award and Zagat's "Top 40 Food" list make the ordinal ranks explicit.

This is one key. Scores are constructed to measure performance in a few simple categories. The scores are a symbolic frame. The frame identifies stereotyped categories that are used by audiences to make sense of the product under review. So long as the categories match the interests of a particular audience, extremely simple categories can be successful. Certainly the simple category frames used by Zagat's have been wildly successful.

A second key is that the scores are closely tied to performance of certain tasks. The test scripts, the audience scores, or other procedures are designed to produce the scores directly. In this sense, the symbolic frames of the categories are closely linked to detailed, specific practices (or procedures, in our language). The specificity of the procedures eases the task of transferring them to new settings. Unlike Collins and his laser-builders, reviews don't deal with cutting-edge science. They work with applied tools using off-the-shelf equipment. In this setting, written descriptions suffice to teach procedures. *PC Magazines* test scripts are based on the assumption that a competent reviewer can follow them without coaching from the editor.

In summary, three elements combine so that procedural reviews can be performed and received in a wide variety of settings. Formal, institutionalized practices create stable environments. Frames constructed of simple, globally available categories can be more readily imported into local situations. So long as the specific practices are followed in the local setting, the simple, ordinal ratings emerge reliably. Procedural knowledge travels well because it is well-standardized, simple, and closely linked to practice. Procedural reviews are a technology that produces trust.

If procedural knowledge spreads because it is simple and closely connected to procedures, what about connoisseurial knowledge? Connoisseurial knowledge is not simple and not linked to detailed practices. How can it travel at all?

## How Does Connoisseurial Knowledge Spread?

The nature of a connoisseurial review—the premium on sensitivity to nuance and complex understanding—suggests that connoisseurial knowledge should be immobile. It is probably less mobile than procedural knowledge. However, this does not mean that it is narrowly limited to local settings. The fact that large numbers of people buy and use connoisseurial restaurant reviews suggests that the argument that restaurant meals were locally situated was wrong. The more general questions are, how do connoisseurial reviews escape the trap of solely local relevance, and how can connoisseurial reviews produce credible knowledge applicable in a wide range of settings for many people? I think that there are five reasons for the success of the connoisseurial route to credible knowledge.

Consistent performance in the execution of its tasks is a goal of every organization. In reviews, consistency is an important evaluation criterion. For example, it is the major reason that reviewers visit restaurants more than once. Inconsistency—the inability to serve identical dishes on different evenings—is a mark of a bad restaurant. The more successful the organization, the more likely it will give the same performance regardless of who occupies the roles of server and cook. What is true of restaurant reviews is also true of other performances, like theater or music.[17] A goal of any organization is to provide consistent products to an audience. Further, the more highly skilled the organization, the more likely it will be able to deliver a consistent performance, and the more likely it will be highly rated by the reviewer. The fact that high skill and high consistency frequently occur together is one reason connoisseurial reviews work. People depend on organizations being consistent for connoisseurial reviews to work. If, for example, the restaurant delivers a consistent experience, then readers can count on an experience similar to the reviewer's. The fact that organizations often are consistent is one reason why connoisseurial reviews are successful.[18]

Second, an important characteristic of connoisseurial reviews is that audiences learn to judge credibility using iterative trust building. Audiences use their prior experience with publications and individual reviewers to help them understand each new review. A short way to say this is that publications and connoisseurial reviewers develop fine-grained reputations that audiences use to assess the credibility of a review. Because audiences learn to make allowance for the point of view of each reviewer and publication, people in widely varying settings can make use of the same connoisseurial reviews.

Third, many audiences do not need quantified precision. When choosing, for example, a major appliance like a dishwasher it is sufficient to know which one is the best (given your needs and budget). Being able to quantify how *much* better it is compared to the second-ranked product won't improve your decision. The point is that a rank order is often all that is needed, and ordinal ranks have many of the characteristics of simplicity that make procedural reviews useable in widely varying settings. Connoisseurial reviews are often sufficient for ordinal ranks.

Fourth, alternative sources of information have serious problems. Many information sources are linked to product makers, and the people who produce them will benefit if a customer buys the product. This conflict of interest makes them potentially biased and, in principle, suspect. Examples include advertising, trade shows, product brochures, web sites, and store salesclerks. An independent source of information is rare and, for that reason, valuable. Further, even an audience that understands numbers and prefers procedural reviews may not always find one available. A connoisseurial review may be sufficient and satisfactory, if it is the only independent source of information available. Taking advantage of the experience of others in the form of a review may be a sensible strategy when the benefits and costs are difficult to quantify.

Finally, when we say connoisseurial reviews are statements of personal reactions to a product, this does not mean that their content is arbitrary. Connoisseurial reviews have rules. They have a conventional structure. They have conventional parts. Broadly speaking, a standard review has two parts: a summary and an evaluation. The reviewer briefly summarizes the capabilities of the product—the plot, music, capacity, speed; whatever is relevant for the particular product or performance. Then the reviewer evaluates these capabilities. Usually, the relevant categories for evaluation are conventional and well understood by any culturally literate person. For example, we saw evidence in chapter 5 that among gastronomes there are common standards for the evaluation of good restaurant food that are understood worldwide.

Not every category is mentioned in every connoisseurial review. One reviewer explained, "I have *so* little space. I have to write very selectively. . . . I write what is noteworthy about the restaurant. It can be either good or bad. . . . This is simple to say but not so easy in practice." Most categories are omitted from most reviews. The convention is to mention only those categories where the restaurant stands out as unusually good or unusually bad. Not to mention a category means that there was, as the saying goes, nothing to write home about.

The point is that connoisseurial reviews have rules, just like procedural reviews. The rules are not expressed as mechanical procedures, but they nonetheless constrain the discretion of the reviewer. They allow an appropriately knowledgeable audience to interpret the text of the reviewer. Although the judgment may be personal, the categories in which it is expressed are not. They are given by the conventions of the review genre and by the interests of the audience. They limit the characteristics of the product that the reviewer may discuss. In this sense, connoisseurial reviews are not as subjective as they may seem. It is possible that most could be reproduced by another person, at least in terms of the broad ordinal ranking of products. Credibility depends, in part, on whether the reviewer followed the rules. In terms of standard sociological theory, I am describing how credibility depends on following conventions.[19]

This issue is related to the fact that the credibility of review knowledge is usually based on reading a stream of reviews. Although a set of standard categories can be constructed to evaluate every product or performance, this doesn't mean that every reviewer uses the categories in the same way. The rules for connoisseurial knowledge are not as rigid as they are for procedural knowledge. Different reviewers have different priorities. One way to distinguish reviewers is that they assign different priorities to categories. Audiences develop a sense of how the reviewer prioritizes over the course of a number of reviews. They can see how—to use a film example—a reviewer may always respond to a particular director or actor, or the reviewer may never seem to think very much about the soundtrack. A respondent described one Chicago movie reviewer:

> [He] brings so much more film history and theory into his reviews than [another reviewer]. [He] has more substance. . . . I know that [he] speaks to the things that I care about in movies. He has little to say about slasher movies or romantic comedies. My teenage son thinks he is long-winded and boring.

Readers who trust a reviewer writing about intellectual films may ignore comments about comedies. These sorts of judgments were common in my interviews. The ability to make allowances for the characteristics of the reviewer assists audiences in their credibility judgments. In a connoisseurial review, credibility judgments can be very fine-grained.

In summary, both connoisseurial and procedural knowledge are technologies of trust.[20] Although they have different strengths, both can produce mobile knowledge, and they are both in frequent, common, contemporary use.

## TWO ROUTES TO CREDIBLE KNOWLEDGE

The study of credible reviews has led us to the larger issue of the nature of credible knowledge. The chapter argues that credibility is a product of organizational processes. There is a parallel here to the production of culture. The production of culture research (e.g., Crane 1992; Hirsch 1972; Peterson 1976, 1978, 1994) applies organizational theory to the production of cultural objects. One important insight has been that the actual content of the cultural objects is strongly influenced by the characteristics of the organization that does the production. This book approaches reviews from a "production of knowledge" perspective. One theme is that the form of the production organization influences the substantive content of the knowledge produced.

Credible knowledge, then, is the result of particular organizational processes. I found two distinct sets of organizational practices by which reviewers produce credible knowledge. Connoisseurial reviews invoke the experience, talent, and personal sensitivity of the expert reviewer. Procedural reviews point to their explicit procedures and add that anyone could, in principle, follow the procedures and duplicate the results. Connoisseurial and procedural reviews are different answers to the question, "Why do you believe

**Table 6.2.  Characteristics of Routes to Credible Knowledge**

|  | *Connoisseurial route* | *Procedural Route* |
| --- | --- | --- |
| **Production** | | |
| Division of labor in review | Simple | Complex |
| Resources needed for production | Few | Many |
| Methodology | Not explicit | Explicit |
| Number of products | One | Many |
| Comparison to similar products | Left to audience discretion | Explicit in review |
| Goal of review | Text recommendation | Relative ranking of all products in review |
| Source of knowledge | Reviewer personal response | Quantitative measurements |
| Core production process | Craft production | Mass production |
| **Reviewers** | | |
| Qualifications | Refined aesthetic sensitivity | Technical training |
| Reviewer discretion | Much | Little |
| Formal credentials | None required | Yes |
| Most important person | Reviewer | Editor |
| **Review Text** | | |
| Length | Long | Short for single product; longer for entire review |
| Primary presentation | Discursive text | Summary statistical tables |
| Writing focus | Engaging readers | Clarity, often at expense of engaging readers |
| Dissemination | Mass media | Mass media |
| **Ethics** | | |
| Conflict of interest | Single person | Multiple people |
| Basis of conflict of interest | Conflicting interests of individual reviewer | Outdated or biased procedures |
| Policies | Usually informal, unwritten | Usually formal, written |
| **Audience** | | |
| Primary interests | Complex | Simple |
| Most important criteria | Unknown, varying | Known, clear |
| Number of criteria | Many | Few |
| Alternative criteria weights | None | Many possible |
| Cognitive processing | High | Low |
| Rhetorical argument of publication to readers | Summary and evaluation of personal experience | Procedures produce evaluation without human intervention |

this is true?" The answers emphasize two different kinds of credible knowledge that I call *credibility routes*. The word *route* emphasizes that credible knowledge is the result of a process. Connoisseurial and procedural are more than just rating systems. They are also two different approaches to producing credible knowledge. There are diverse issues involved in the answers. The two different answers lead to differences in the production of reviews, the qualifications and role of reviewers, the characteristics of audiences, and in the review text itself. As a conclusion to this chapter, table 6.2 summarizes the important differences in the two different answers.

Connoisseurial and procedural reviews create incentives and pressures that press upon organizations. Some pressures are from audience expectations or standards of fairness; others are internal logics that control organizational activity. Although the initial effects may be limited, over time, these pressures lead organizations to become more firmly connoisseurial or procedural. In the end, the rating system—connoisseurial or procedural—influences all levels of organization: hiring, editorial roles, costs, content, audiences, reviewer choices, and others. In this sense, the distinction between connoisseurial and procedural reviews becomes much more than just a simple difference in rating system. It totally shapes the organization and its audience.

## NOTES

1. This information is drawn from news articles by Storch (1993) and Miner (1993), and from my field notes. The Carla Kelson quote is from Storch. The reader quote is from my field notes.

2. Opening night at the theater is the exception that proves this rule. Everyone knows all the critics will be there. If the reviewers are influential, success or failure may ride on that single performance. No wonder actors have opening night jitters.

3. Shapin (1994) discusses knowledge and trust among the seventeenth-century English gentlemen-philosophers who were pioneers in empirical science. A final chapter describes the modern equivalents and it includes a discussion of trust in small communities of scientists. Since my research site is reviews, not small groups, I would never observe this credibility mechanism. This book studies the credibility of public knowledge like that published in mass media.

4. The term "research network" is from Barnes and Edge (1982:19). It refers to the relatively small groups of scientists who work on similar research problems and are in active communication and dialog. There is no standard term; they also go by the names "invisible colleges" (Crane 1972) and "clusters" (Mullins 1972), among others.

5. Many of the examples studied by Porter are legally mandated as part of government policy making, such as cost-benefit analysis or environmental-impact statements. In these cases, the debates are between organizations and groups of experts representing the organizations. These complex situations are beyond the scope of this

book. Porter also studies examples where there is a large, self-interested audience, like accounting. This is much closer to the situation in reviews; in fact, the numbers vetted by independent accountants in corporate annual reports are a form of procedural review. Investors and potential investors could ignore the financial data if they want. The question is, why do they pay attention if they don't have to? The accounting scandals of 2000–2002 certainly suggest reasons to ignore those data.

6. In recent years, personal computer use seems to have become more important. *PC Magazine* is aware of its diverse readership. Its recent "Perfect PC" issues illustrate the perfect computer for ten different audiences (*PC Magazine* 2003).

7. There are, of course, people who do not like a given publication; but they will not read it, and the credibility of its reviewers will not be an issue for them.

8. A former *Gourmet* reviewer echoes this, affirming that the magazine assumed that its "well-heeled, self-indulgent readership was interested only in those restaurants that could be recommended with confidence" (Jacobs 1990:11).

9. Portions of this paragraph paraphrase Swidler and Arditi (1994).

10. The credibility of knowledge has been the subject of recent books and articles, notably Shapin (1994, 1995a, 1995b) and Swidler and Arditi (1994). Reading these authors helped clarify this section and I am indebted to them.

11. This may seem too simple because newspapers can produce both connoisseurial and procedural knowledge. However, when we look deeper it becomes clear that organizations that produce both kinds of knowledge use different people for each. The extensive division of labor used in procedural reviews is ill-suited for connoisseurial reviews, and connoisseurial reviewers tend not to have the specialized technical knowledge needed for procedural reviews.

12. This distinction between the arguments of the reviewers and the acceptance of the argument by an audience is somewhat similar to Shapin's (1995a) distinction between credibility and validity of knowledge. They share a dimension dealing with credibility judgments. There are three differences. Shapin does not consider alternative ways to make credible arguments. Validity would be yet a third dimension. And, unlike this distinction where dimensions are firmly attached to reviewers and audiences, respectively, Shapin's dimensions are not attached to social actors.

13. This is the issue of institutional isomorphism eloquently described by DiMaggio and Powell (1991). This discussion shows reviews as a case of mimetic isomorphism.

14. As noted in chapter 2, this statement should be qualified by noting that there are probably no pure examples of connoisseurial or procedural reviews. Real reviews almost always mix both connoisseurial and procedural elements. For example, even book reviews—among the most consistently connoisseurial of all reviews—often include procedural characteristics, like the length and the price of the book. Financial reviews, for example mutual fund ratings, and computer hardware reviews—both strongly procedural reviews—include text to help readers interpret the tables of numbers and rankings.

15. The possibility of manipulation is not the same as inaccuracy. For instance, Nielsen TV ratings have a variety of serious problems and, for certain TV shows, numbers as small as two or three households may make a significant difference in the rat-

ing (these are shows on less popular cable channels, see Jensen 1999). However, TV networks and advertisers must have a way to measure popularity and there is no alternative to the Nielsen ratings. So, despite all the suspicions of inaccuracy, they continue to use Nielsen's numbers. Nielsen argues that it could produce a more accurate TV rating system but that broadcasters have been unwilling to pay higher costs for greater accuracy. Money is not the only reason broadcasters are unwilling to change. The errors tend to favor big, established networks and stations. Nielsen spokesman Jack Loftus says, "It's not a medium friendly to cable or independent stations" (quoted in Jensen 1999:900–901). The existing rating system tends to reinforce the existing hierarchy of broadcasting power and prestige. The Nielsen families are confidential and, as long as they remain so, no one argues that the ratings can be manipulated.

16. Bruno Latour (1987, 1988) supplies one answer to this question. Briefly, he argues that knowledge becomes embodied in technology, which is stable and performs consistently. Technological objects become "black boxes" that, in combination with standards, form durable, standardized contexts. The spread of science, then, is due to the successful spread of standardized contexts for generating or confirming knowledge. Latour has developed an entire language to describe these issues including "enrollment" of allies, "control" of allies, "points of passage" for groups that wish to benefit from scientific developments, and other terms. Although this material is very interesting, a full discussion is unneeded for the points that I wish to make here.

17. Consistent performance is an issue in procedural reviews as well. In products like cars or computers, an inconsistency is called a "defect." The number of defects is simple to count and meaningful to anyone who has had to bring in a product for repair. *Consumer Reports* always reports the number of defects in every car review. *PC Magazine* hardware reviews report results from user surveys of frequency of repairs and customer support.

18. To relate these issues back to the sociology of science: In terms of these concepts, laboratory science is a performance. If experimental mastery has been achieved, then the laboratory performance can be brought to the same outcome everywhere — that is, the performance is universal — and it is consistent. If only a skilled expert in a local setting can successfully complete the performance, and others are unsuccessful, then it is inconsistent. From this point of view, the question of moving from local to universal is a question of ability to create a consistent performance.

19. Much of Becker's (1982) discussion of conventions in art worlds is relevant here.

20. This is Porter's (1995) felicitous phrase, although he applies it to quantification.

# Chapter Seven

# "Dining Is My Sport": Reception and Hierarchies

> I don't care about what Michael Jordan and the Bulls did last night. Dining is my sport and Wheaton is my coach.

Saying that Michael Jordan's basketball performance wasn't important was almost heresy in Chicago during the mid-1990s. For some, however, dining has the same appeal as sports: it engages their attention, provides a point of contact with other people and a topic of conversation, and it adds excitement and meaning to their lives. Quoted above, a committed gastronome makes the analogy explicit. He goes on to describe why he reads reviews.

> Dining changes. I'm not just talking about trendy stuff; of course that is always changing. I mean on a more fundamental level: whole new cuisines. . . . Wheaton tells me about them and he tells me what to expect or he warns me to avoid some foods. Critic's comments help me understand what I eat and add meaning to my experience.

He was typical of many respondents who followed current interpretations of the arts through reviews. Like consumer products, arts products change constantly. People with jobs, spouses, families, and lives can't easily keep up with current developments. For many, the arts are a source of relaxation and indulgence. Reviews help these people understand changes and thereby add depth and interest to their experiences.

The connoisseurial-procedural distinction describes the production of reviews and it has a major influence on reception. However, it does not fully describe the motives for reception. People read reviews for surprisingly diverse reasons. Reviews are complex products and reception is correspondingly complex. People respond in multiple ways. This chapter begins by describing some typical reasons people read reviews. Then it examines a common theme running through all the responses: the importance of the evaluation. Readers strongly respond to the evaluations and the hierarchies that evaluations create.

The reader below describes a common reason for reading reviews: following the fortunes of people he knows or admires.

> They help me keep up with my friends. . . . I worked as a waiter when I was an undergraduate . . . [and] as a maître d' for three years after. I know many of the maître d's in Chicago and some of the chefs and owners. Since I started law school, I don't have time to eat out or socialize as much but I want to stay in touch. The reviews keep me abreast of how my friends and their restaurants are doing.

Notice that he's also interested in their restaurants. He was a participant in the restaurant scene for many years. Although his career has taken another path, he retains an active but somewhat nostalgic interest in restaurants and restaurant people.[1] His comment was echoed by others who read reviews as a way to follow their interests in people and organizations.

> I was a drama major in college. . . . I once dreamed of making it on Broadway or the movies. I tried that for a year but it wasn't working so I went to my backup plan. . . . I buy the *New York Times* mostly to read the theater coverage. I'm still interested in acting, staging, and interpretations of plays. The *Times* reviews help keep me in touch with the theater. They tell me what's good or bad and who's up and down.
>
> *Question*: Do you get back to New York very often?
>
> Oh no! I haven't been back since I left and that's been now 12 years. I'm not reading reviews to see the plays. . . . I read so I'm connected with the theater.

This person isn't reading her beloved theater reviews to help her decide which plays to attend. She uses them to keep track of the current trends in New York theater. This sort of motivation was very common. Reviews may provide a partial substitute for actual experience with the product, as in this case. Reading the reviews becomes the experience more than any actual experience itself. This seems to be particularly true for reading reviews of books. Here is one typical explanation of reading book reviews.

> In college I wrote an American history paper comparing Ulysses Grant and Robert E. Lee. It was an ordinary paper in retrospect, but I studied the Civil War closely for the first time. I was fascinated and I took a course. . . . I've never lost my interest but I've never had time to do much with it. One thing I do is read reviews of new books on the Civil War. . . . For example, Grant's reputation

seems to be improving as it undergoes something of a reevaluation right now. I learn enough that I feel like I could pick up again where I left off.

People often read reviews to keep up with a topic. One interviewee had been a car fan as an adolescent. Now in his forties, he told me, "I still subscribe to *Car and Driver*. The articles and reviews help me feel in touch." For other people, reading reviews gives them a way to compare their experiences with those of an expert reviewer. In the last chapter, we talked about how readers judge credibility by repeatedly comparing their experiences with reviewers'. Some people want to know how their taste and sensitivity compare. The comparison tells them something about themselves and their identity.

> Eating in different restaurants has always been fun. But I don't have the breadth of knowledge or experience of a professional. . . . I read reviews to compare what I notice to what the reviewer notices. Sometimes I go back to eat the same food again to try to understand what a reviewer is saying. . . . I learn about how things should taste from the evaluations. The more I understand, the better my taste has become. It is a little self-improvement project I've been working on.

Self-improvement was a common theme. It is linked to a more familiar sociological concern with social mobility. Reviews may form part of a social mobility strategy.

> As I've been promoted I need to manage the social parts of my career. I think there is a certain polish you need in some higher circles. When you go out [to eat] you need to be able to comment on the food. You want to sound intelligent and sophisticated. The knowledge and criteria are all in the reviews. . . . They help me fit in better in those circles. . . . They helped my career.

The quote above suggests some of the complexity of motivations. Within a few sentences the respondent talks about two different personal goals that reviews foster: gaining social status ("higher circles") and enhancing social mobility ("helped my career").

The preceding pages briefly describe six varied reasons for reading reviews.[2] These reasons have at least two things in common. First, everyone pays attention to the evaluation. Look back at the quotations and every one mentions the evaluations in the reviews. The evaluations are unusual. Readers were often aware that the evaluations were important and several self-consciously commented on their value. One reader understands the importance of reviewer's evaluations because of their thoughtful analysis.

> Reviews are analytical in a way that is unusual in newspapers and magazines. Good reviews have explicit comparisons that tell me what is good or what is bad

about a restaurant or something else. You won't find that in a news story. If you find criticism in a news story, it is almost always in a quote and negative quotes are usually paired with positive quotes. This seems to be some sort of journalistic norm to always report both positive and negative sides. . . . Good reviews don't talk about both sides. They take a clear, unambiguous stand and they explain why. It is refreshing and very attractive.

Evaluations are one reason why reviews are different from other text. The evaluations place products in a larger context of other, similar products and tell readers about that context. Regular readers find this to be one of their most appealing characteristics.

Second, these reasons are personal: reviews keep individuals in touch with interesting product categories, with other people, with organizations, with ideas, or help their personal mobility. This shows some ways in which public elements of culture can be used for private purposes. Reviews enhance the agency of the readers by helping them pursue private goals.

But there is a distinction between private uses of reviews and another set of uses where people read reviews as a prelude to action. The archetype of action is reading reviews to help decide whether to buy a product or attend a performance. When reviews shape a reader's actions, they influence others who are touched by the consequences of those actions, such as the makers of the products they may buy. Because of this influence, action-oriented uses are where reviews have their largest impact. The remainder of this chapter and the next chapter focus on how reviews influence actions and the consequences of that fact. In particular, this chapter examines how reviews create hierarchies and in turn help create whole status systems.

## STARS AND STATUS HIERARCHIES IN REVIEWS

Some critics use star ratings to summarize the overall quality of the dining experience at a restaurant. In the United States, stars were first awarded by Claiborne in the early 1960s. They originated in the Michelin Red Guides, which began awarding stars in 1926.[3] The stars create one of several hierarchies constructed by reviews. We begin by looking at stars ratings and the hierarchy that they construct, then we examine more complex hierarchies.

There are several systems for awarding stars. Restaurant critics award stars differently than many other review genres. Film critics, for example, typically use a scale ranging from one to four stars and award an average movie two stars. A really bad movie might receive one star or less. Restaurant critics tend to follow Michelin: the average restaurant receives no stars and is not even reviewed. Only exceptional restaurants are honored with stars. This sometimes confuses readers who think that one star means a bad restaurant. Michelin uses a three-star system. Michelin guides were written to encourage travel (on Michelin tires, of course). The system used in Michelin guides is related to travel: one star means "very good cooking," two mean "cooking worth a detour" and three mean "cooking worth a special journey." Michelin is sparing with its awards; there are fewer than twenty-five three-star restaurants in France. Almost all American critics use a four-star system. The stars do not have the same carefully distinguished meaning as the Michelin stars but, like Michelin, four-star restaurants are exceptional and most critics award them rarely. William Grimes, the current (2003) *New York Times* restaurant reviewer, judges only six restaurants in New York are worth four stars: Alain Ducasse, Bouley, Daniel, Jean Georges, Le Bernardin, and Lespinasse.[4] Wheaton awards four stars to eight Chicago restaurants: Charlie Trotter's, Everest, Les Nomades, Ritz-Carlton Dining Room, Spiaggia, Topolobampo, Trio, and Tru.

One value of stars is that they summarize the entire prestige hierarchy of restaurants. Table 7.1 contains all 154 restaurants listed in the September 2003 issue of *Chicago* magazine, ranked from one to four stars (*Chicago* 2003).[5] The hierarchy generally resembles a pyramid, with the fewest restaurants in the top and the most in the lower categories. Although this distribution was constructed largely by one person, Dennis Ray Wheaton, we know from the analysis in chapter 5, especially figure 5.3, that it is consistent with the distribution constructed by Zagat's survey respondents. In this sense it can be seen as a reflection or measurement of a broad consensus about the distribution of restaurant status.[6]

A certain logic suggests that many cultural hierarchies resemble a pyramid.[7] One reviewer said, "A memorable, excellent meal is unusual and very hard to do. As you go to fewer stars, meals become easier and less complex, and more restaurants can do them." If the criteria mean something, then it must be difficult and unusual to achieve the highest level, and this suggests few cultural products will receive the highest ranking. This looks like a fairly

**Table 7.1.  Chicago Restaurant Status Hierarchy**

| Star Ranking | Number of Restaurants | Percent |
|---|---|---|
| ★★★★ | 8 | 5.2 |
| ★★★½ | 3 | 1.9 |
| ★★★ | 13 | 8.4 |
| ★★½ | 19 | 12.3 |
| ★★ | 40 | 26.0 |
| ★½ | 44 | 28.6 |
| ★ | 27 | 17.5 |
| Total | 154 | 100.0 |

conventional social stratification system: Very few restaurants on top; the vast majority on the bottom. The simple pyramid echoes the shape of many systems of inequality.

Stars are controversial. Proponents of stars argue that they offer a service to readers by summarizing the overall evaluation. Readers use them as a convenient screening device. Publishers like stars because they are an excellent source of free advertising. They allow product makers to put the stars in ads with a line identifying the publication that made the award. Most reviewers don't like stars. They argue that pretending there is a single scale on which one can evaluate an entire restaurant experience is so distorted as to be useless. They echo Claiborne's comments on the proliferation of ethnic dining (quoted in chapter 3), saying there is no way that the experience of diners in a French restaurant can be compared to, say, a Burmese restaurant in a single summary. Reviewers point out that reviews are short; readers should read the entire review, which contains a much more nuanced picture of the restaurant, rather than relying on the capsule summary of stars. Critics find it very difficult to assign the stars. It is often easier to write the review than to award stars.

In sociological terms critics point to a problem of incommensurability between the categories of restaurants. If the restaurant categories are not comparable, then any attempt to arrange them on a single scale is a distortion. Such a move obscures the real distinctions that are relevant to audiences. In table 7.1 we observe a simple, unidimensional distribution of prestige. Given its simplicity and the objections raised by reviewers, we can reasonably ask, is this all? Does this simple stratification structure define the qualities that are important to diners (and reviewers)? This is a question about the distribution of prestige for a class of cultural products. Here we're asking about the shape of the field of restaurants. But the question can be asked of any class of products, including various categories of art or music, not to mention computer hardware or home appliances. This question is particularly relevant for reviews because these are the sorts of judgments that reviewers make every day. It is a broader question because it is the sort of judgment that everyone makes when they assign high or low prestige to a particular product in a larger class. It is an important question because one of the most important contemporary theorists of culture, Pierre Bourdieu (e.g., 1984), argues that cultural prestige is distributed throughout entire societies on a single, unidimensional scale of cultural capital.

## When Is Cultural Status Unidimensional?

From a theoretical point of view, a single distribution is an accurate description of the prestige hierarchy of a field of cultural products if the following conditions are true.[8]

1. There must be a consensus regarding the criteria to be used to evaluate the product class. In this case, all audience members must believe that food quality is the single most important criterion by which to judge the status of a restaurant.
2. There must be another consensus regarding the characteristics of each position in the distribution. In this case, there must be consensus about what characteristics of a restaurant qualify it to be a two-star restaurant, or a three-star restaurant, or whatever.
3. Audience members must have similar abilities to judge all levels of prestige. Here, the audience members must be able to judge one-star restaurants as well as four-star restaurants.
4. There must be yet another consensus about how the different attributes of the product will be weighted. Since the distribution in table 7.1 is based primarily on judgments of food quality, there must be agreement on how to weight freshness, texture, visual appeal, and all the other attributes of restaurant food quality.
5. Finally, the key criterion should have equal salience for all members of the audience. In this case, food quality must be equally important to every person.

If these conditions are true, then a unidimensional scale accurately describes the status hierarchy of a cultural product. How well do these five points fit the status hierarchy of restaurants?

A single criterion—food quality—is the basis for *Chicago* magazine restaurant evaluations, and Zagat's respondents are specifically instructed to rate food quality, so the consensus about criteria is a fact by definition. For restaurant audiences there is little controversy that food quality is of central importance (but see below for qualifications). For other products there may be less consensus. In statistical software, for example, ability to handle the general linear model is often seen as the most important criterion. But the general linear model is only applicable to certain kinds of data. For other data—like sample surveys or time series data—other statistical procedures are more important. Complex products have multiple audiences and each may place different criteria at the center of its ranking.

Is there consensus about each position? When I asked restaurant reviewers to describe the characteristics of, for example, a two-star restaurant, they gave two answers. One simple answer was that a two-star restaurant is clearly not as good as a three-star restaurant but it is better than a one-star restaurant. This is obvious to even casual observers and it is not very satisfying. When pressed for a more informative description, a typical reviewer's response referred to other restaurants: "I gave [this restaurant] two stars because the food [quality] was like [several other restaurants]." A common variation was "It's not quite as good as [another higher-ranked restaurant]." I concluded from these conversations that the characteristics of each star stratum are not easy to articulate in the abstract. The system seems to depend primarily on knowing how other restaurants rank and doing comparisons. The stratum that everyone understands is a four-star restaurant. One critic summarized: "Superb food, a great wine list, flawless service, elegant décor." The star scale is anchored by its highest value. The characteristics of other strata are unclear even to those who award the ratings, and any consensus is likely to cover a wide variety of beliefs about which characteristics are important to each stratum.

The comparison in figure 5.3 showed that, on average, critics and diners make similar judgments of restaurant food quality. But we also saw some notable differences. Zagat's audience surveys showed several systematic biases: new restaurants tended to rank lower, long-time restaurants tended to rank higher.[9] These were biases attributable to the fact that diners were not all one audience. Different audiences tended to rate restaurants differently. This means that audiences are not equally able to judge occupants of different positions in the hierarchy. Or, stated differently, when rating restaurants on food quality, they tend to introduce factors that are not related to food quality into their judgments. This, of course, relates to point 1, and suggests a lack of consensus about the evaluation criteria.

The weights assigned to different components of food quality tend to depend on the cuisine. A typical reviewer comment is "Restaurants are so diverse. You have to judge them by their own standards, by what are they trying to do. . . . French restaurants don't do the same things to food as Contemporary American and I judge them differently." The evidence in chapter 5 suggests that food quality weights are broadly similar across audiences. The various mechanisms that generate this consensus are readily apparent. Similar education: major cooking schools teach similar technique. Eating in restaurants that others have rated highly gives a common experiential basis. One critic noted, "Anyone who is well-connected with other foodies can easily find the short list of good restaurants in any city in the country." Others validate opinions; there is a constant circulation of people traveling around the country and eating in good restaurants. Reviewers regularly dine with traveling gastronomes. Competitions like the James Beard Awards highlight current trends and provide exemplars of fine dining. Finally, everyone reads the same publications: *Gourmet*, *GQ*, *Food and Wine*, *Wine Spectator*, and others.

Even if there is consensus, there is still a problem. The problem is indicated by reviewers' objections to assigning stars: Restaurants are very hard to compare. Reviewers tend to object to stars because cuisines can be so different.

This is, in part, a technical objection: a problem of acquiring expertise in various world cuisines. The variety in a full-time restaurant reviewer's life can sometimes resemble one of those "if today is Tuesday this must be Brussels" packaged tours: Today a Thai restaurant, tomorrow Soul Food, on Friday Argentinean. Reviewers have found solutions to the technical problem: usually, doing research and inviting along someone who knows the cuisine. From our point of view, a more significant objection is that each cuisine has its own standards and it is most appropriately judged by what it tries to do. If they are judged by their own standards of excellence, then the dining experience in a four-star Japanese restaurant will be completely different from the experience in a four-star French restaurant. Ranking them on the same scale tends to give the impression that they are somehow the same. This means that a single status hierarchy can be too simple and, as a result, be confusing and misleading.

The weights issue is related to the last question. Is the key criterion equally salient to all audiences? In the case of restaurants, is food quality equally important to everyone? Critics' star ratings are based primarily on food quality, but reviewers are well aware that readers have multiple reasons for consulting the review. In addition to the overall evaluation, reviews often contain explicit information about cuisine, price, wine lists, credit cards accepted, location, and child-friendliness, among others. Reviews often contain lists of restaurants in various categories.

We conclude that the status hierarchy of restaurants is not unidimensional. It does not meet even one of the five criteria. The fact that restaurant status hierarchy is multidimensional raises another series of questions: How many dimensions are there? How are they divided? Are they all equally important or are some more important than others? How, in general, are the different dimensions related? We turn to these questions next.

## Restaurant Status in Multiple Dimensions

*Chicago* magazine (2003) cross-indexes its restaurants by food quality, price, cuisine, location, and adds a list for weekend brunches. Zagat's has many, many cross-indexes: eighty-nine different categories of "Types of Cuisine," sixty-eight categories of "Neighborhood Location," and there are twenty-five pages listing restaurants by "Special Features." This last list contains no less than forty-seven different categories, ranging from the formal ("jacket required") to the trendy ("cigars welcome"); see table 7.2. Although many categories are simple listings of restaurants and so indicate boundaries, they are all linked to Zagat's reviews and their evaluations.[10]

In the front of each book, Zagat's lists the "Top Ratings" in sixty-six categories (see table 7.3).[11] These sixty-six lists are explicitly rank-ordered by

**Table 7.2.   Zagat's Lists of "Special Features"**

| | | |
|---|---|---|
| Bathrooms to visit | Hotel dining | Private rooms |
| Breakfast | "In" places | Pubs/bars/microbreweries |
| Brunch | Jacket required | Quick bites |
| Buffet served | Jury duty | Quiet conversation |
| BYO | Kosher | Raw bars |
| Celebrity chefs | Late-afternoon dining | Romantic Places |
| Cheese trays | Late dining | Senior appeal |
| Chef's table | Meet for a drink | Singles scenes |
| Child friendly | Natural/organic | Sleepers* |
| Cigars welcome | Noteworthy newcomers | Sunday—best bets |
| Entertainment | Noteworthy closings | Tasting menus |
| Entertainment/dancing | Outdoor dining | Tea service |
| Fireplaces | People-watching | Theme restaurants |
| Game in season | Power scenes | Transporting experiences** |
| Gracious hosts | Pre-theater menus/Prix | Visitors on expense account |
| Historical places | Fixe menus | Winning wine lists |

\* Defined as "good to excellent food but little known."
\*\* Defined as "like traveling to another time and place."

food quality ratings, so not only are boundaries marked but also there is an explicit hierarchy within each category. Each hierarchy is very visible and highly accessible. There is no single hierarchy in restaurants.

In my interviews Zagat's readers responded strongly to the lists of restaurants. Many referred directly to using the lists. Many diners cited the various categories and lists as the main reason they used Zagat's. Three typical comments: "The lists are really helpful when you want to find a restaurant." Or, "I originally bought Zagat's for the ratings, but when you combine them with a list in the front you have a super way to find a good restaurant . . . that fits your preference. . . . Now I mostly turn to the lists first." Or, "I kind of agree with the criticism that Zagat's . . . [is] superficial, but the lists of restaurants are so useful. I buy it for the lists."

The lists address several issues that are important to diners. My interviewees described at least six reasons. Convenience was an important reason. "I can find good restaurants quickly." "The reason I like Zagat's is that I can decide what kind of food I want to eat, look it up, and pick the top restaurant on the list. It's *so* easy." The lists help people find restaurants easily.

The lists also help people match their preferences to restaurants. "Zagat's has always had the right categories for me. . . . When I was single I used Zagat's to find the best singles places and romantic restaurants. Now I use Zagat's to find restaurants that can handle children and have good food, both."

Diners find the comparative value of the lists useful. "I showed my friend where [a new restaurant] was on the list. He knew immediately that it was better than [one restaurant] but not as good as [another restaurant]." "When

**Table 7.3. Zagat's Lists of "Top Ratings"**

| | | |
|---|---|---|
| Top 50 Food | Noodle shops | Private rooms |
| Top by Cuisine | Pizza | Pub dining |
| American | Seafood | Quick bites |
| American (regional) | South American | Sleepers |
| Barbecue | Southern/Soul | Tasting menus |
| Brasseries | Spanish | Trips to the country |
| Cafés | Steakhouses | 24-hour |
| Caviar & champagne | Tapas | Top by Location (followed |
| Chinese | Thai | by 38 categories) |
| Coffeehouses | Vegetarian | Top 50 Decor Ranking |
| Continental | Vietnamese | Gardens |
| Delis | Wild cards | Old NY |
| Dessert | Top by Special Feature | Romance |
| French | Breakfast | Rooms—classic |
| French (Bistro) | Brunch | Rooms—modern |
| Greek | Hotel dining | Views—city |
| Hamburgers | Improved | Views—water |
| Indian | Kosher | Top 50 Service |
| Italian | Late dining | Best Buys |
| Japanese | Lunch ($20) | Full-menu restaurants |
| Korean | Newcomers/rated | Specialty shops |
| Mediterranean | Newcomers/unrated | Bargain Prix Fixe menus |
| Mexican/Tex-Mex | People-watching | Lunch |
| Middle East | Power scenes | Dinner |

I'm going to a new restaurant, knowing where it fits on the lists is a way to set my expectations. I compare it to restaurants that I know." "I like to know what I'm going to eat. . . . How good is the food? The lists of restaurants tell me how a restaurant compares to others . . . and give me a sense of what kind of experience I'm going to have." The ratings provide explicit comparisons.

Even when diners are not making an explicit comparison, the ratings supply implicit relative statements about restaurants. These are often helpful in conversation. "My favorite restaurant has a [food] rating of twenty-two. When I say 'Zagat's rates it a twenty-two,' people know how good it is." "We talk about restaurants using Zagat's as a sort of handy reference. We say 'That's an eighteen.' Or 'That's a twenty-five.' It's a quick way to communicate about the restaurant." "When I say one of Zagat's numbers, people know a lot about the restaurant." The numerical ratings are a convenient shorthand that helps diners talk about different restaurants. There is a simple, implicit comparison built into the numerical values that gives diners an easy way to compare restaurants.

Zagat's lists are particularly valuable when traveling. "I buy Zagat's when I fly into new cities so I can find the good restaurants near my hotel." "When

I'm in a city where I don't know many people the best way to find a place to eat is Zagat's lists." In a strange city people don't know the restaurants and they need guidance.

People go out to restaurants for many reasons. Food, of course. But sometimes for convenience, sometimes for something familiar, sometimes for the exotic, sometimes to please friends or business associates. The eighty-nine types of cuisine, sixty-six categories of "Top Ratings," and the forty-seven "Special Features" reflect this reality. Here is a typical comment from a diner reflecting on what she looks for in a restaurant.

> Of course we want good food, but there are always other considerations. Last summer I wanted to eat outdoors as often as possible. In the winter I like fireplaces. Sometimes we're in the mood for a French Bistro; sometimes we want Chinese; sometimes we like formal dining; sometimes casual. . . . I can find all this in Zagat's and it's easy.

This diner and others like her say that good food is not the only consideration. In this sense the large number of categories is a closer representation to what really interests diners. Dining choices are always conditional on food plus other things. The cognitive maps that people form of good restaurants seem to include multiple cuisines and a host of other considerations. Many considerations are visible in the quotes in the past two paragraphs. Other concerns include cuisine:

> I love Chinese. . . . When I'm a host I take guests to Chinatown. I've taken Chinese cooking classes and studied the history of Chinese cuisine. I love to show friends and business associates how excellent Chinese food tastes. If the only Chinese they've eaten is take-out, they are amazed.

Age: "Our [eighteen-year-old] son wouldn't know what to do with the food at Topolobampo. When he and his friends want Mexican food they go to Taco Bell [laughter]." Noise: "A noisy restaurant is exciting and energizing . . . [but] my fiancée and I go to quiet places when we are planning our wedding. We're still foodies though, so they have to be good restaurants." Who you are dining with: "When I eat out with my husband we go to a different kind of restaurant than when I'm eating with business associates. . . . I wouldn't be me if I wasn't looking for an excellent dinner no matter where I eat." What you want to display: "I take out-of-town visitors to one of the restaurants with a view. It showcases what a marvelous city I live in. . . . If you know where to go you can get such good food, too." This is far from an exhaustive list but it is clear that diners take much more than good food into consideration when they choose a restaurant.[12] When choices require that multiple conditions be satisfied, audiences want simple access to all the conditions. This is one key to the success of Zagat's and its enormous lists of categories.

A final reason may be the most important: Throughout the quotes there is a continuous stress on the importance of finding the best food, finding the best restaurant, finding the best experience. Reread the quotes and you'll see that the diners are frequently intensely aware of differences in quality, especially food quality. Part of Zagat's appeal is that it gives them an accessible method that assures them a certain level of quality. These people use the hierarchies to enhance their experiences at restaurants. That so many hundreds of thousands of people buy Zagat's guides every year says there is a huge audience for the status hierarchies that they make visible. In short, audiences find the value of the lists to be in the hierarchies that they make visible. Audiences use these hierarchies to help them make choices.

This means that the single status hierarchy in table 7.1 is incomplete. People rank and evaluate restaurants in more complex ways. If they are asked only to evaluate food quality, they will happily oblige. Respondents are eager to please; they are intellectually capable of evaluating restaurants using one criterion. But such a methodological technique obscures a theoretical error. When the question asks respondents to use one criterion, all other criteria will be ignored. The problem is that a researcher cannot conclude from this that a single dimension is the only important basis on which people judge restaurants. In the language of survey research, the result lacks validity. People have a complicated view of the status of a restaurant. There are several dimensions. Diners care about food quality but they consider it in the context of a larger picture that includes cuisine, location, who they are dining with, and a host of other concerns.

## How Reviews Help Individuals Achieve High Status

How do individuals achieve status in this world of many dimensions? Recent work in this area emphasizes an apparent decline in the cultural snobbery that Bourdieu discusses in *Distinction*. Cultural differences are still a major basis for stratification, but there is a significant difference. High status is not a result of knowing only high-prestige cultural capital; instead, it is a result of being able to accurately perceive the cultural needs of the moment and find the appropriate solution. This requires familiarity with *many* forms of cultural capital. To emphasize the breadth of knowledge required, the contemporary high-status person is called a "cultural omnivore."[13] In the case of restaurants, multiple status hierarchies create the environment where omnivores flourish. The data used for the univore-omnivore research—questions about music preferences in the General Social Survey—cannot show multiple status hierarchies, but I suspect that music looks much like restaurants: Each music genre has its own status hierarchy, most performers specialize in particular genres, and most competition is within largely separate genres. Like restaurants, music also supports large numbers of status hierarchies: The 2004 Grammy awards recognized 105 categories arranged into 30 musical genres! In a complex environment of multiple status hierarchies, reviews help people achieve high status as omnivores. One respondent described this mechanism:

> Several managers discovered I know restaurants and now they ask me before they entertain traveling VIPs. . . . Once I realized this I read restaurant reviews much more carefully. The reviews tell me about restaurants that I haven't visited: wider knowledge. . . . I've been invited to dinners where no one would ever have thought of me except for my restaurant knowledge. Career-wise it's been helpful.

Given the constant turnover of chefs as well as frequent openings and closings, restaurant knowledge becomes obsolete quickly. Several respondents described reviews as a way to keep up in a dynamic field, for example: "Restaurants change constantly. I want to eat at good restaurants but I want to avoid the declining restaurants. Reviews help me stay in touch; I couldn't do it without reading reviews." Reviews facilitate being an omnivore. They expose the good and bad to public view. The person who reads them can find valuable tools to sustain omnivore status.

Reviews often contain discussions of what Erickson calls the "rules of relevance." Erickson (1996:224) says that "the most useful cultural resource is a . . . working knowledge of a lot of cultural genres combined with" rules about "which culture to use in which context." The Zagat's categories are exactly that: they provide guidance that explains where a restaurant fits into its context. Explicit discussion of which audience dines at a restaurant is a common element in connoisseurial reviews. Audiences are fully aware of this issue and they regard it as of some importance. One respondent explains: "I host business dinners two or three evenings a week. An embarrassment could ruin a good business contact. I want to go to the right place. If I haven't been there before how can I know if it is the right restaurant unless I read a review?" Another respondent says, "On our first date I asked my girlfriend where she liked to eat and she said 'Thai food.' I didn't know anything about Thai restaurants, but Zagat's did. We had a stellar date." These mechanisms and others like them show how a complex society pushes people to become omnivores. Almost a century ago, Simmel (1955) pointed out that complex societies spawn a wide variety of social circles so that few share the same knowledge. For individuals who have to operate in this environment, wide knowledge is valuable because it helps them make connections.[14] Reading reviews gives people some of the tools to become an omnivore, which is a path to success.

Size matters:

> We lived in Lawrence, Kansas . . . and everyone went to the same five or six restaurants. . . . Chicago is just too big and there are too many interesting restaurants. If you enjoy dining and want to eat well, you have to read the *Chicago* [magazine] reviews.

The preceding quote indicates an important qualification to the omnivore literature. Omnivores and reviews are especially important in large fields. It is significant that prior studies have been based on national samples of music preferences (Peterson, Bryson) and a large city (Erickson). Only in large fields can there be multiple dimensions that make mastering the field a problem without an obvious solution. Only under this circumstance can being an omnivore be something distinctive.[15]

To rank restaurants on a single scale is valuable only for limited purposes. In particular it is valuable for the single purpose of judging food quality. Since food is so important for connoisseurial restaurant reviewers, this is a sensible thing for them to do. But researchers cannot conclude from this that review readers use only food quality to judge restaurants. It only demonstrates that one can judge restaurants on a single scale; researchers cannot use this scale for the purpose of understanding how people perceive the stratification of restaurant prestige. Pierre Bourdieu has a different opinion and we turn to a critique of his theory next.

## Reviewers and Hierarchies of *Distinction*

Bourdieu's example of Parisian theater (1984:234–40) is particularly interesting because he discusses critics. Theater is organized around two opposite poles: the binary opposition of boulevard theater (the "bourgeois" pole) and avant-garde theater (the "intellectual" pole) has exact binary parallels in theater audiences, the press, critics, and readers. The "bourgeois" pole occupies the position of high economic capital but low cultural capital. The "intellectual" pole reverses that: low economic capital but high cultural capital. Reviewers, according to Bourdieu, "reproduce . . . the space in which they are themselves classified" (1984:235). They exist primarily as products of classes and class fractions and their comments reflect the perspective of the class fraction to which they belong. A class only listens to a reviewer to the extent that the reviewer is a member of the class. "In accordance with the law that one only preaches to the converted, a critic can only 'influence' his readers insofar as they grant him this power because they are structurally attuned to him in their view of the social world, their tastes and their whole habitus" (1984:240). The vision of reviewers that emerges from Bourdieu's example shows that they obey the same rules as every other actor in his world of distinction-based social status.

Do restaurants work the same way? Restaurants should be a good test since restaurants were invented in Paris and gastronomy is so quintessentially French. In fact, cuisine is not just important; it is central to the French national identity (Ferguson 1998, 2004). Thus the mechanisms of distinction should work with particular effectiveness. Instead, restaurants pose problems for Bourdieu. In the first place, economic and cultural capital are closely related, but in exactly the opposite way than Bourdieu expects. Far from separating high cultural and economic capital, cuisine joins them: *haute cuisine* is high-cost cuisine. Using restaurants in Paris, the same city as Bourdieu's example, figure 7.1 shows the relationship in the 2004 Michelin Red Guide between meal cost and stars. The median cost of a dinner at a three-star restaurant in Paris is over 190 euros. Only the wealthy can afford this sort of high cultural capital. Since high cultural and economic capital are closely associ-

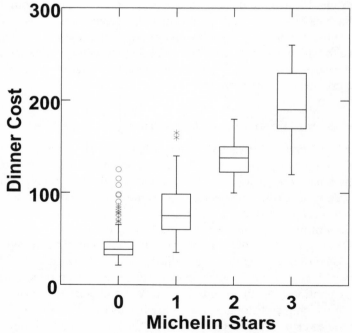

**Figure 7.1.    Relation Between Dinner Cost and Michelin Stars in Paris**
Source: Tabulated from Michelin (2004).

ated, there is no equivalent to the binary contrast between boulevard and avante-garde theater.

Like Bourdieu's theater critics, restaurant reviewers are embedded in both a larger public world and the narrower world of the cultural product they review. Unlike his description of theater critics, class divisions of the wider public world have relatively little influence. The criteria reviewers use are not class-based, instead they derive from theories of gastronomy, which have a strong ethnic component and an even stronger component defined by "good food." The "good food" component is specific to restaurants. Restaurant critics are far more autonomous than the theater critics Bourdieu describes. For them, the characteristics of restaurants as a cultural product are the most significant part of their evaluation.

The social field of restaurant criticism is organized, not by a single binary contrast, but by many hierarchies. There are hierarchies of restaurants, audiences, reviewers, and publications. Zagat reflects the complex boundaries and hierarchies of restaurants by listing no less than forty-seven different restaurant categories. In restaurants (and software) a binary tension exists, but it is between critics, as consumer advocates, and product makers (restaurateurs or software vendors). This is the reason that ethics are so important for critics. Ethical standards give reviewers a way to manage that tension and clarify whose side they are on. Restaurants, restaurant reviewers, and diners inhabit a far more complex environment than Bourdieu's Parisian theatergoers.

Bourdieu describes a world where individual products, reviewers, audiences (class fractions), and even publishers in the case of Parisian theater are aligned together. As a result of this comprehensive alignment Bourdieu maps the social space as a *single* hierarchy of social status. In contrast, the world of restaurants described here breaks down this identity. It is a much more open world, where multiple hierarchies are visible and high-status individuals display their status by being involved in and knowledgeable about a wide variety of fields.


## THE FOODIES

It is also a world of foodies. Foodies are people who spend a large portion of their lives thinking about food, talking about food, eating, and anticipating eating. Some are professional members of the restaurant industry, like chefs or others working in restaurants, but more interesting to us are the nonprofessionals. They have day jobs but, like the person quoted at the beginning of the chapter, "dining is their sport." Most interviewees who thought of themselves as sport diners estimated they spent ten to fifteen thousand dollars per year on dining for pleasure.[16] The amount of money involved implies that these people have a large impact on restaurants. Their impact is enhanced by the fact that friends use them as resources and so they influence other people's dining choices as well.

Foodies are linked by mass media like *Chicago* magazine or *Gourmet*. Probably more significant are the networks linked by informal dining clubs. These are small groups of friends who get together regularly to enjoy restaurants. A conversation conveys some of the passion of these informal groups of foodies.

*Wife*: We have so much fun at restaurants!

*Husband*: A good new restaurant is exciting. I mean that literally. I feel excited and all my senses feel sharper and clearer when we go out to a new restaurant.

*Wife*: We get ready by reading reviews and articles. We look them up on the web. We try to get an advance copy of the menu.

*Question*: Can't you do that without the club? Why do the club?

*Husband*: [My wife] and I eat out together a lot but eating with the club is better. Members bring different perspectives to the food. They make the meal more interesting.

*Wife*: Some of them know food better than we do. They notice things that we wouldn't.

*Husband*: They know *some* cuisines better than you and I.

*Wife*: Yes, *some*. Restaurants always have so much to notice and talk about. Eating with the club is pure entertainment. After a meal and wine we come home excited and happy.

They enjoy the food more when they eat with knowledgeable friends. This is not unlike groups of friends who gather to watch sports. The clubs were a serendipitous discovery and I found three as part of my search for people who read restaurant reviews.[17] For most participants the goal is more than just eating interesting food with friends. They were explicitly interested in experiencing the best that they could. One particularly articulate person explained his motives.

When I am interested in something I buy only the best. The best that I possibly can. I can't afford a Picasso but I can eat at the best restaurants in the world.

*Question*: How do you know what is the best?

Critics like Wheaton here in Chicago or Reichl or Sheraton in New York. You match your tastes against them. The Michelin Red Guide in France. Food writers like MFK Fisher or Trillin. I've gone to some cooking schools. Many, many meals. You learn to know what good food tastes like.

There are, in short, a group of people who are interested in the best food they can find. They have the money, the time, and the interest to search for it. Where other people might remember important sports games or art exhibitions, they mark memorable meals. Reviews construct this sort of person. Reviewers challenge readers with the implicit promise, "Follow my advice and you can be the sort of person who understands and appreciates the best." Some readers respond by deciding that that is exactly the kind of person they want to be.

Bourdieu's emphasis on the development of the habitus in childhood and formal schooling highlights the origins of restaurant dining knowledge. How did foodies learn? The first point is that no one I interviewed had been raised in a family that dined for fun. They learned as adults.[18] Learning required a lot of eating, but that was part of the fun. Often they became interested and pursued their interest systematically through eating and reading. They were able to add food knowledge to their habitus as adults. Reviews play an important role by making dining accessible. A typical story is told by a lawyer.

> I never had the time or money until after I made partner [at my law firm]. When I became interested in restaurants I found the entry was easy. The best restaurants are all laid out in *Chicago* magazine. The criteria are in the reviews. You have to learn a whole vocabulary of foreign words to describe dishes and ingredients but it is all accessible in books, articles, and reviews. Then you have to eat a lot of meals and remember what you ate.

Respondents repeatedly mentioned the accessibility of dining. One said, "Learning about good food and drink requires only time, a little money, and a personal interest. I learned the difference between Château Margaux and Merlot. Anyone could do it." Reviews democratize access to high status objects.

Our analysis of reviews suggests a dynamic system. Restaurants change constantly: we saw how hard it was to maintain consistent service and food quality. The number of hierarchies is also not fixed. Whole new cuisines can emerge: Heartland cuisine in the 1970s, Thai in the 1980s, Fusion in the 1990s; some persist while others disappear as quickly as they emerged. The same is true in software: constant new versions change the position of existing products. The cultural inequalities are dynamic, changing from year to year, sometimes from month to month. The composition of the hierarchies and the position of individual products is in constant motion. Movement within the hierarchy and the emergence of new hierarchies means that to the extent that the habitus is fixed, it is also obsolete. Reviewers publicize the in-equalities in the system as they chronicle movements of products and emer-gence of hierarchies. The result is a society in which consumption and taste are less neatly tied to class and are more complex.

Instead of a tightly restricted system where cultural differences align with differences between class fractions and stratification is based on users and nonusers of certain cultural objects, this vision suggests a more open, acces-sible, and contingent system. Using the criteria and information openly avail-able in reviews, individuals can formulate social mobility strategies to ac-quire high-status cultural capital. Not the least interesting aspect of foodies is that they suggest that the class-based, self-reproducing culture of distinction is not as important as Bourdieu thinks.

Sport dining foodies are a Weberian status group, defined by their aesthetic sensibility and in contact via mass media and networks of informal dining clubs. I suspect such status groups exist in many areas of culture. User groups are the computer equivalent of dining clubs, and computer magazines like *PC Magazine* are the computer mass media equivalent of *Gourmet*. Such sta-tus groups operate outside of the distinction-based culture. To the extent that the spread of reviews democratizes access to any form of culture, Bourdieu's distinction-based culture may be in retreat in some areas of contemporary so-ciety.

To the extent that reviews invite readers to develop a refined sensitivity, they tend to work independently of standard socioeconomic stratification. Computer user groups are composed, in part, of people who build their own equipment and do not want to pay commercial prices. Even restaurant din-ing, which can be very expensive, can be pursued at low cost. One unusual group of foodies was a group of impoverished graduate students whose goal was to eat the best meal they could for under fifteen dollars per person total (including tip and taxes). Obviously this didn't allow them to drink alcohol, and they ate at a lot of Chinese and Thai restaurants, but they also found a number of non-Asian restaurants where they could eat excellent food at that price. Reviews construct an audience interested in optimal use of its assets of time and money. It is an audience that actively seeks the best use of its re-sources; for example, the mutual fund with the best return on investment, the best restaurant meal, the best bicycle, the best computer, or the best experi-ence at a theater. Reviews create stratification systems based around under-standing the nuances of particular products. This stratifying work is to a large extent independent of the standard stratification system. It can be a very attractive system. The existence of foodies (and others) suggests that many people like being members of an elite composed of the sort of person who appreciates and consumes the best.

One might think that this world of multiple hierarchies is difficult or complex for audiences. Ironically, the added complexity is not a weakness; rather, it is valuable. We see in chapter 8 how audiences use this system of multiple hierarchies to help them make choices. It turns out that the complexity is more apparent than real: audiences use the inequalities to simplify their decisions.

## NOTES

1. This reader provides an interesting twist on Becker's (1982, chapter 2) categorization of major participants in the arts. Former *employees* of arts organizations, like this respondent, are an audience overlooked by Becker, although it may overlap with his category of "serious audience members."

2. Chapter 5 describes another reason: reading reviews because the reviewer writes so well, such as John Kenneth Galbraith and George Bernard Shaw.

3. Andre Michelin introduced the Michelin Red Guides on Easter 1900. They were an instant success, selling 35,000 copies in 1900. The initial Red Guide was pocket sized, 939 pages, and listed services for motorists in alphabetical order by the French town in which they were located. Initially Michelin stars were awarded for hotels. In 1926 Michelin began awarding a single star to good restaurants and the 1931 guide first used the three-star system (Chelminski 1986).

4. When I showed Wheaton this list he immediately noticed, "New York is just *foie gras* this and *foie gras* that." All six restaurants are French.

5. Rating 154 restaurants does not mean that there are no more good restaurants in Chicago. The number is a result of the limited number of pages the publisher is willing to allot to the listing. See appendix C for full details on the number of cases in this table.

6. Restaurant reputations and audiences are primarily drawn from a single metropolitan area. Thus status distributions exist largely within a metro area and not across areas. One exception is the effort by various international publications to give awards to the best restaurant in the world, for example, *Wine Spectator*'s Readers' Choice awards. Even here reputations are clearly more limited: "If you break out voters based on where they live, [a majority of respondents in] every region voted for one of its own restaurants" (Mathews 1998:73).

7. The reason there are more restaurants with one and a half stars than one star is an artifact of page limits. Wheaton says *Chicago* lists the best restaurants in the city and there are too many one-star restaurants to include them all.

8. This discussion was inspired in part by Shils's (1968) analysis of deference.

9. The fact that these biases are due to the self-selection of Zagat's respondents is not relevant to this point. All diners select the restaurants where they eat. The fact that groups of diners tend to be biased in these ways simply underscores two points: food quality is not the only important criterion, and there is incomplete consensus about what constitutes good food.

10. The lists of categories in tables 7.2 and 7.3 are from Zagat's New York guide (Zagat and Zagat 2002:10–22 and 258–83). New York was the first guide published and the categories are best developed there. These categories are similar in every Zagat's guide, regardless of the city. Less complex cities than New York have generally fewer categories. Because of cross-indexing, the same restaurant may appear in multiple categories.

11. In addition to the sixty-six "Top Ratings" in table 7.3, an additional thirty-eight "Top by Location" categories are on pp. 14–16. The back of the guide lists sixty-eight additional location categories.

12. There is also evidence that product makers think of restaurants in the context of a large number of hierarchies. In my interviews with restaurateurs they were very self-conscious that the appeal of their restaurant was linked to a fairly narrow category. Several referred spontaneously to particular Zagat's categories to illustrate their point. The relevant categories were not just cuisines but also nonfood issues like location, view, and décor.

13. The initial work here is Peterson's studies of cultural omnivores and univores (Peterson and Kern 1996; Peterson 1997a). Enhancements were contributed by Erickson's (1996) study of occupations and Bryson's (1996) study of music.

14. Erickson (1996) makes a similar point in the context of a discussion of variety in networks.

15. This suggests a general point about the emergence and stability of cultural categories. Many categories may emerge and persist only in large environments. As environments become smaller they have successively fewer categories. When studying cultural categories, size matters. This is particularly easy to see in the case of restaurants, where the relevant environment is the metropolitan area. We can study multiple cases by studying several metro areas. Where the environment is a national market, like it is for many genres of music, this may be harder to see. This underlines the importance of choosing a research site carefully.

16. Dining for pleasure excludes business-related dining. I asked Chicago interviewees how much this would cost in New York; one said, "You know Manhattan prices: multiply by three." Below I describe a group of impoverished graduate student foodies who do not follow this pattern of expensive dining.

17. Only one called itself a "club"; the others simply thought of themselves as people who enjoyed restaurants together. The clubs were solely for pleasure. They were composed of well-paid professionals. Each club had four to six core participants and another eight to ten occasional participants. They spent one or two evenings each month dining at a restaurant that had attracted their attention.

18. It is significant that all major restaurant reviewers did not develop the restaurant portion of their habitus as children. Like Wheaton, they learned good food as adults; see Claiborne (1982), Jacobs (1990), Reichl (1997c), Sheraton (2004), and Wine (1993).

## Chapter Eight

# Reviews and the Status Culture

*Question*: Why do you read reviews of books?

To find out if it is a good book, a book I want to read.

*Question*: Why not use other ways, like the name of the author?

I can only do that if I know the author. There are authors that I read every book they publish. Patrick O'Brian was like that until his death. I read Larry Mc-Murtry and Jim Lehrer. . . . But there are too many books where I don't know the author. Then the review is important.

*Question*: Does the price ever matter?

Cheaper is better but, really, the price doesn't tell you if the book is any good. . . . Price never matters.

In most contexts that last sentence would be absurd: "Price never matters." The person making the statement is no eccentric multimillionaire; he is a middle-class professional with small children and a wife who is currently staying home to care for them. He is financially pressed. The fact that it is reasonable to de-clare that price doesn't matter says something important about books. Books are emblematic of a number of product categories where price does not supply useful information. Deprived of useful price information, audiences use re-views to help them make decisions about these products. Because price is ir-relevant, reviews are important.

Reviews of these products are particularly influential. To the extent that re-views have a transformative effect on the social world, their uses must have a significant impact not just on readers but also on other actors. This occurs when readers use reviews to guide action, such as guiding the choice of a product. In such product categories reviews influence product makers, and reviewers are significant and influential. Considering these issues leads us to explicate a sociological theory of choice, which we contrast to the price-based economic theory of choice. Through their effect on choices, reviews have a major influence on contemporary society. Chapter 7 discusses the effects of the hierarchies created by review rankings. This chapter extends that discussion to encompass the effects of reviews on society as a whole.

## REVIEWS AND SOCIOLOGY

Reviews are common to aesthetic, humanistic, consumer, and scientific fields. Reviews produce rankings that contribute to the stratification of these fields. Review evaluations and judgments lead to public pronouncements of status and position in a hierarchy. This ties stratification directly to reviews. It also ties directly to sociology: the core of sociology is the study of inequality and stratification. In this sense, the study of reviews can contribute to the core of the sociological project.

Reviews contribute to stratification in many ways. They are public pronouncements of status judgments. The pronouncements include the status of individual products and the criteria used to make judgments. They can make entire stratification hierarchies visible. This includes not just static hierarchies; they also draw attention to changes in status. They provide a forum for debate and discussion of status and the criteria used as the basis for status rankings. In all these ways they make status much more transparent and public.

### Inequality and Transparency

Transparency has not been a major concern in the study of social stratification. It is worth considering briefly the circumstances under which transparency is valuable in a stratification system. Most prior research that underlines the value of transparency studies economic systems or institutions (e.g., Carruthers and Stinchcombe 1999). Transparency in an economic system like a stock market ensures that all participants have the same information and they participate on an equal footing. Transparency ensures that investments are what they appear to be, that investors are not being defrauded without their knowledge. If every stock is a potential swindle, then people are very reluctant to invest. Since access to capital is improved by a large and liquid market, discouraging potential shareholders is against the interests of the sellers as a whole, and so stock markets tend to have rules that foster transparency; for example, rules about disclosure of information, conflict of interest, and auditing. Indeed, one of the major causes of the corporate accounting scandals of 2000–2002 was the failure of transparency mechanisms like auditing and disclosure requirements, leading to widespread distrust of crucial financial information like reports of debt obligations and earnings. This is a very brief summary of the value of transparency in economic systems. But what about social and cultural systems? What value does transparency have for them?

Let's approach this question via a classic sociology of art subject: painting, particularly French painting. Throughout most of the nineteenth century, French painting was controlled by what White and White (1993) call the Academic system. The system consisted of approved training, proper subjects, competitions, and prizes directed by the Royal Academy. Why does this institutional arrangement make sense? Consider the situation of French nobility or newly wealthy capitalists who wanted to buy art or participate in discussions of art. A painting is a complicated and subtle product. How could nonartists know what is good art? How could they know the value of what they buy? How could they know they were not being swindled? White and White are very explicit; the Academic system was a "system oriented to the needs of high-placed buyers" (p. 43). These people were not art professionals and did not have the time or commitment to go through a long personal training process to learn how to recognize good and valuable art. Academy definitions of artistic excellence and Academy certification via training and awards supplied a shortcut. The Academic system functioned to designate what was good art.[1] The effect was to simplify how much one had to learn in order to recognize good art, and that in turn expanded the number of potential art buyers. Although artists hated the rigidities and competitions of the Academic system, they had to sell their paintings to support themselves economically. If the only people who knew the value of their product were fellow artists, they could never successfully reach a wide audience. Artists needed to reach a wider and wealthier audience for economic success. Thus in this system, both product makers (artists) and audience members benefited from an institutional mechanism to judge the value of the product. The need for cultural evaluation and certification of quality was so strong that when the status and prestige hierarchy of the Academic system broke down it was replaced with a new set of institutions to certify the quality of painters and paintings, the dealer-critic system.

The dealer-critic system was different in many ways: it was more flexible, more complex, and more open to new subjects and new artistic techniques than the Academic system. Both systems featured an identical core function:

to produce status hierarchies of product makers (artists) and products (paintings). The hierarchies that the dealer-critic system produced were more complex and there were more of them, but hierarchies were as important in the dealer-critic system as they had been in the old system; a shared purpose was to produce inequality.

This example illustrates the value of making a status hierarchy more transparent. Both potential audience members and product makers benefited. The audience benefited because it received assurance that it was buying or viewing quality art. This is the cultural equivalent of avoiding a financial swindle. The artists benefited because the certifying institutions defined quality. When artists met that definition the institutions connected them to wealthy and prestigious audiences, and they became professionally and economically successful. Given the complexity involved in judgments of art, it could be argued that the presence of reviews is a necessary condition for painting to emerge as a modern occupation. Painting as an occupation is only possible because reviews make it more transparent to audiences of (potential) buyers.

Thus the sociological study of reviews is, in part, a study of transparency: who benefits and why they benefit. Evaluations are a mechanism that makes social hierarchies more visible, but reviews are more than evaluations. They support inequality in at least two additional ways. First, they frequently discuss criteria for making evaluations. The reason reviews discuss criteria is to help consumers understand the review and the resulting evaluation. These discussions make the criteria for choice more visible. As we've seen, readers use these criteria for their own purposes, or modify them to better fit their interests. Furthermore, open discussion of criteria makes the principles on which hierarchy and status are based visible and accessible. Attending to the criteria helps audiences sustain their status as cultural omnivores (see chapter 7). Making the criteria visible democratizes access to the product. Any literate person can learn to appreciate it. Second, at a very basic level reviews contain information about the product, including summaries of its value, performance, or capabilities. In a way that self-interested advertising never would, this information exposes flaws and comparative weaknesses in products. This clarifies the hierarchy of products, which are better and which are worse. Much of the material in the case studies (chapters 3 and 4) can be read as a description of what is being made visible and how audiences respond. A key difference between connoisseurial and procedural reviews is that they make different things visible.

As chapter 6 points out, connoisseurial and procedural reviews are different routes to knowledge. The evaluations, criteria, and summaries of reviews are all newly created knowledge. The special value of this knowledge stems from the fact that it is credible because it is from an independent source. The sociological study of reviews is also a study of knowledge, its characteristics, how it is produced, and how it is understood.

## TOWARD A SOCIOLOGY OF CHOICE

We've looked at many reasons for producing and reading reviews. The last two chapters described strengths of different forms of credible knowledge and the advantages of hierarchy and status. Status is not just about prestige. It is not prestige for prestige's sake. It is about access to desirable things, including resources, and knowledge of desirable things. These are some of the issues at stake when people make choices.[2] For many audiences, reviews— through the production of credible rankings—assist their choices. This is a sociological approach to choice. There is an alternative theory of choice: neoclassical economics. From some points of view economic theory is the social science success story of the last generation (Fourcade-Gourinchas 2001). Considering a simple economic theory illuminates some important characteristics of reviews. We develop such a theory in the next section and contrast it to a sociology of choice.

### When Price Fails

One simple theory of choice is the theory taught in basic economics courses. Such a simple economic theory would argue that all the necessary information for making a decision is incorporated in the price of the product. In a competitive market the equilibrium price takes into account all relevant differences including the quality and features of the product, the desirability of the product, the reputation of the seller, and the need of the buyer, among others. Price is so accessible and simple. If all relevant information needed for a purchase decision is collapsed into price, why are there reviews? What is it about products that makes price inadequate and requires reviews?[3]

Let's begin to answer these questions by considering some price-related examples that point us in the right direction. Our simple theory suggests that when demand increases, product makers have two choices. Either they can produce the same amount and the price of each item will rise, or they can produce a larger amount and the price will be stable.[4] In a number of common circumstances product makers choose a stable price. When a book becomes a popular best seller, publishers do not raise the price; instead they print more copies.[5] Similarly, popular plays add performances rather than increase prices. Popular movies stay in first-run theaters longer and their video release is delayed.[6]

In the event of high demand in such markets, product maker strategy is to increase the volume sold and sell to larger audiences, rather than increase the price and sell to smaller audiences. Consequently, products are not distinguished by price. The audience pays exactly the same price for a mediocre product as for an outstanding product. That is the core of the problem: Price carries no information about product quality. Therefore audiences need other information in order to understand what to buy and how to compare products. This is a fundamental characteristic of many cultural products like books, music CDs, movies, theater, and dance. The reader will notice that these are products where reviews are often important. The point is simple: Cultural evaluations in the form of reviews are important when price does not supply adequate information to audiences.[7]

Restaurant food prices are similar in certain respects but with an interesting additional complexity. Price is related to restaurant food quality. We saw this for Parisian restaurants in figure 7.1.[8] No one is surprised that food quality and price are related. Each additional increment of quality is expensive. It requires better-quality ingredients, better-trained staff, more staff, and a better (and more expensive) chef. One chef said to me,

> Fine dining takes special care and work, and that means a big staff. Not everyone knows how to make and serve really good food, so when you find good people you try to keep them. If you want them to stay then you have to pay them. . . . For good food, everything just costs more.

A larger and broader group of restaurants is the full collection of restaurants included in Zagat's. Figure 8.1 uses Zagat's Chicago rankings to plot price estimates on the vertical axis against food quality ratings on the horizontal axis. To help us see the overall pattern more clearly, a line is drawn through the center of the data at each food rating.[9] The line "smoothes" out the local variations in the data, so it is called a smoothed line or a smoother. The first thing to notice about the plot in figure 8.1 is that the line is concave upward. Looking closely at the smoothed line is the best way to see the overall pattern in the plot. Notice that the plot can be divided into two sections. For the restaurants with a food rating of eighteen or less, the line is almost horizontal, indicating no relationship between price and food. Actually, the median price for restaurants with a food rating of twelve is $20; for a food rating of eighteen it is almost identical: $20.50. For restaurants rated nineteen or above, the line is clearly sloped, indicating a positive relationship.[10]

This two-part pattern was not what we saw in figure 7.1 using Michelin ratings of Paris restaurants. What does it mean? The second category—restaurants with food quality rated nineteen and above—looks like figure 7.1. No surprise here; these are restaurants with high food quality. For food quality of eighteen

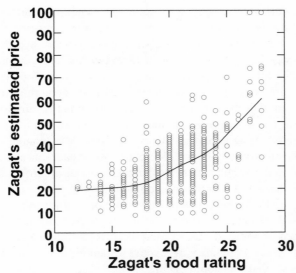

**Figure 8.1. Comparison of Zagat's Price and Zagat's Food Quality**
Source: Tabulated from van Housen (2003)

and below, the smoothed line is horizontal, indicating no apparent relationship between price and quality. Why? What is different about these restaurants? Looking at the names of restaurants at this lower price level offers a clue: Some are sports bars and microbreweries that serve food. Another clue is that Rain Forest Café and the Hard Rock Café fall into this category. For these restaurants, food quality and price are unrelated because the primary reasons diners visit them do not always include food. They go for other reasons: to meet people, to watch sports, to drink, or to enjoy the rainforest décor. (A similar plot [not shown] of the Paris Zagat's [Lobrano and Deschamps 2004] price versus food quality reveals an identical two-part pattern.)

Thinking about why people dine in restaurants quickly leads to a long list of reasons: Zagat's list of "Special Features" has forty-seven categories (table 7.2). People go to restaurants for dozens of reasons, but what does this say about price? A single price doesn't tell diners much about the restaurant. Figure 8.1 shows that at any price between fifteen and twenty-five dollars per meal there are many, many restaurants. Diners have many, many choices. At almost any price, diners could be paying for good service, a convenient location, a great view, a raw bar, special food for children, or dozens of other things, possibly including a particular cuisine. Price tells consumers very little about any of these things. Price doesn't give enough details about the restaurant.

Reviews are the only independent source of this nonprice information. One of the most important characteristics of restaurant audiences is that they are heterogeneous and restaurants themselves are correspondingly diverse. Each audience weights the attributes of the product (in this case, restaurant dining) somewhat differently and each looks for a product that delivers what it wants. Under these circumstances, price doesn't contain enough information to match audiences with their preferred product. Price is too simple; it summarizes too much. Reviews are important when price fails.

Nobel Prize–winning economist Gary Becker (1996, chapter 9) also addresses the question of why people do not choose restaurants as a simple economic theory predicts. His paper has the narrow goal of explaining how adjacent restaurants with the same food quality and the same prices may differ in popularity. To do this he develops a formal model of restaurant pricing that includes overall demand for restaurant meals as part of the model.[11] Intuitively this makes sense if people dine in a restaurant partly because the restaurant is popular. Popularity makes the restaurant more attractive. Becker (p. 197) suggests that this could occur,

> perhaps because a person does not wish to be out of step with what is popular or because confidence in the quality of the food . . . is greater when a restaurant . . . is more popular. This attitude is consistent with Groucho Marx's principle that he would not join any club that would accept him.

Similarly, lack of popularity will deter diners from visiting a restaurant. Formally, Becker proposes that the demand for restaurant meals by any individual depends on both price and the overall demand for meals. If diners select restaurants partially based on popularity, one restaurant may be extremely popular while an adjacent restaurant may be almost deserted.

Becker's theory is not inconsistent with what I propose. We agree that a popular restaurant attracts people simply because it is popular. People may not want to be thought out of step or they may be curious as to what all the fuss is about; whatever the reason, popularity feeds on itself. Many people have noticed that certain restaurants acquire a reputation as trendy, which means that diners visit the restaurant simply because desirable others also dine there. It is valuable to have a formal economic model of how trendy restaurants work.

However, there are several significant differences between Becker's point of view and mine. The argument that I am making implies that there is no such thing as an aggregate demand in the sense of demand from undifferentiated, identical consumers.[12] What matters is not overall demand, but demand by specific, bounded audiences, each with a specific and different collection of criteria for a good restaurant meal. These are similar arguments, except that in my case I am arguing that the key question is which group of people (i.e., which audience) goes to a restaurant, not whether people in general dine at the restaurant. Although there are many audiences (see tables 7.2 and 7.3), the effect of multiple audiences is easiest to see in the case of trendy restaurants. Each year there are some three or four restaurants in Chicago that attract a trendy audience.[13] Trendy audiences can be fickle. When I asked why a particular trendy restaurant was not listed in *Chicago* magazine, a reviewer told me,

> I don't think the food there is very good. . . . Now what will happen to this restaurant is one of two fates. Either the food will improve and people will start coming for the food, or, when the trendy people go elsewhere in a year or two, it will go out of business.[14]

An analysis based on multiple audiences has an implication for the shape of the demand curve. For any particular audience the demand curve is probably a smooth, downward sloping curve like those typical for most other commodities. For any particular restaurant the demand for meals, however, shows sharp discontinuities as entire audiences stop eating at one restaurant and move to another.

A further difference is that people choose restaurants for many reasons. Audiences described by Zagat include visitors on an expense account, parents, yuppies, and forty-four others. There is no reason to think that Zagat's forty-seven categories are an exhaustive list. This suggests that analyses based on price are too narrowly focussed to be of value in understanding restaurant audiences' choices. They leave out too many elements in the choice process.

## When Are Reviews Important?

Personal experience is often limited by lack of time, money, or other resources. The complexity of modern society frequently creates situations where such limits are important. Using the experience of others is a strong, even optimal strategy to overcome these limits. Under these circumstances the study of reviews supplies the basis for a sociological model of choice. Although we are almost always limited by lack of time or money, we don't look at reviews for everything we buy. Under what circumstances will audiences use reviews? Phrased differently, when does price fail? The answer is in three parts. We look first at the broad characteristics of contemporary society that foster high demand for products. Then we describe the circumstances under which audiences lack crucial knowledge about the products they buy. Finally, we examine the characteristics of products for which price information tends not to be useful as a guide for purchase decisions. These circumstances lead audiences to search for third-party product information and evaluations; that is, for reviews.

## *High Demand for Products*

Centuries ago, most people lived in a subsistence economy where they produced almost everything that they needed for life in their own household. Comparatively few goods were bought or traded; trade tended to be based on luxury items rather than products needed for everyday life. By contrast, today we live in a more complex, much wealthier society where we personally produce almost none of the items we use in our daily lives. We produce for others—often as members of large corporate organizations—and buy what we need to maintain our lives. One name for this change is an increasing refinement of the division of labor: our work becomes more specialized.[15] To fill our needs for durable goods, foodstuffs, professional services, and entertainment, we depend on organizations and other individuals for services and for products. This is one reason for the demand for a wide variety of products. The consequences of this are well known and have been extensively studied. They require no extensive discussion here, so this discussion is brief and is intended mostly as a reminder to readers.

One consequence of the extensive division of labor is that people have become much more productive.[16] Productivity increases have lead to enormous increases in income. Between 1820 and 1998, median real income in the United States has increased from $1,257 to $27,330 in constant 1990 dollars.[17] The consequences of this are vast, extensively studied, and well known, so that I need not repeat them here. I draw attention only to one consequence: increased income gives people the ability to buy many more goods. In developed countries most people live well above subsistence levels. They buy most commodities by choice, not out of necessity. This factor contributes to the demand for a wide variety of goods and services.

A consequence of high incomes is an increase in leisure time. The average manufacturing work week has declined from around sixty-six hours per week in the mid-1800s to under forty hours by the end of the twentieth century (Whaples 2001). Increased leisure leads to demand for other products. Examples include tennis racquets, golf clubs, vacation homes, boats, and all the other goods that accompany participation in leisure activities.

Although we need to buy quantities of goods, the complexity of the economy creates situations where we will lack necessary information on which to base our choices. Our ability to gather information on products is often limited by lack of time, money, or other resources. The next section specifies social structural characteristics that make limited information a virtual certainty.

## *Audiences Lack Product Knowledge*

Although high incomes and leisure time allow access to desirable things, the contemporary world can still be a bewildering and frustrating place. The production of culture literature describes structural characteristics of the contemporary capitalist economy that result in audiences lacking personal knowledge about many of the products that they buy. Production of culture theory is primarily a theory of the structural characteristics of cultural production (Hirsch 1972; Peterson 1976, 1994, 1997b; Peterson and Berger 1975) and it pays little attention to audiences. The theory can afford to pay little attention to audiences because the dominant fact about audiences is that their preferences are inscrutable: "All hits are flukes" in the language of Bielby and Bielby's (1994) research into successful television programs. Since corporations do not know what audiences will like, they cannot predict which products will be successful.

This view of audiences has two important implications. First, since no one can reliably predict what audiences will like, production organizations respond by producing many more new products than can succeed. Although such overproduction guarantees that most products will fail, product makers hope that they will stumble on the Next Big Thing. Most products don't even recover the cost of production; almost all profits come from a few unusually successful products.

Second, culture-producing industries must produce new commodities. Product makers such as television networks, movie studios, or recording labels generate a constant stream of new (if very similar) products (DiMaggio 1977): it is the very core of the corporate mission. Even industries not usually considered cultural, like computer software, appliances, or automobiles, generate a constant stream of new products. Capitalist firms seeking to maximize profits are driven to introduce new and revised products at frequent intervals, thereby persuading consumers to buy additional quantities, thus increasing revenue. The combination of a competitive environment along with the value of the revenue boost obtained from consumers who buy the new, revised, or "improved" products creates a constant pressure for product innovation and differentiation.

Related to these characteristics is the fact that some products are infrequent purchases. Often these are durable products that last for many years. Typical examples include cars, personal computers, and major appliances. When products are purchased at long intervals, much knowledge that audiences gained during the previous purchase will be outdated and useless. Familiar products will no longer be available and new products will be unfamiliar: they will have different characteristics and capabilities. This forces audiences to find ways to update their information. For products like these, reviews are a convenient source of the information that they lack.

These characteristics distance audiences from product knowledge. Continuous production of new products coupled with product revision and differentiation make existing consumer knowledge constantly and rapidly obsolete. Large audiences are put in situations where they want to buy products that they know little about. Before they buy, many consumers feel compelled to spend time, money, and energy researching which products meet their needs. This is time-consuming and hard. Reliable information is hard to find and reliability itself is difficult to assess. In this way, contemporary society creates situations where most of us lack the necessary information on which to base our choices.

Using reviews is a strong, even optimal strategy to overcome these limits. In the niches where these limits are common, institutions develop to publish reviews. Thus we see reviews of painting, music, books, computer software, appliances, cars, and many other products. Although we are almost always limited by lack of time or money, we don't look at reviews for everything we buy. We can be more specific about the products where audiences typically use reviews to help them make choices. These are products for which price information is not useful.

## Price Information Is Not Useful

Prices can be a convenient way to judge and compare products, but not always. Under what circumstances will price information be inadequate? These are the circumstances under which reviews are important. A sociological theory of choice applies under these circumstances. I have identified five characteristics under which reviews are likely. Not all of these characteristics will be true for every product that is reviewed, but most will be true for most products, and the more that are true, the more likely a product is to be reviewed.

First, for some products price is unrelated to experience. There are products where the entire category has the same price. For example, all first-run movies are priced alike, regardless of their appeal, their stars, the quality of their writing, or any other characteristics. Other examples where price differences tend not to reflect differences in quality include Broadway shows and books. Under these circumstances price doesn't help audiences make choices.

Second, crucial characteristics of some products are not accessible before purchase. Easily accessible information such as prices, brand names, or reputations are not reliable predictors of product desirability or quality. Important information is not readily accessible. Information from product makers is typically an incomplete description of important aspects of products. There are three kinds of products where key characteristics are especially difficult to judge. First, some products require consistency for a high-quality audience experience. This is especially important for performances, such as theater, restaurants, ballet, or live music. If you are assured of a high-quality performance, your choice is easier. But how can a person know about quality of the performance without attending? There are several answers to this question—including talking to friends, and making judgments based on reputation and genre—but one common answer is to read reviews. Second, for some products repair and reliability are important. This is typical of products such as cars or major appliances. Since reliability only becomes apparent over years of use, it is very difficult to assess before purchase. Finally, in certain categories each product is often one of a kind—such as books, music CDs, and films. For these products, audiences can't easily judge the product without purchasing it. Reading reviews is a solution.

Third, potential buyers have difficulty learning about the product before purchase. Audiences have no easy way to try out some products, at least not under realistic conditions. This problem is particularly significant for "experience products."[18] These are products whose value lies in the experience, not in the functional use of the object. Since no one knows what experience they will have before attending a performance, reading a review is a valuable way to help decide if it may be worthwhile. Examples include art, music, dance, opera, theater, or fine dining; all classic high-culture products. Some non-high-culture products have this problem as well; for example, movies. Since many experience products are performances and they are only available for a limited time, informal mechanisms—like word of mouth—may not be sufficiently timely and formal sources of information—like reviews—are important. The point of reviews is, as so many reviewers say, "I do this so you don't have to."

Fourth, the alternatives may not be clear. Without clear alternatives audiences won't even know what choices are possible. This situation occurs under several circumstances. In some cases the products are so new that audiences won't know that the product category exists. This occurred repeatedly in computer software, computer hardware, and telecommunications markets during the 1980s and 1990s. Second, audience members may simply lack information about alternatives and they may not want to incur the search costs. Reviews can dramatically reduce search costs. Third, some products tend to be one of a kind, like paintings or books, so that appropriate comparisons are difficult without a great deal of effort, prior experience, or training. Audiences lacking the necessary background may be willing to depend on a review to guide them.

Finally, differences between alternative products may be hard to detect. This is a particular attribute of product categories that have not been standardized. It is a characteristic of the early life of a product. An example is personal computer databases. In 1986 *PC Magazine* reviewed commercial databases (Krasnoff and Dickinson 1986), finding 130 products. There were major differences between these products. Seventeen years later, a *PC Magazine* review of personal databases found the commercial market had only seven products (Dreier 2003), and they were quite similar. In the circumstances of personal computing in the 1980s, audiences had enormous difficulty finding the characteristics and suitability of the alternatives for databases, word processors, spreadsheets, and other software. Price contained little information and reviews were extremely important. As the products age, they become more standardized and homogenized, prices decline, and the number of products and product makers declines precipitously; in short, they become commodity products.[19] Commodity products are unlikely to be reviewed. Audiences can buy on price and that's all they need to know.

Product standardization cuts both ways. If there is no standardization at all, every product maker will tend to be in a category by itself. Every product maker will produce a different alternative product. Reviewers cannot easily compare a diversity of products and there will be no reviews. This explains why, despite obvious audience interest, there are few reviews of many service industry categories, such as auto repair shops, physicians, dentists, lawyers, and the like.[20] There are *so* many product makers and each one tends to have a somewhat different skill set. Satisfaction often depends on the match between a set of particular personal skills and the problem that the product maker is being asked to solve. Reviews are very difficult.

When they are deprived of useful price information, audiences search for alternative ways to judge the potential value of a product. One alternative mentioned in the preceding paragraphs is to depend on friends' advice to help you choose. If friends recently bought a similar product they can explain the alternatives and help you choose the one you need. They are, however, subject to significant limits. They may not have personal experience that is relevant; their experience may be out of date or too narrow; you may not trust the quality and reliability of their advice; or you may not like their taste or style. Still, within limits friends are a good source of help. Another alternative is to seek information from advertisements, salesmen, or product brochures. These sources suffer from a conflict of interest that limits their credibility: they will benefit if you follow their recommendation. This weakens the value of ads and other information provided by product makers.

Reviews are not self-interested. Reviews make the quality of a future experience more transparent, they list the alternatives, they can supply information about reliability, and explain the key attributes of each product. In short, they can overcome every one of the five difficulties we discuss here. This is why they are so important for choice.

Under these circumstances audiences search for visible indicators of the potential value of a product. They can find them in published reviews. The reviews make the quality of a future experience more transparent. This summarizes the conditions under which we expect to find reviews. These conditions supply the basis for a sociological model of choice.

## Toward a Sociological Theory of Choice

If the core of sociology is the study of inequality, then a sociological model of choice should also have inequality at its center. This model is based on the premise that understanding hierarchical stratification is the key to understanding certain choice behavior. This is why it is a sociological model of choice and not an economic model; economists tend not to focus on stratification when they think about choice behavior. A summary of this theory includes eight propositions.

1. The extensive division of labor, large incomes, and extensive leisure time characteristic of contemporary society assures that people must buy large numbers of products.
2. Certain attributes of capitalist production tend to separate people from the details of most products. These include the constant stream of new and revised products, overproduction of new products, and the fact that certain products are infrequently bought. This guarantees that almost no one has detailed information about the products they need to buy.
3. For certain products price information will not be useful. These products have one or more of the following five characteristics: The price of the product is not closely related to the quality of the buyer's experience, important features of the product cannot easily be judged, it is difficult to learn about the product before purchase, alternative products that fulfill the same function are not clear, and there are significant differences between alternatives. The more of the above characteristics a product has, the less helpful will be the price information for people trying to decide which product to buy. When prices are not good indicators of the desirability of a product, then audiences search for other sources of information.
4. The incentives described in the preceding three points create a demand for independent, third-party product information about products.
5. Credible reviews are an independent third-party source of product information. Other sources, such as advertisements, product brochures, web sites, or salespeople are undesirable because they are self-interested in the sense that they will benefit if a person follows their advice.

6. Reviews establish criteria, and describe and evaluate products.
7. Review evaluations create hierarchies that rank the desirability of products. The effect of published reviews is to publicize these hierarchies, thereby making them available to broad audiences.
8. The public availability of status hierarchies allows them to be used by people who are not in touch with characteristics of the products they need. Audiences use review-created product hierarchies to help make choices.

   In summary: audiences use status hierarchies to help them make choices when price information is inadequate or unavailable. Figure 8.2 summarizes the theory.

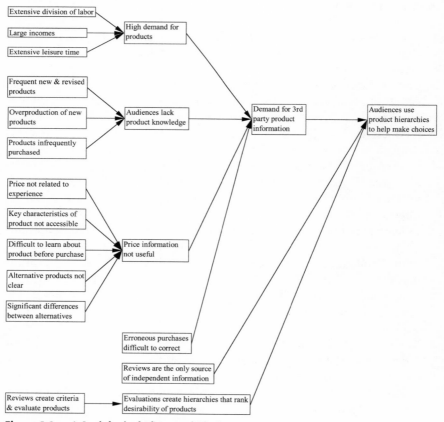

**Figure 8.2.    A Sociological Theory of Choice**

## REVIEWS AND THE EDITORIAL ACTIVITY OF BUSINESS

Audiences measured in the millions respond strongly and positively to hierarchies of cultural products. We've suggested that a sociology of choice is important for large classes of products: Everything from painting and restaurant meals to cars and appliances. If this is true, why aren't these issues—reviews and their effects—more widely noticed and studied?

The answer is that the full importance and effect of reviews is concealed by certain characteristics of modern society. Consider a natural experiment: we contrast the characteristics of the non-Internet world to the world of the Internet, using the case of books and Amazon.com. The non-Internet world is occupied by well-developed, hierarchically organized pyramids of commerce: producers, distributors, retailers, and customers. The Internet is often seen as antithetical to these business models. It is described as a medium that flattens hierarchical models by making distributors and possibly retailers superfluous. Pioneering businesses such as Amazon.com seem to be harbingers of this new organizational form. From the point of view of a consumer these new forms have advantages and disadvantages. The advantages have been widely noticed: lower costs, elimination of the need for customers to physically travel from store to store, easy price comparisons, wider selection, and others. Some disadvantages have been less widely recognized. The simplest way to see some of them is to consider Amazon's inventory: it currently claims around 6 million books. If you know the book you want to buy, Amazon can surely sell it to you. Amazon has worked hard to make the sales process simple and easy. But what if you aren't so certain? Unlike a physical store you can't browse the books. Amazon is out at the end of a long wire and very distant. Think about the distance combined with 6 million choices and e-commerce begins to look less gloriously liberating and more like an overblown, confusing mess.

To solve this problem, Amazon has imposed several different kinds of structure on its books. Some of these are nonhierarchical. Books are categorized by author and by many standard categories: fiction, nonfiction, poetry, history, science fiction, travel, and so on. More interesting is the hierarchical structure generated by reviews. The hierarchy is created when the reviews tell readers which are good books. Amazon uses reviews everywhere. Amazon.com currently lists the award winners from fifty-eight different book awards, including winners in previous years. For example, the Caldicott medal is given annually by the American Library Association to the illustrator of the most distinguished American picture book for children, and Amazon.com lists winners beginning in 1938. The Pulitzer Prize winners are listed since 1965. Nobel Prize for Literature winners start in 1901. Amazon.com lists books reviewed in eighteen media outlets including the *New York Times Book Review*, the *New York Review of Books*, *Atlantic Monthly*, *Time*, *Wired*, National Public Radio, and *Oprah*. For most of these outlets its archive of reviews dates back to 1996. There are best sellers from its own "Amazon.com 100" list ("Updated Hourly," the web page explains), selections by Amazon.com customers, and Amazon's own editor's reviews. In addition, "Movers & Shakers" is a category of books with the biggest gain in Amazon.com sales rank over the past twenty-four hours (also "Updated Hourly"). Amazon encourages readers to write reviews and to summarize their reviews with a star rating (one to five stars). It even prints the average star rating of each book. If you are too busy to remember to check the Web, Amazon will email you reviews of exceptional books in categories that interest you. All this structure simplifies choices and helps match readers with books. The reviews supply an editorial function for Amazon audiences. They inform the audience which products are worth paying attention to and which are less important.

To understand why this is especially important for Internet retailing, contrast Amazon to a physical bookstore. A large bookstore may have over 100,000 titles, but an average store has 10,000 to 20,000. Just like Amazon, these 20,000 books have been categorized but each category has many fewer books. The bookstore has filtered the books to offer only a limited selection of those books it believes of greatest interest to its audience. This is a classic editorial activity. In this sense the bookstore—like every other retail store— is not just a commercial operation; it is also an editorial organization.

Of course many bookstores also make use of reviews. Reviews like the current *New York Times* best seller list are often posted in prominent locations. Award-winning books often receive special displays. But no physical bookstore uses reviews as extensively as Amazon. The reason is that their most important editorial effort occurs when bookstores select the books to keep in stock. This is true of all retail stores. Audience choices are limited by sheer physical distance to the product selections available in local stores. Since the choice you can never make is the choice you've never heard of, this form of review (thumbs up or thumbs down) has the most powerful influence on an audience.

In newspapers, editors are commonly responsible for accepting the mass of news that arrives each day and arraying it in a priority order. Items of greatest interest to their readers are placed prominently on the front page; items of less interest are printed on an interior page. Some items are deemed uninteresting and they are not reported at all. This is commonly seen as an editorial function. It is not just something that happens in newspapers, magazines, and other communication media. Retail organizations decide which products to stock and where to place them. In business-to-business commerce, organizations decide to buy from some suppliers and not others. These decisions result in arrangements of products and suppliers into explicit hierarchies. Editorial decisions of this sort are standard operating procedure in many institutions.

Outside the Internet the effects of reviews are concealed by alternative stratification systems. Outside the Internet both the physical constraints of distance and the editorial activities of stores stratify products. Neither factor exists on the Internet, so the full effects of reviews and the hierarchies they create become visible. In a world of limited time, limited money, and limited energy, hierarchical stratification is a requirement for people to use the Internet effectively. Audiences respond so strongly to reviews on the Internet because reviews create stratification systems that make the Internet usable.

This issue is broader than the Internet. *Chicago* magazine, *Zagat's*, and others define a universe of meaningful distinctions with their star ratings, numerical scores, and lists of good restaurants. Striking because of their comprehensive thoroughness are *Zagat's* lists of eighty-nine types of cuisine, forty-seven "Special Features," and, most important, sixty-six "Top Ratings." By printing these categories *Zagat's* gives them a distinctive reality. The lists and ratings define what are the appropriate restaurants to which any restaurant is to be compared and they say explicitly where each restaurant ranks in its comparison group. All this is done in a visible, public way that draws attention to the winners and losers. Some of these distinctions would not exist without the reviewers' lists; certainly most of them would not be as visible. In short, by their public nature, reviews create and disseminate distinctions and rankings, thereby creating new cultural objects. Audiences respond because the new objects help them make sense of their world.

## REVIEWS AND THE STATUS CULTURE[21]

Reviews are common to aesthetic, humanistic, consumer, and scientific fields. This very breadth makes them an intriguing object for study. What is shared among these diverse fields that they use reviews as a common institution? To answer this question, we examine some of the broad, macro characteristics of modern society.

Among the standard contrasts between premodern and modern society is the observation that modern life has become less local. Once most people lived most of their lives within small communities: people were not geographically mobile, travel was slow and difficult, communications were limited. Consequently, most people had comparatively little contact with the rest of the world. In the modern world people are more mobile, transportation has become dramatically easier and faster, and easy, instantaneous communications are widespread. Physical distance has become much less important. Consequently, social life has become less restricted to local contexts and is now embedded in a global context.[22] This change has been extensively discussed for over a century. Several implications are relevant here.

It has been widely noticed that the limits of physical distance constrained people's access to products. The difficulty of physically moving products limited choices to what was locally available. The section above describes the editorial activities of retail businesses as they choose the products they will offer to customers. Despite the enormous variety of available products, relatively few are offered for local sale. The paradox of abundant production but limited local access and choice presents an entrepreneurial opportunity in a capitalist society. Many solutions attempt to overcome the limits of distance. For consumer goods, mail-order catalogs were an early innovation. For cultural goods, the mass media successfully overcame local limits. For current events, mass circulation newspapers (and later radio; still later television) delivered news, politics, weather, and sports, as well as cultural items.[23] All these solutions help people transcend the limits of locality in modern society. The Internet, email, and instant messages are only the latest advances in a centuries-long trend toward the declining importance of physical distance.

As people have access to an ever-wider collection of product choices, a different constraint becomes steadily more important. The removal of physical distance has created many, more diverse choices but it also creates more confusion and complexity. How can anyone decide? For millions of people and for certain products, a solution is to use reviews. Reviews create status hierarchies that people use to sort and limit their choices to make decisions easier and faster. The location of a product in a status hierarchy becomes of central importance. Products are differentiated by their location in a status hierarchy rather than by physical accessibility.[24] This is the mechanism that makes reviews work: *reviews replace physical distance with status distance.*

Thus, two inherent components of contemporary society combine to boost the importance of reviews. The first component is the increasing number of products and people's increasing awareness of those products. The second is the decline in distance. This is the reason reviews have been a growth industry since World War II. It is also the reason why reviews will become even more important in the future. The issues of status are central to contemporary society. In this context, credible public declarations of winners and losers, coupled with reasons and criteria, make reviews powerful. Reviews help define status hierarchies and play a major role in the creation and maintenance of status distinctions.

Reviews can successfully create status hierarchies only if they produce credible knowledge. This links the dual sections of this book: credible reviews are a prerequisite for hierarchies. How is credible knowledge constructed? The answer to this question occupied us from chapter 2 through chapter 6. The issue of physical distance raises a related question: If reviews create status hierarchies in an environment where distance is becoming less important, then they must work across long distances. This is a problem because reviews are local productions. This is particularly problematic for connoisseurial reviews, which are not only local but personal statements. In chapter 6 we ask, what could be more locally situated or more idiosyncratic than dinner in a restaurant? The answer has two parts. First, connoisseurial reviews have norms, standard conventions governing what reviewers write. Knowledgeable readers used the norms to interpret the experience described by the reviewer and apply it in a broader context. Second, readers make fine-grained judgments of credibility. Individual reviewers can be credible only on specific narrow issues and ignored on other issues. For procedural reviews the question can be answered more directly. The reason they work is the standardization and simplicity of the measures used, yielding high reliability.

Two further issues are relevant in the context of our discussion of the characteristics of modern society. As an example, consider writing. In the literate, bureaucratic, modern world, almost everyone around the world needs to write and everyone can see the advantages of being able to write easier and faster. If a product like a word processing program promises to help you do just that, then most people can see clear reasons to buy it. If, as during the 1980s, there are many word processing programs for sale, then which one will you buy? A credible review could help solve this problem. So far this tracks what we assert in this book, but there is a larger point connected to modern bureaucratic institutions. The institutions of the modern nation-state and modern capitalism (both global and local) create environments that are standardized no matter where you live. These similar environments create common needs, like the need for word processing programs. The point is that the institutions of modern societies have created standardized contexts with common problems and dilemmas.[25] The worldwide success of reviews is a result of the success of certain institutional contexts becoming standard around the world. This is one reason why reviews are able to transcend the local context in which they were written.

A second reason has to do with the nature of the knowledge that reviews create. The simplest result of a review is a rank order of products or an even simpler thumbs up/thumbs down for a single product. The simple, standard rank order de-emphasizes the local context of production and it can easily be used without regard to the specific groups or people who created it.[26] It is a very abstract form of knowledge. The rating of a bond in New York can be used by a potential investor in Los Angeles, London, or Tokyo. The rank order is easy to transmit and easy to understand. Such an abstract form fa-

cilitates use of reviews across long distances. Reviews make possible trans-
actions between people who are widely separated in space.

The abstract form of review knowledge also helps them to cross time. Consider reading a review to guide your choice of a product. The guidance will
be valuable if you, as a result, buy a better product, the same product for a
lower price, or a product that more closely fits your needs, or obtain some
other advantage. These qualities of a purchase are not of interest in themselves. Instead they are valuable because they bring future rewards. Such rewards could include increased satisfaction, enhanced prestige, or more resources. Being able to pick the right restaurant to host a client, boss, or date
can be instrumental in securing a contract, being promoted, or cementing a relationship. In this sense, reviews create knowledge that links present and future. Again, they can do this because review knowledge is abstracted from the
local environment where it was created.

This book looks at reviews on many levels, from the micro-processes of
production to the mezzo-processes of audience reception and interpretation,
to the macro-processes of global capitalism. The goal was to situate reviews
at all these levels and to begin to point out some of the ways that reviews relate to sociological issues at each level. Reviews create institutionalized
forms of abstract knowledge. Their content depends on both the qualities of
the product being reviewed and also on the organization producing the review. Organizations specialize in either connoisseurial or procedural reviews.
Audiences respond by using the ranks and status hierarchies for their own diverse purposes, including helping them make choices.

The macro characteristics of reviews place them in a global economy. In a
market economy, product differentiation is the key to successfully attracting
the attention of an audience of consumers. Faced with many seemingly differentiated choices, consumers—including consumers of cultural products—
may find it difficult to know which distinctions are meaningful. This is what
makes reviews powerful. Reviews exist to define choices and to hold good
and bad examples up to public attention. The need for these distinctions is
ubiquitous in contemporary life; it occurs in the fine arts, in the humanities,
in popular culture, in high culture, and in consumer products. Thus, reviews
occur in many social fields. Understanding reviews and their effects requires
that we take account of social structure, status, organization, and culture.

The goal of this chapter is to contextualize reviews in their local and global
context. At the center of reviews lies the same subject that is the core of sociology: status and inequality. A sociology of reviews offers opportunities that
would enrich sociology as a whole. It would attend to the conditions where
status, stratification, structure, and culture override the prosaic, price-oriented
realm of economic life.

The study of reviews and rating systems has been neglected in sociology. The goal of this book is to begin to remedy that neglect. The first steps that I have taken here begin with rich, detailed descriptions of reviews. The conceptual distinction between connoisseurial and procedural reviews clarifies two commonly seen forms of reviews. These forms help organize the production of reviews as well as audience reception. I have attempted to sketch the implications of reviews for different areas of sociology, including the sociology of knowledge, the sociology of scientific knowledge, social stratification and inequality, economic sociology, and, above all, for the sociology of culture. The sociological theory of choice sketched here is preeminently a cultural theory. This book only skims the surface of the possibilities inherent in the study of reviews and rating systems. Studies of reviews, their organization, causes, and effects would benefit all of sociology.

## NOTES

1. In general, the Academic system was a network of gatekeepers, not reviewers. I discuss it here because it illustrates the value of transparency. The dealer-critic system has reviewers at its core.

2. This chapter emphasizes the role of reviews in making practical choices. I fully appreciate that many reviews are read for reasons that have nothing to do with choices. For example, one may read a review of a Broadway performance of a Shakespeare play for many reasons, none of which depends on actually going to see the play. The history of Shakespeare productions, the careers of the celebrity actors or directors, the values currently dominant in New York theater are of interest to many readers, and these are largely independent of the choice to see the play. Similar reasons play a role in one's choice to read reviews of restaurants, painting, sculpture, and other products including cars, personal computers, and software. This use of reviews is much more common in the rich text of connoisseurial reviews than in the spare, predominantly numerical approach of procedural reviews. These are interesting issues and they are discussed in chapter 7.

3. Two notes about this theory. First, no economist believes such a simple theory. It is useful as a null hypothesis to make the point about reviews in the following paragraphs. Second, I realize that I've oversimplified many things. For example, there is no such thing as a unique price; price is only relevant at a certain quantity. Both price and quantity determine the equilibrium. This is clear from supply and demand curves. This simple theory also assumes all buyers are identical. Once buyers are heterogeneous, then price reflects the value of the product to the marginal buyer.

4. Yet a further alternative: if production is sufficiently large, price will decline.

5. This analysis is too simple for books. There are several price levels: hardbound books, book club editions, quality paperbacks, trade paperbacks, and remaindered and used books. A typical strategy of publishers is to start with the most expensive books,

the hardcover editions, and when sales begin to wane, to bring out successively cheaper editions. Popular books tend to stay at higher-priced levels longer; nonetheless, one cannot judge a book by its price: At best, price conveys limited information about the important qualities of a book.

6. In the case of movies, there are in fact several price levels, starting with first-run theaters, then second-run theaters, ending with video and DVD rentals and sales. Like books the usual strategy is to release the film initially at the high-priced theaters and, as each price category becomes exhausted, to release the film into the next lower priced category. Blockbuster movies, like *Titanic*, stay at high-priced levels longer and theaters schedule extra showings, but the price of a ticket does not rise. Again, price contains little information about the qualities of a movie.

7. Certain cultural products are often bought at least partially as investments; examples include painting and sculpture. For them, price over time is a kind of a review. If the price rises it means that the community of buyers is reviewing it more positively. A written art review or art appraisal is a kind of prediction about the direction of the market. For many other cultural products like movies or restaurants, there is no price fluctuation that gives an independent, readily available evaluation whether or not to go to the movie or eat at the restaurant. Reviews are the only major source of independent information.

8. A plot (not shown) of *Chicago* magazine stars against Chicago Zagat's price estimates shows a pattern identical to that in Paris: better restaurants are more expensive.

9. The line is a LOWESS smoother using a tension of 0.5.

10. As an aside, note that the plot shows some visual evidence of heteroscedasticity; the variance becomes larger on the right side. This is another indication of the difficulty of using price as an indicator of food quality. Since I do not attempt to generalize to a population or test statistical significance, possible heteroscedasticity is irrelevant to the interpretations offered here.

11. I'm avoiding some economic jargon here. In the language of economics, Becker's model includes aggregate demand for restaurant meals as an endogenous variable.

12. To be fair, Becker is unlikely to believe that there is only one kind of consumer. He's playing a standard economics game: Let's construct the simplest possible model that explains the outcome.

13. One can reasonably ask, "trendy for whom?" It is true that there are probably several trendy audiences. The trendy audience that I am referring to is the audience of affluent, fairly young people who follow trends in fashion and dining. They were called "yuppies" in the 1980s. It is an identifiable audience, especially when it deserts a restaurant. Trendy restaurants are those where celebrities passing through Chicago often eat. They are always new restaurants and this distinguishes them from longtime favorite restaurants like the Pump Room in the Omni Ambassador East Hotel.

14. Becker's analysis implies that popular restaurants will always remain popular. That is, he explains why people go to a popular restaurant. His model does not show how such a restaurant might lose popularity. Becker's model is a static model and not a dynamic model.

15. A sharp increase in the division of labor has been one major source of the enormous increase in productivity commonly called the Industrial Revolution, exemplified by Adam Smith's famous example of pin-making (Smith 1976 [1776]).

16. The increased use of capital is another cause of the increase in productivity. See Denison (1974) for an extended discussion of the causes of economic growth.

17. Author's calculations from tables B-10 and B-18 in Maddison and Johnston (2001).

18. This useful term is from Caves (2000). Note that experience products are defined from an audience perspective.

19. For a discussion of this pattern, see Carr (2003). Carr's article is aimed at product makers and large corporate users of information technology; he does not discuss reviews.

20. There are two exceptions to this sentence: *Consumer Checkbook* publishes reviews of services including auto repairs, plumbers, physicians, and hospitals in seven metro areas including Chicago, San Francisco, Minneapolis–St. Paul, and Washington D.C. In sixty-two cities www.angieslist.com publishes reviews and ratings by consumers for about 250 categories of local home improvement companies and contractors. Angie's List is an innovative use of the Internet to supply Zagat-style ratings.

21. The term "status cultures" is used in the title of an article by Randall Collins (1992), a Weberian analysis of the role of women in the production of status groups. He does not define the term and does not use it in the text. The article describes the increasing importance of status in the Weberian sense of lifestyle and status display, what Collins refers to as "Goffmanian labor" on the part of women. This is related to my use of *status culture* but my analysis concerns status as prestige and the importance of status as a way of guiding choices. I am not aware of any other uses of this term.

22. Giddens (1990) refers to this as "disembedding" and "reembedding," terms that I find confusing. Modern social life is not "disembedded"; it remains fully embedded but it is embedded *differently* than it was in premodern times. The embeddedness is not as local as it once was.

23. To this list one can also add transportation advances that improve access to products: railroads; air travel; and multilane, divided, limited-access highways.

24. Reviews provide three kinds of information to audiences. This paragraph emphasizes the comparative information in the status hierarchy. Other important information is about the characteristics of the product itself and which criteria are important in evaluating the product (see chapters 2–4, and earlier sections of this chapter).

25. This is not an argument that all societies are converging on a single form. It is simply a note that bureaucracies and other social institutions exist in many contemporary societies.

26. In this sense, review results are an example of Giddens's (1990) "symbolic tokens"; mechanisms that make it possible for people to be disembedded from local settings. Giddens's primary example of a symbolic token is money. Although reviews are not nearly as important as money, reviews and money share many similar characteristics as specific social forms closely linked to the development of modern social institutions.

# Appendices

## APPENDIX A

**Methods**

The research design is based on a four-part design of cultural study. The model, from Griswold (1987b), suggests that in order to obtain a complete grasp of a cultural object one must study four aspects: production, content, reception, and the larger social environment.[1] *Production* is the collection of activities and the interests of the actors who create the object. *Content* refers to the thematic, narrative, and textual characteristics of the phenomenon. In this case, I pay particular attention to how and why reviews become credible. *Reception* involves understanding how those who are involved with the object use it and interpret it. The *social environment* refers to the social context in which the phenomenon exists.

The reasons for choosing the major case studies of restaurant reviews and software reviews are outlined in chapter 1. For both cases I had access to backstage information. For computer software and hardware, especially statistical software, I have written and edited reviews and I knew editors, publishers, and many other reviewers. I have been a part of the discussions surrounding issues such as choosing products for review, appropriate review criteria, fairness, how the content of the review is shaped, and how different audiences respond, among others. As a software consultant, I personally worked for several product makers during times when a major product was being reviewed. I attended marketing meetings where strategies for handling software reviews were discussed. I attended product-planning meetings called to discuss the reasons for not getting a stellar rating in the last review.

I have participated in the discussions surrounding reviews from the perspective of a reviewer, an editor, and an employee of a product maker. In addition, I was fortunate to find a key informant: Ted Stevenson, then senior editor (software) for *PC Magazine*. We did five interviews over the course of three years. Since I use statistical software extensively, and have been frequently asked to recommend individual products, I am an avid reader of statistical software reviews. Thus I am also a member of the audience.

Unlike software reviews, I had not actually written restaurant reviews. Since my personal restaurant review experience did not extend to the backstage, I depended on another key informant, Dennis Ray Wheaton, chief restaurant critic for *Chicago* magazine, and the premier restaurant reviewer in Chicago. Over the course of four years, I ate over twenty working meals with him. This gave me the invaluable ability to compare his experiences with the food, service, and décor at these restaurants with the final text of published reviews. Further, we talked extensively about all aspects of his work as a restaurant reviewer; everything from the process of selecting restaurants, the criteria he used, how he made judgments, to how various audiences like his editors and restaurateurs as well as *Chicago* magazine readers responded to his reviews. These meals and conversations gave me access to the backstage events in restaurant reviews, similar to the backstage information that I had about software reviews.

Restaurants turn out to have a number of other advantages as a research site. Compared to most commercial products they are less expensive and, since their primary audiences are located in a single metropolitan area, they are more accessible. The cost and difficulty of gaining access create significant barriers to the study of many other commercial products. A researcher cannot as easily gain wide experience with them and interviews with product makers would be more difficult. Further, restaurants are not as ephemeral as some fine arts like dance, theater, or musical performances.[2] They can be visited by researcher-sociologists, who can make their own evaluation. The chef, owner, and staff are available for interviews, and they are often eager to describe their experiences to an informed, interested listener. Thus, compared to reviews of art, music, dance, or other fine arts, restaurant reviews offer some unique advantages that simplify and enrich data collection and analysis.

To supplement my personal experience as a software reviewer, editor, and consultant, and my conversations with Stevenson and Wheaton, I interviewed people involved with software and restaurant reviews. For the production side of reviews, I gathered information from diverse sources. I conducted interviews with over thirty-six people involved in reviews. They included representatives of all actors concerned with production: reviewers, editors, chefs, software developers, marketers, corporate executives, and others. To understand reviews of commercial products I conducted several interviews at Consumers Union and I interviewed the editor of a major automotive review publication. In addition, I read extensively in commentaries on stock, bond, and mutual fund reviews, reviews of bicycling equipment, and credit ratings. To improve my understanding of arts reviews, I interviewed a University of Chicago Press editor, a television critic, a movie critic, and a jazz critic. For yet another perspective on reviews, I interviewed Lorri Cox, manager of the Ratings Program of Lettuce Entertain You Enterprises, a Chicago-based restaurant development corporation, which managed thirty-four restaurants at the time of the interview. The ratings program is the in-house secret dining program for Lettuce Entertain You Enterprises. Finally, Roger Ebert, *Chicago Sun-Times* movie critic and, at the time, the only person to win a Pulitzer prize for film criticism, taught a course on film criticism at the University of Chicago in which I enrolled.

To understand audience responses, I interviewed thirty-three review readers—a mix of age, race, gender, and social class—and I conducted three focus groups with a total of twenty-two review readers. (The focus group discussion guide is printed below.) These interviews covered what reviews the respondents read, how often, why they read them, why they believed what they read, how they used reviews, and friends' use of reviews, among other items. Most interviewees were chosen because they were intensely interested in reviews, read reviews frequently, and often used the information in reviews. They read many kinds of reviews: art, automobiles, books, bicycles, computer and electronic games, computer software, computer hardware, consumer appliances, consumer electronics, dance, movies, music (both popular and classical), restaurants, and theater. I interviewed several because their unusual positions in corporate or academic settings gave them a noteworthy perspective on reviews.

I organized a session on Software Reviews at the 1994 Conference on Computing for the Social Sciences, June 3, 1994, College Park, Maryland. The other three participants—Ted Stevenson, then senior associate editor, software, *PC Magazine*; Richard Goldstein, software reviews editor, *The American Statistician*; and Randy Pitzer, marketing, SPSS, Inc.—described statistical software reviews from the perspective of an editor, a reviewer, and a product maker.

I read dozens of commentaries about reviews, focusing particularly on controversies. I read autobiographies of restaurant reviewers (no software reviewer has published an autobiography). I also read marketing brochures, reviewer packets, written histories of restaurants and software companies, company annual reports, mission statements, and restaurant and software trade journals.

## Interview Subjects

The position and organizational affiliation at the time of the interview identify each of the thirty-six people. Several others agreed to be interviewed only if I did not mention their names at all. I promised anonymity to all review readers whom I interviewed, including focus group participants.

Rona Arons, public relations, Consumers Union
Eric Asimov, restaurant reviewer ($25 and under), *New York Times*
Richard Babcock, editor, *Chicago* magazine
Mark Battaglia, vice president of marketing, SPSS, Inc.
John E. Booth, author of *The Critic, Power, and the Performing Arts* (1991)
Ellen Braitman, writer, Consumers Union
Pat Bruno, restaurant critic, *Chicago Sun-Times*
Lorri Cox, manager, Ratings Program, Lettuce Entertain You Enterprises
Jan Deckenbach, associate editor, University of Chicago Press
Tom Deutsch, engineer, Consumers Union
Andrew Dornenburg and Karen Page, authors of *Dining Out* (1998)
Pat Fleury, director of Technical Support, SYSTAT, Inc.
Jack Fuller, publisher and occasional jazz reviewer, *Chicago Tribune*
Richard Goldstein, software reviews editor, *The American Statistician*
Phyllis Issacson, James Beard Foundation
Steve Johnson, TV critic, *Chicago Tribune*
Susan McCreight Lindeborg, executive chef, *Morrison-Clark Inn*, Washington, D.C.
Paul Lingenfelder, director of evaluation, MacArthur Foundation,
Stan Loll, software books editor, Wadsworth
Mark Melikian, former editor, *Consumer Reports*
Pamela Narins, marketing, *SPSS Inc.*
Penny Pollack, dining editor, *Chicago* magazine
Rick Popely, Sr., editor, *Consumer Guide Auto*
Robin Raskin, former editor, *PC Magazine*, and editor in chief, *FamilyPC*
Ruth Reichl, restaurant critic, *New York Times*
Phyllis Richman, restaurant critic, *Washington Post*
William Sanders, director of marketing, BMDP Statistical Software
Mike Sheinfield, public relations director, ZagatSurvey LLC
Ted Stevenson, senior associate editor, software, *PC Magazine*
Kathy Stolley, sociology guide, About.com
Lisa Strong, marketing, Net Shepherd
Charlie Trotter, executive chef and owner, *Charlie Trotter's*, Chicago, Illinois
Phil Vettel, restaurant critic, *Chicago Tribune*

Dennis Ray Wheaton, chief restaurant critic, *Chicago* magazine
Leland Wilkinson, former president of Systat, Inc., senior vice president of
   SPSS, Inc.
Michael Wilmington, movie critic, *Chicago Tribune*

All the reviewers I interviewed work for elite print publications. These reviewers differ in some respects from reviewers for other publications like radio, television, weekly newspapers, suburban newspapers, or magazines that do not focus on food. Where these differences are important, I drew attention to them. A particularly important difference is between small and large publications, where small publications' lack of resources and dependence on single advertisers influence policy and practice.

## Sample Reviewer Interview Schedule

I felt that it was very important to be able to ask specific questions and keep the interviews focussed on specific events. Thus, the schedule was customized for each reviewer and each review genre. I did extensive preparation to be able to ask about specifics. In preparation for each interview, I read at least one year of reviews; I read every nonreview article written by the reviewer that I could find in the Lexis/Nexis database; and I ate a meal in at least two restaurants recently reviewed by each reviewer. For editors and publishers I read the prior year of the publication. In preparation for product maker interviews, I read every review of the product that I could find. In the case of restaurateurs, I ate at each restaurant. In all cases of statistical software, I personally used the product. This activity gave me a great deal of information about products and product makers in action. Using the information gathered by these means I converted the general questions in the sample interview schedule into specific questions about reviews or a product. The interviews were usually about two hours long, ranging from one to four hours.

1. General work experience
   How did you become a reviewer? What makes reviewing a desirable job?
   How did you come to review [this product]? Do you like reviewing [this
      product]?
   What are your strengths as a reviewer?
2. Experience at [publication]
   Where else have you worked?
   How did you come to work for [journal/magazine/newspaper]?
   Do you have other responsibilities at [publication]?

3. Constructing reviews (macro-production of text)

Walk me through the steps a review goes through at [publication].

How do you decide what to review? How do you decide when to re-review a [product]?

Is there a [product] you wouldn't review? What are their characteristics?

Are there [products] that no one would review? What are their characteristics?

How are reviewers assigned or chosen for [product] reviews?

Describe the procedure(s) for actually collecting information for the review. Number of visits/products? Describe how you test/act when testing/visiting. Do you use sources of information other than your personal impressions? Which ones?

Do you check facts mentioned in the review with each vendor before publication? Who does this? How extensively?

Other than you, how many people are involved in the review? Describe what each person does.

What is the production schedule at [publication]? Does it influence your reviews?

4. Writing the review (micro-production of text)

Have you written a recent review that has been particularly successful?

What are the characteristics of a good review of [product]?

An unsuccessful review? What made it unsuccessful? Characteristics of an unsuccessful review?

How do you order and organize the text of your reviews? How do you choose what to put in and what to leave out?

How much time do you need to write a typical review?

How long is your typical review?

5. Standards

Describe how you decide whether a [product] is good or bad? Have you ever written about your personal preferences to your readers? Where do your standards or criteria for your reviews come from?

If [publication] gives some sort of summary ratings like stars, what are the advantages? If not, what are the strengths of not awarding stars? What are the criteria for 1, 2, 3, etc. stars? How did you arrive at those criteria?

6. Credibility

Do you think that readers believe your text? What are the characteristics of your reviews that make them believable?

Do you do anything to make your text more convincing to readers? What?

7. Bias

Do you know of cases where a reviewer pulled his/her punches to give favorable review? What did/would you do?

Do you know of cases where a reviewer had an ax to grind? What did/ would you do?

8. Publication

   What benefits does [publication] receive from publishing [product] reviews?

   How important are [product] reviews to [publication]?

   What, if anything, has changed over the years about the way [publication] does reviews?

9. Who reads the review?

   For whom do you write reviews? Characteristics of *ideal* reader you envision? What characteristics of the [product] interest them?

   Do you have any information on who actually reads your reviews? What are characteristics of people who actually read your reviews? What characteristics of the [product] interest them?

10. Criteria & standards

    How do you know you are choosing the [products] your readers want reviewed?

    How do you know you are using the criteria and standards that your readers share?

11. Feedback?

    How much feedback do you receive?

    What kind of influence do readers have on the review process?

    What is the quality of the feedback?

    Do some readers tell you they don't believe your text? What do they say?

12. Editors, relations with

    Describe your relationship to your [editor/manager].

    From your perspective, what makes a good [editor]?

    Has any [editor] ever made substantive changes to your text?

13. Vendors, relations with

    How important are your reviews to [vendors]?

    How much feedback do you get from [vendors]? What is the quality of the feedback?

    Have [vendors] ever complained to [publication] about your reviews? What happened?

14. Contact with vendors

    How much contact do you have with [vendors]?

    During the review, what contact do you have with [vendors]?

    Does the [publication] have rules about contact between reviewers and vendors? Are the guidelines written? Are the guidelines printed?

    *Restaurant only.* What do you do to avoid being recognized? Have you ever been recognized? What did you do then? Have you ever written about this experience?

Under what circumstances would you accept something free from a vendor? Does the [publication] have guidelines about accepting gifts?

Is accepting marketing literature or private product briefings considered a "free gift"?

15. Other reviewers, relations with

What other reviewers of [product] do you admire? What do they do particularly well?

Do they influence your work? How?

How much contact do you have with other reviewers of [product]?

16. Competition

Who are your chief competitors?

Do you have the same audience as [competitors]? If different, how?

How would you compare your strengths and weaknesses to your competitors?

How would you compare the quality of your work to that of your competitors?

How much contact do you have with other reviewers in [your publication]? What is the relationship between their reviews and yours?

17. Reviews and Reviewers in general

Who is the best [product] reviewer you know? What makes him/her so good?

What do you think of Internet reviews (e.g., IMDB, etc.)? Do you read them? How influential are they?

To whom are your reviews most important? To readers? To your career? To your editor? To [publication]? To [vendors]?

Is there anything else you want to say to me? Anything important that I've omitted?

## Focus Group Discussion Guide

The focus groups had two goals: to establish how readers used reviews and to explore the characteristics of reviews and reviewers that readers were aware of. Most interviewees, including focus group participants, were chosen because they were intensely interested in reviews, read reviews frequently (four or more reviews per week, at least two different products—this eliminated people who only read book review sections of newspapers), and often used the information in reviews. The kind of reviews they read was not important. They were asked to note the reviews they read in the week prior to the meeting. Again, this helped keep the discussion concrete and specific.

*Introduction and Ground Rules*

Thanks for coming.

Purpose of group: discuss reviews and your experiences with reviewing.

Logistics

Time frame: about two to two and a half hours

Room setup: tape recording, taking notes

Ground rules: You are free to express opinions openly without repercussions. There are no "right" or "wrong" answers and everyone's opinion is important. My role is to encourage comments and facilitate the discussion.

Comments made in this room will be kept confidential and your names will never be associated with anything that you say.

*Participant Introductions*

Please tell us your first name and the kinds of reviews you read regularly?

*1. Background: Review reading*

I want to ask about the reviews you've read recently. Tell us about one that was particularly good or bad. [Probe: Did something in particular strike you about any recent review? What?]

What are your favorite publications where reviews are published? Are there publications whose reviews you would not read?

Over the time you've been reading reviews, are there particular reviews that were unusually significant to you? What made them so valuable? In general, how important are reviews? [Probes: purchase, discussion with others, general knowledge about a product]

*2. Reviewers*

Let's talk about your favorite reviewers. Who are your favorite reviewers? What makes them good? [Probe: Are there reviewers whom you would not read?]

*3. Credibility and reviews*

Do you particularly trust some reviewers? What makes them trustworthy? [Probes: Are there reviewers whom you particularly distrust? What makes them untrustworthy?]

What about publications? Are there publications that you particularly trust? What makes them trustworthy? [Probes: Think about publications you distrust; what are they like?]

Some reviewers award summary ratings like stars. Are they important or
valuable? What makes them valuable? [Probes: Do you read them instead
of the review text? Would you miss them if a reviewer stopped using them?
Would you notice if a reviewer started using them?]

Some people are skeptical about reviews. They say that reviewers aren't fair
or impartial, and they pay too much attention to products from heavy advertisers. Can you recall reviewers or reviews that you believe weren't
fair? What made them unfair? [Probes: Do you know of publications that
favorably review products from advertisers? What makes you think
that?]

## 4. Conclusion

Summarize main points of discussion.
Is there anything else you want to add? Anything important that I've omitted?
Thank you!

## APPENDIX B: PRIOR STUDIES OF
## RESTAURANT REVIEWS

The three academic studies of restaurant reviews have generally similar
methodologies. Jolson and Bushman (1978) study diners, restaurant owners, and food critics. Their description does not make clear whether their
"food critics" are employed as restaurant reviewers. The way they talk
about them suggests that they are. They used convenience samples throughout and received responses from 628 diners, 100 restaurant owners, and 80
food critics. Response rates were, respectively, 68.4 percent, 24.0 percent,
and 72.1 percent. The diners are drawn from "consumers who reside in affluent sections of two major eastern cities" The owners run "well-known,
gourmet-type restaurants in 13 cities." Critics are from "throughout the
country" (p. 68).

Schroeder (1985) studied restaurant critics using a convenience sample. He
received 22 responses out of 30 mailed questionnaires containing a 40-item
survey; a response rate of 73 percent. Critics "write for daily newspapers published in the top metropolitan areas of the United States" (p. 57).

Finally, Barrows et al. (1989) studied diners using yet another convenience
sample. They received 390 responses out of 1,000 surveys—a response rate
of 39.0 percent—mailed to randomly selected faculty and staff of "a large
university in the New England region" (p. 86).

The nonacademic study that I use in table 3.2 is the "Tastes of America" study conducted by *Restaurants and Institutions* magazine. It reports results of a market research survey conducted yearly from 1980 through 1988, and every two years since then. Like most nonacademic studies, the sample and methodology are never described in detail but the description of the 1988 study is typical. "The market research firm of National Family Opinion sent out questionnaires to 2,000 representative households. Participants returned 1,309 replies for a 65 percent response rate" (Bertagnoli et al. 1988: 42). The sample appears to be stratified although there is no explicit statement saying so. The 1980 study says, "Within the major geographic regions, the households conform to the typical patterns of population density, age of members, household income, and household size and configuration" (Ashton 1980:54), although this sentence is not repeated in later years. Since 1990 the sample size and composition have not been reported, except that the 1992 survey reported polling 4,000 households which returned 2,502 questionnaires (McCarthy and Strauss 1992:24). Sampling error is never reported. The questions asked in the surveys are sometimes not repeated from year to year. The questions we are interested in—how diners choose restaurants—have not appeared since 1985.

Various Tastes of America surveys contain similar tables comparing the influence of different factors on dining decisions, for example Ashton (1980:84), Liesse (1981:112), Faulkner (1982:82), Gullickson (1983:144), and Pratscher (1985:106). I chose to use the 1981 data because the other years have various problems. The 1980 data contain thirteen categories, including such categories as "Quality of food" and "Atmosphere." The question is confused. Since readers haven't been to the restaurant and they have no personal knowledge about, say, the quality of the food, I did not trust the data. The 1982 and 1983 comparison tables do not report results for the entire sample, only for selected subsets. In 1985 the data for ads are broken down by newspaper, radio, and TV ads.

## APPENDIX C: DISENTANGLING THE NS FROM ZAGAT'S AND *CHICAGO* MAGAZINE

The comparison of Zagat's ratings and *Chicago* magazine stars in chapter 5, chapter 7, and chapter 8 is complicated in that both publications list restaurants that they do not rate and some restaurants have multiple locations. Further, they do not always use identical restaurant names, which complicates combining two different datasets so that the restaurants match correctly. The

**Table C.1.    2003 Zagat's Restaurant Ns**

| Category | N | Description |
|---|---|---|
| Overlap with *Chicago* magazine | 127 | Food rating in Zagat's and star rating in *Chicago* magazine* |
| | 28 | Food rating in Zagat's, appearing in *Chicago* with no star rating |
| | 425 | Food rating in Zagat's, not in *Chicago* magazine |
| Ratings: | 580 | Total restaurants with food ratings |
| | 138 | No food rating because "an important newcomer or a popular write-in" |
| | 1 | No food rating because of recent chef change (Founders Hill Brewing) |
| Restaurants reviewed in Zagat's: | 719 | Total separate restaurants listed. This is the number of unique Chicago restaurants listed, disregarding multiple locations |
| | 342 | Multiple locations (e.g., the Corner Bakery has 10 locations. All 10 are listed in Zagat's, but they are all awarded the same rating. The 9 duplicates are counted in this row; the 1 remaining is counted in the previous row.) |
| States: | 1,061 | Grand Total number of restaurants reviewed in Zagat's |

* The key to reading this table is to understand that the Ns sum downward from the top row by sections: thus, 127 + 27 + 426 = 580 Total restaurants rated, and 580 + 138 + 1 = 719 Total number of separate restaurants listed in Zagats, etc.
Source: Compiled from van Housen (2003)

result is that the number of cases (Ns) on which the statistical results are based are not intuitively obvious. The tables in this appendix provide a complete description of how the ratings and listings are categorized and how the datasets combine. Table C.1, below, shows how the 719 restaurants listed in the 2003 Chicago Zagat's (van Housen 2003) are divided. Table C.2 shows how the 201 restaurants listed in the September 2003 issue of *Chicago* magazine (*Chicago* magazine 2003) are divided. Since not all restaurants had Zagat's food ratings or *Chicago* magazine stars, the actual numbers used for the analysis in chapters 5, 7, and 8 are smaller. The tables below show that because of multiple locations Zagat's actually reviewed 1,061 restaurants and *Chicago* magazine reviewed 271 restaurants. Multiple locations do not enter the tables in the text above because the unit of analysis is the review, not the restaurant.

**Table C.2.   2003 *Chicago* Magazine Restaurant Ns**

| Category | N | Description |
|---|---|---|
| Overlap with Zagat's | 7 | Restaurants with star ratings appearing only in *Chicago* magazine* |
| | 20 | Star rating in *Chicago,* appearing in Zagat's without Zagat's food rating |
| | 127 | Star rating in *Chicago* magazine and food rating in Zagat's |
| Star ratings: | 154 | Total restaurants with star ratings |
| | 1 | No stars, pending rating because of a chef change (Green Dolphin) |
| | 3 | No stars, but given full-length reviews (about 750 words each) |
| | 12 | No stars, listed in sidebars beside the regular restaurant listings |
| | 31 | No stars, listed as "Chicago classics and hot spots" |
| Restaurants reviewed in *Chicago* | 201 | Total separate restaurants listed. This is the number of unique Chicago restaurants listed, disregarding multiple locations. |
| | 70 | Multiple locations (e.g., the Carson's has 4 locations. All 4 are listed, but they are awarded the same rating. The 3 duplicates are counted in this row; the 1 remaining is counted in the previous row.) |
| Total: | 271 | Grand total number of restaurants listed in *Chicago* magazine |

* The key to reading this table is to understand that the Ns sum downward from the top row by sections: 7 + 20 + 127 = 154 total restaurants with star ratings; 154 + 1 + 3 + 12 + 31 = 201 total separate restaurants listed in *Chicago* magazine, and 201 + 70 = 271 Grand total number of restaurants.
Source: Compiled from *Chicago* magazine (2003)

# NOTES

1. See Mukerji and Schudson (1991; also Gamson 1998) for a discussion of a tripartite model including production, content, and reception. These models differ from Griswold by omitting the social world. Bourdieu's theory of fields (e.g., 1983) suggests a similar four-part model including the characteristics of the cultural object, the conditions of production and reception in the field, and the position of the field compared to other fields.

2. The characteristics of restaurant meals make them similar to arts like theater, opera, or dance and different from painting or sculpture. Specifically, restaurant meals are performances. The goal of any restaurant, like other performing arts, is to provide an audience (i.e., diners) with an experience that is both attractive and consistent. Chefs and kitchen staff take raw food, which varies in taste and appearance, and transform it into a finished dish with an attractive but standardized appearance and taste.

Wait staff attend to the varying needs and requests of customers in a way that again provides a consistent, attractive experience. In nonperforming arts, like painting, once a canvas is finished the cultural object is fixed and there is relatively little the artist can do to alter the aesthetic experience of the reviewer. In restaurants, like other performance arts, the experience is reconstituted at every performance—for restaurants that means every dish served to every diner—and this raises issues like consistency and the possibility of manipulating the experience to improve the reviewer's opinion.

# References

Adelson, Alan. 1995. "How 'Hoop' got blackballed." *Entertainment Weekly* 285: 5–6. July 28.

Adler, Jerry. 2003. "A review to die for?" *Newsweek*. 141(10): 53. March 10.

Adler, Mortimer J., Charles van Doren. 1972. *How to Read a Book*. Rev. and updated ed. New York: Simon and Schuster.

Aikman, Becky. 2003. "After expansion, Zagats returns to basics." *Newsday*. January 27.

Allen, Michael Patrick, Anne E. Lincoln. 2004. "Critical discourse and the cultural consecration of American films." *Social Forces*. 82(3): 871–94.

Allen, Ted. 1996. "Going solo at Trio." *Chicago* 45(11): 92–96, 112. November.

Alsop, Stewart. 1993. "We're just doing what we perceive to be our job, Microsoft." *InfoWorld* 15(19): 4 May 10.

———. 1994a. "Our new set of modern colorful clothing hasn't changed our principles." *InfoWorld* 16(46): 194. November 14.

———. 1994b. "Despite our mistake, we're standing by the review and award we gave OS/2 Warp." *InfoWorld* 16(48): 130. November 28.

Alter, Jonathan. 1993. "The incendiary aftershocks." *Newsweek* 119: 65. March 15.

Alva, Marilyn. 1992. "Have restaurant reviewers gone soft?" *Restaurant Business Magazine* 91(9): 92. June 10.

———. 1994. "Does he still have it? Lettuce Entertain You Enterprises Inc. founder Richard Melman." *Restaurant Business Magazine* 93(4): 104. March 1.

Armstrong, David. 1994. "Ziff happens." *Wired* 2(5): 41–47. May 1994.

Arons, Rona. 1997. Personal interview. October 29.

Ashton, Robin. 1980. "Eating out: 1981." *Restaurants & Institutions* 87(12): 49–62, 82–86. December 15.

Associated Press. 1993. "3 'Dateline' staffers fired over GM report." *Chicago Tribune* 146(80): 14. March 21.

Barberian, Harry, David Kingsmill. 1992. "The food critic: Trouble by the barrel." *Nation's Restaurant News* 26(23): 22. June 8.

Barnes, Barry, David Edge, eds. 1982. *Science in Context*. Cambridge, MA: MIT Press.

Barnhart, Bill. 1998. "Star power: Inside the ratings." *Chicago Tribune* 151(60): 3, section 5. March 1.

Barrows, Clayton W., Frank P. Lattuca, Robert H. Bosselman. 1989. "Influence of restaurant reviews upon consumers." *FIU Hospitality Review* 7(2): 84–92.

Baumann, Shyon. 2001. "Intellectualization and art world development: Film in the United States." *American Sociological Review* 66: 404–26.

Becker, Gary S. 1996. *Accounting for Tastes*. Cambridge, MA: Harvard University Press.

Becker, Howard S. 1982. *Art Worlds*. Berkeley: University of California Press.

Becker, Penny Edgell. 1999. *Congregations in Conflict: Cultural Models of Local Religious Life*. New York: Cambridge University Press.

Beisel, Nicola. 1990. "Class, culture and campaigns against vice in three American cities, 1872-1892." *American Sociological Review* 55(1): 44–62.

Beisel, Nicola. 1993. "Morals vs. Art: Censorship, the politics of interpretation, and the Victorian nude." *American Sociological Review* 58(2): 145–62.

Bell, Daniel. 1973. *The Cultural Contradictions of Capitalism*. New York: Basic Books.

Berberoglu, H. 1981. *The World of the Restaurateur*. Toronto: Kendall/Hunt Publishing Company.

Berk, Kenneth N. 1987. "Effective microcomputer statistical software." *American Statistician* 41(3): 222–28.

Berlo, David K., James B. Lemert, Robert J. Mertz. 1969. "Dimensions for evaluating the acceptance of message sources." *Public Opinion Quarterly* 33: 563–76.

Bertagnoli, Lisa, Brian Quinton, Jeff Weinstein. 1988. "The changing tastes of America." *Restaurants & Institutions* 98(30): 42–82. December 9.

Betts, Paul. 2003. "The tourists' bible looks to evolve." *Financial Times*. p. 11. July 12.

Bielby, William T., Denise D. Bielby. 1994. "'All hits are flukes': Institutionalized decision making and the rhetoric of network prime-time program development." *American Journal of Sociology* 99(5): 1287–1313.

Binder, Amy. 1993. "Constructing Racial Rhetoric: Media Depictions of Harm in Heavy Metal and Rap Music." *American Sociological Review* 58: 753–67.

Birmele, Ricardo. 1986. "WordPerfect 4.1." *Byte* 11(9): 311–12. Sept.

Blank, Grant. 1986. "Reviewing statistical software on microcomputers: Methods and vision." *Computers and the Social Sciences* 2(1/2): 1–10. January–June 1986.

———. 1989a. "Bias in statistical software reviews." Pp. 14–20 in Kenneth Berk and Linda Malone, eds., *Proceedings of the 21st Symposium on the Interface: Computing Science and Statistics*. Alexandria, VA: American Statistical Association.

———. 1989b. "CSS." *PC Magazine* 8(5): 123–24. March 14.

———. 1989c. "Finding the right statistic with Statistical Navigator." *PC Magazine* 8(5): 97. March 14.

———. 1993. "Statistica/DOS." *PC Magazine* 12(9): 283–84. May 11.

Blume, Marshall E. 1997. "An anatomy of Morningstar ratings." Unpublished manuscript. October.

Boger, Carl A., Jr. 1995. "Food labeling for restaurants: Fact versus fiction." *Cornell Hotel & Restaurant Administration Quarterly* 36(3): 62–70. June.

Bond, Michael. 1986. *Monsieur Pamplemousse on the Spot*. New York: Ballantine.

Booth, John E. 1991. *The Critic, Power, and the Performing Arts*. New York: Columbia University Press.

Bourdieu, Pierre. 1983. "The field of cultural production, or the economic world reversed." Richard Nice, trans. *Poetics* 12(4–5): 311–56.

———. 1984. *Distinction: A Social Critique of the Judgment of Taste*. Richard Nice, trans. Cambridge, MA: Harvard University Press.

———. 1985. The market of symbolic goods. R. Swyer, trans. *Poetics* 14: 13–44.

Brill, Steven. 1993. "NBC fraud shows media double standard." *Chicago Tribune* 146(115): 41. April 25.

Brillat-Savarin, Jean Anthelme. 1971 [1825]. *The Physiology of Taste or Meditations on Transcendental Gastronomy*. M. F. K. Fisher, trans. New York: Harcourt Brace Jovanovich.

Bryson, Bethany. 1996. "Anything but heavy metal: Symbolic exclusion and musical dislikes." *American Sociological Review* 61(5): 884–99.

Burns, Elizabeth. 1972. *Theatricality: A Study of Convention in the Theatre and in Social Life*. London: Longman.

*Business Week.* 1995. "The Business Week best seller list." *Business Week* 3440: 16. Sept. 4.

Canter, Sheryl. 1993. "Stat of the art." *PC Magazine* 12(9): 227–30. May 11.

Canter, Sheryl, Charles Kadushin. 1993. "Systat for DOS, Systat for Windows." *PC Magazine* 12(9): 284–87. May 11.

Caro, Mark. 1999. "In numbers we trust (too often)." *Chicago Tribune* 152(24, section 7): 1, 10. January 24.

Carpenter, James, Dennis Delora, David Morganstein. 1984. "Statistical software for microcomputers." *Byte* 9(April): 234–64.

Carr, Nicholas G. 2003. "IT doesn't matter." *Harvard Business Review*, pp. 41–49. May.

Carruthers, Bruce G., Arthur L. Stinchcombe. 1999. "The Social Structure of Liquidity: Flexibility, Markets, and States." *Theory and Society* 28(3): 353–82.

Caves, Richard E. 2000. *Creative Industries: Contracts between Art and Commerce*. Cambridge, MA: Harvard University Press.

Chelminski, Rudolph. 1986. "Chez Michelin its tubby tires and a cachet of symbols; history and use of the Michelin guide." *Smithsonian* 71(6): 56.

*Chicago* magazine. 2003. "September restaurants." *Chicago* 52(9): 222–41. September.

*Chicago Tribune.* 1991. "Guess you had to be there." *Chicago Tribune* 146(151): 22. May 31.

———. 1994. "Lawsuits put fire under steakhouse feud." *Chicago Tribune* 148(314): 43. November 8.

Christiansen, Richard. 1998. "Deadlines, discoveries, and three basic questions." *Chicago Tribune* 151(144): 1, 7. May 24.

Claiborne, Craig. 1959. "Elegance of cuisine is on wane in U.S." *New York Times* 108(104): 1, 24. April 13.

——. 1963. "Directory to dining." *New York Times* 112(145): 34 May 24.

——. 1982. Craig Claiborne's a feast made for food: A memoir with recipes. New York: Doubleday.

Clark, Priscilla P. 1975. "Thoughts for food, II: Culinary culture in contemporary France." *The French Review* 49(2):198–205.

Coffee, Peter. 2002. "JMP sifts insight from mountains of data." *eWeek* 19(40): 48, 52. October 7.

Collins, H. M., R. G. Harrison. 1975. "Building a TEA laser: The caprices of communication." *Social Studies of Science* 5: 441–50.

Collins, Randall. 1992. "Women and the production of status cultures." Pp. 213–31 in Michele Lamont and Marcel Fournier, eds., *Cultivating Differences: Symbolic Boundaries and the Making of Inequality.* Chicago: University of Chicago Press.

Consumers Union. 1996. "Buying tires: Three easy steps." *Consumer Reports* 61(1): 35–39. January.

Cooper, Arthur. 1973. "Critic as superstar." *Newsweek* 82(26): 96–98.

Corse, Sarah M. 1997. *Literature and Nationalism: The Politics of Culture in Canada and the United States.* New York: Cambridge University Press.

Corse, Sarah M., Monica D. Griffin. 1997. "Cultural valorization and African American literary history: Reconstructing the canon." *Sociological Forum* 12(2): 173–203.

Coser, Lewis A., Charles Kadushin, Walter W. Powell. 1982. *Books: The Culture and Commerce of Publishing.* Chicago: University of Chicago Press.

Council of Economic Advisors. 2002. *Economic Report of the President.* Washington, DC: U. S. Government Printing Office.

Cox, Lorri. 2000. Private interview. June 13.

Crane, Diana. 1972. *Invisible Colleges: Diffusion of Knowledge in Scientific Communities.* Chicago: University of Chicago Press.

——. 1992. *The Production of Culture.* Beverly Hills, CA: Sage Publications.

Cranor, Lorrie Faith, Paul Resnick, Danielle Gallo. 1998. "Technology inventory: A catalog of tools that support parents' ability to choose online content appropriate for their children." www.research.att.com/projects/tech4kids/t4k.html.

*Current Biography.* 1969. "Claiborne, Craig." *Current Biography 1969.* New York: H. W. Wilson, pp. 95–98.

Dallal, Gerard E. 1988. "Statistical microcomputing—Like it is." *American Statistician* 42(3): 212–16.

Darling, Harriet. 1994. "Survey results point InfoWorld testers in the right direction." *InfoWorld* 16(50): 104–7. December 12.

Davids, Meryl. 1995. "A long—but rewarding—day in the life of a restaurant manager." *Cosmopolitan* 218(5): 162. May.

Denison, Edward F. 1974. *Accounting for United States Economic Growth, 1929–1969.* Washington, D.C.: Brookings.

de Nooy, W. 1988. "Gentlemen of the jury ... The features of experts awarding literary prizes." *Poetics.* 17: 531–45.

——. 1989. "Literary prizes. Their role in the making of children's literature." *Poetics* 18: 199–213.

DeVault, Majorie L. 1990. "Novel readings: The social organization of interpretation." *American Journal of Sociology* 95: 887–921.

Dickinson, John. 1990. "Tomorrow's word processors today." *PC Magazine* 9(14): 95–147. July.

Dickstein, Morris. 1992. *Double Agent: The Critic and Society*. New York: Oxford University Press.

DiMaggio, Paul. 1977. "Market structure, the creative process, and popular culture: Toward an organizational reinterpretation of mass culture theory." *Journal of Popular Culture* 11: 436–52.

———. 1982a. "Cultural entrepreneurship in nineteenth-century Boston, part I: The creation of an organizational base for high culture in America." *Media, Culture, and Society* 4: 33–50.

———. 1982b. "Cultural entrepreneurship in nineteenth-century Boston, part II: The classification and framing of American art." *Media, Culture, and Society* 4: 305–22.

———. 1987. "Classification in Art." *American Sociological Review* 52: 440–55.

———. 1991. "Social structure, institutions, and cultural goods." Pp. 133–55 in Pierre Bourdieu, James S. Coleman, eds., *Social Theory for a Changing World*. Boulder, CO: Westview Press.

———. 1992. "Cultural boundaries and structural change: The extension of the high culture model to theater, opera, and the dance, 1900–1940." Pp. 21–57 in Michele Lamont and Marcel Fournier, eds., *Cultivating Differences: Symbolic Boundaries and the Making of Inequality*. Chicago: University of Chicago Press.

———. 2000. "The production of scientific change: Richard Peterson and the institutional turn in cultural sociology." *Poetics* 28: 107–36.

DiMaggio, Paul J., Walter W. Powell. 1991. "The iron cage revisited: Institutional isomorphism and collective rationality in organizational fields." Pp. 63–82 in Walter W. Powell and Paul J. DiMaggio, eds., *The New Institutionalism in Organizational Analysis*. Chicago: University of Chicago Press.

Dornenburg, Andrew, Karen Page. 1998. *Dining out*. New York: Van Nostrand Reinhold.

Dowd, Timothy J., Maureen Blyler. 2002. "Charting race: The success of Black performers in the mainstream recording market, 1940 to 1990." *Poetics* 30: 87–110.

Dowd, Timothy J., Kathleen Liddle, Kim Lupo, Anne Borden. 2002. "Organizing the musical canon: The repertoires of major U.S. symphony orchestras, 1842 to 1969." *Poetics* 30: 35–61.

Dreier, Troy A. 2003. "Databases for all reasons." *PC Magazine* 22(1): 116–32. January.

Dyck, Timothy. 2002a. "State standing up for users." *eWeek* 19(8): 58. February 25.

———. 2002b. "Clash of the titans." *PC Magazine* 21(6): 122–38. March 26.

Ebert, Roger. 1994. *Roger Ebert's Video Companion*, 1995 ed. Kansas City: Andrews and McMeel.

———. 1995. "Anatomy of a snub: Critic who cried 'foul' compares 'Hoop' to nominated documentaries." *Chicago Sun-Times* 49: 7. February 26.

Ebony. 1998. Top black films of all times. *Ebony* 54 (1): 154–62.

Echikson, William. 2003a. "Wish upon a star." *Wall Street Journal* pp. A8. Feb 28.

———. 2003b. "Death of a chef." *New Yorker* 79(11): 61. May 12.

———. 2004. *Noble Rot: A Bordeaux Wine Revolution*. New York: Norton.

Eisner, Elliot W. 1985. "On the uses of educational connoisseurship and criticism for evaluating classroom life." Pp. 103–119 in *The Art of Educational Evaluation: A Personal View*. London: Falmer Press.

Entman, Robert M. 1991. "Framing U.S. coverage of international news: Contrasts in narratives of the KAL and Iran Air incidents." *Journal of Communication* 41(4): 6–27.

———. 1993. "Framing: Toward clarification of a fractured paradigm." *Journal of Communication* 43(4): 51–58.

Ephron, Nora. 1968. "Critics in the world of the rising soufflé (or is it the rising meringue?)." *New York* 1(26): 34–39. Sept. 30.

Erickson, Bonnie H. 1996. "Culture, class, and connections." *American Journal of Sociology* 102(1): 217–51.

Escoffier, Auguste. 1981 [1907]. *Le guide culinaire*. London: Heineman.

Espeland, Wendy Nelson, Mitchell L. Stevens. 1998. "Commensuration as a social process." *Annual Review of Sociology* 24: 313–43.

ETesting lab. 2003. www.etestinglab.com/benchmarks/. June 7.

Etzioni, Orem. 1996. "The world-wide web: Quagmire or gold mine?" *Communications of the ACM* 39(11): 65–68. November.

———. 1997. "Moving up the information food chain." *AI Magazine* 18(2): 11–18. Summer.

FamilyPC. 1996. "Home publishing software." *FamilyPC* 3: 85–89. July/Aug.

Faulkner, Elizabeth. 1982. "Lifestages." *Restaurants & Institutions* 91: 82–100. December 1.

Faulkner, Robert R. 1971. *Hollywood Studio Musicians, Their Work and Careers in the Recording Industry*. Chicago: Aldine-Atherton.

———. 1983. *Music on Demand: Composers and Careers in the Hollywood Film Industry*. New Brunswick, NJ: Transaction Books.

Ferguson, Priscilla Parkhurst. 1998. "A cultural field in the making: Gastronomy in 19th-century France." *American Journal of Sociology* 104(3): 597–641.

———. 2004. *Accounting for Taste: The Triumph of French Cuisine*. Chicago: University of Chicago Press.

Foster, Ed. 2002a. "Some call it fair play." *InfoWorld* 24(49): 64. December 9.

———. 2002b. "The silent treatment." *InfoWorld* 24(50): 68. December 16.

Fourcade-Gourinchas, Marion. 2001. "Politics, institutional structures, and the rise of economics: A comparative study." *Theory and Society* 30: 397–447.

Fox, Richard, Alan Joch, Chandrika Krishnamurthy, Stephen Platt, and Leonard Presberg. 1993. "126 Printers." *Byte* 18 (June): 146–75.

Francis, Ivor. 1981. *Statistical Software: A Comparative Review*. New York: North-Holland.

Francis, Ivor, Richard M. Heiberger, Paul F. Velleman. 1975. "Criteria and considerations in the evaluation of statistical program packages." *American Statistician* 29(1): 52–56.

Franey, Pierre, with Richard Flaste and Bryan Miller. 1994. *A Chef's Tale: A Memoir of Food, France, and America*. New York: Alfred A. Knopf.

Fridlund, Alan J. 1990a. "Number-crunching statistics software." *InfoWorld* 12(9): 59–69. February 26.

———. 1990b. "The next generation of Mac statistics." *InfoWorld* 12(12): 1–10. March 19.

———. 1994. "Tests grow with statistics technology." *InfoWorld* 16(24): 75–84. June 13.

———. 1997. "'SPSS' improved Systat leads the statistics pack." *InfoWorld* 19(18): 120. May 5.

Fridlund, Alan J., Serge Timacheff. 1990. "Crunching the number crunchers: A complex task." *InfoWorld* 12(9): 60, 69. February 26.

Galvan, Manuel. 1989. "Dionne's a French outpost." *Chicago Tribune* 142(265): 26. Sept. 22.

Gamson, Joshua. 1998. *Freaks Talk Back: Tabloid Talk Shows and Sexual Nonconformity*. Chicago: University of Chicago Press.

Gamson, William A., Andre Modigliani. 1989. "Media discourse and public opinion on nuclear power: A constructionist approach." *American Journal of Sociology* 95(1): 1–37.

Gans, Herbert J. 1957. "The creator-audience relationship in the mass media: An analysis of movie making." Pp. 315–24 in Bernard Rosenberg and David Manning White, eds., *Mass culture: The Popular Arts in America*. Glencoe IL: Free Press.

———. 1979. *Deciding What's News*. New York: Random House.

———. 1999 [1974]. *Popular Culture and High Culture: An Analysis and Evaluation of Taste*. 2nd ed. New York: Basic Books.

Geertz, Clifford. 1973. *The Interpretation of Cultures*. New York: Basic Books.

Getzels, J. W., M. Csikszentmihalyi. 1969. "Aesthetic opinion: An empirical study." *Public Opinion Quarterly* 33: 34–45.

Giddens, Anthony. 1990. *The Consequences of Modernity*. Palo Alto, CA: Stanford University Press.

Gioia, Dana. 1999. "Let's review." *New York Times Book Review* 104(4): 12. January 24.

Gitlin, Todd. 1985. *Inside Prime Time*. New York: Pantheon Books.

Goffman, Erving. 1969. *Strategic Interaction*. Philadelphia: University of Pennsylvania Press.

———. 1974. *Frame Analysis*. Cambridge, MA: Harvard University Press.

Goodlad, J. S. R. 1971. *A Sociology of Popular Drama*. London: Heinemann.

Gray, Herman. 1997. "Jazz tradition, institutional formation, and cultural practice: The canon and the street as frameworks for oppositional Black cultural politics." Pp. 351–73 in Elizbeth Long, ed., *From Sociology to Cultural Studies: New Perspectives*. Malden, MA: Blackwell.

Grazian, David. 2003. *Blue Chicago: The Search for Authenticity in Urban Blues Clubs*. Chicago: University of Chicago Press.

Great Steak Houses. 1997. "Great steak houses of North America." *Northwest Airlines Worldtraveler* 29(3): 12

Greene, Gael. 1987. "Ask Gael." *New York* 20(1): 20–28. January 5.

———. 1968. "Craig Claiborne: The gourmet's gourmet." *Look* 32(17): 70–74. August 20.

Grimes, William. 2003. "On second thought: It's still quite good." *New York Times*. October 20.

Griswold, Wendy. 1981. "American character and the American novel: An expansion of reflection theory in the sociology of literature." *American Journal of Sociology* 86: 740–65.

———. 1986. *Renaissance Revivals: City Comedy and Revenge Tragedy in the London Theatre, 1975–1989*. Chicago: University of Chicago Press.

———. 1987a. "The Fabrication of meaning: Literary interpretation in the United States, Great Britain, and the West Indies." *American Journal of Sociology* 92: 1077–1117.

———. 1987b. "A methodological framework for the sociology of culture." *Sociological Methodology* 17: 1–35.

———. 1992. "The writing on the mud wall: Nigerian novels and the imaginary village." *American Sociological Review* 57: 709–24. December.

———. 2000. *Bearing Witness: Readers, Writers, and the Novel in Nigeria*. Princeton: Princeton University Press.

Gross, John. 1969. *The Rise and Fall of the Man of Letters*. New York: Macmillan.

Gullickson, Betsy. 1983. "Best customers." *Restaurants & Institutions* 93: 136–45. December 1.

Halle, David. 1993. *Inside Culture: Art and Class in the American Home*. Chicago: University of Chicago Press.

Hart, Ellen. 1994. *This Little Piggy went to Murder*. New York: Ballantine.

Herbodeau, Eugène, Paul Thalamas. 1955. *Georges Auguste Escoffier*. London: Practical Press.

Hertneky, Paul B. 1995. "Mastering the media." *Restaurant Hospitality* 79(6): 59. June.

Hirsch, E. D., Jr. 1967. *Validity inIinterpretation*. New Haven: Yale University Press.

Hirsch, Paul M. 1972. "Processing fads and fashions: An organizational-set analysis of cultural industry systems." *American Journal of Sociology* 77(4): 639–59.

Hollander, Geoffrey. 2000. "Forecast Pro presages data." *InfoWorld* 22(8): 59, 62. February 21.

Howard, Bill. 1997. Portable desktops. *PC Magazine* 16(14): 100–195.

Hume, Brit, T. R. Reid. 1990. "PC Magazine warps meaning of independent." *Chicago Tribune* 144: 4. July 15.

Hurley, Jayne, Stephen Schmidt. 1993. "Chinese food: A wok on the wild side." *Nutrition Action Health Letter*. Sept.

InfoWorld. 1994. "New product seal: InfoWorld hot pick." *InfoWorld* 16(46): 170. November 14.

———. 1995. "How we tested." *InfoWorld* 17(46): 111, 114. November 13.

Iyengar, Shanto, Adam Simon. 1993. "News coverage of the Gulf crisis and public opinion: A study of agenda setting, priming, and framing." *Communication Research* 20(3): 365–83.

Jacobs, Jay. 1990. *A Glutton for Punishment: Confessions of a Mercenary Eater*. New York: Atlantic Monthly Press.

Jensen, Elizabeth. 1999. "Meet the Nielsens." *Brill's Content* 2(2): 86–91. March.

Jolson, Marvin A., F. Anthony Bushman. 1978. "Third-party consumer information systems: The case of the food critic." *Journal of Retailing* 54(4): 63–79.

Kapner, Suzanne, David Mack. 1996. "Side dishes." *Nation's Restaurant News* 30(1): 24. January 1.

Karpatkin, Rhoda H. 1999a. "How we choose test projects." *Consumer Reports* 64(3): 7. March

———. 1999b. "Letters to the editor." *Brill's Content* 2(9): 120–21. November.

Katz, Elihu, Paul Lazarsfeld. 1955. *Personal Influence*. New York: The Free Press.

Kawasaki, Guy. 1995. *How to Drive your Competition Crazy*. New York: Hyperion.

Kennedy, Randall. 1994. "OS/2 Warp goes light years ahead of 2.1." *InfoWorld* 16(46): 167–70. November 14.

Kramer, Matt. 1989. "The Times' restaurant critic." *Wine Spectator* 13(19): 21–29. February 15.

Krasnoff, Barbara, John Dickinson. 1986. "Project Database II." *PC Magazine* 5(13): 106–83. June 24.

Lamont, Michele. 1992. *Money, Morals, & Manners: The Culture of the French and the American Upper-Middle Class*. Chicago: University of Chicago Press.

Lamont, Michele, Marcel Fournier, eds. 1992. *Cultivating Differences: Symbolic Boundaries and the Making of Inequality*. Chicago: University of Chicago Press.

Lamont, Michele, Virag Molnar. 2002. "The study of boundaries in the social sciences." *Annual Review of Sociology* 28: 167–95.

Lang, Gladys Engel, Kurt Lang. 1988. "Recognition and renown: The survival of artistic reputation." *American Journal of Sociology* 94: 79–109.

Lang, Kurt. 1958. "Mass, class, and the reviewer." *Social Problems* 6: 11–21.

Latour, Bruno. 1987. *Science in Action: How to Follow Scientists and Engineers Through Society*. Cambridge, MA: Harvard University Press.

———. 1988. *The Pasteurization of France*. Alan Sheridan and John Law, trans. Cambridge, MA: Harvard University Press.

Latour, Bruno, Steve Woolgar. 1986. [1979] *Laboratory Life: The Construction of Scientific Facts*. Princeton: Princeton University Press.

Leathers, Dale G. 1992. *Successful Nonverbal Communication: Principles and Applications*. 2nd ed. New York: Macmillan.

Lessig, Lawrence. 1997. "Tyranny in the infrastructure: The CDA was bad—but PICS may be worse." *Wired* 5(7): 96. July.

Lester, Marilyn. 1980. "Generating newsworthiness: The interpretive construction of public events." *American Sociological Review* 45(6): 984–94.

Levine, Daniel B. 1997. "Entry-level desktop publishing tools." *PC Magazine* 16(8): 157. April 22.

Levine, Lawrence C. 1988. *Highbrow/Lowbrow: The Emergence of Cultural Hierarchy in America*. Cambridge, MA: Harvard University Press.

Levy, Emanuel. 1979. "The role of the critic: Theater in Israel, 1918–1968." *Journal of Communications* 29: 175–83. Autumn.

———. 1988. "Art critics and art publics: A study in the sociology and politics of taste." *Empirical Studies of the Arts* 6(2): 127–48.

Lewin, Kurt. 1947. "Channels of group life: Social planning and action research." *Human Relations* 1: 143–53.

Lieberson, Stanley. 2000. *A Matter of Taste: How Names, Fashions, and Culture Change*. Cambridge, MA: Harvard University Press.

Liesse, Julie. 1981. "Best customers." *Restaurants & Institutions* 90: 102–14. December 1.

Lobrano, Alexander, Mary Deschamps. 2004. *2004/05 Paris Restaurants*. New York: Zagat Survey.

Lu, Shun, Gary Alan Fine. 1995. "The presentation of ethnic authenticity: Chinese food as a social accomplishment." *Sociological Quarterly* 36(3): 535–53.

Lynch, Michael. 1985. *Art and Artifact in Laboratory Science: A Study of Shop Work and Shop Talk in a Research Laboratory*. London: Routledge and Kegan Paul.

Machrone, Bill. 1984. "Project: Database redux." *PC Magazine* 3(18): 81–86. Sept. 18.

———. 1991. "Bang for the buck: A new way to look at PCs." *PC Magazine* 8: 242–46.

———. 1993. "Putting Gateway's new portable machines through their paces." *PC Week* 10(46): 66. November 22.

Maddison, Angus, Donald Johnston. 2001. *The World Economy: A Millennial Perspective*. Paris: Organization for Economic Cooperation and Development.

Manville, William H. 1968. "That anonymous man in the corner can make or break this restaurant." *Saturday Evening Post* 241(25): 34–36, 74–75. December 14.

Mariani, John. 2003. "The agony of the three-star restaurant." *Restaurant Hospitality* 87(4): 24. Apr.

Mathews, Thomas. 1998. "1998 readers' choice awards." *Wine Spectator* 23(5): 58–75. June 30.

McCarthy, Brenda, Karen Strauss. 1992. "Tastes of America: 1992." *Restaurants & Institutions* 102(29): 24. December 9.

McCroskey, James C. 1966. "Scales for the measurement of ethos." *Speech Monographs* 33: 65–72.

McCroskey, James C., Thomas J. Young. 1981. "Ethos and credibility: The construct and its measurement after three decades." *Central States Speech Journal* 32(Spring): 24–34.

Merton, Robert K. 1969. "Behavior patterns of scientists." *American Scientist* 57(1): 1–23.

Metz, Cade. 1999. "The newest value notebooks." *PC Magazine* 18(4): 98–110. February 23.

Michelin. 2004. *Paris 2004*. Paris: Michelin.

Miller, Bryan. 1986. "Romantic dining: What is it and where is it best?" *New York Times* 136: C1. February 14.

———. 1993. "Music du jour." *New York Times* 142(95): 1. April 4.

———. 2003. "Cooking up a storm." *New York Times*, pp. A17. March 15.

Miller, Michael J. 2002. "Why we publish reviews." *PC Magazine* 21(6): 8. March 26.

Miner, Michael. 1993. "Dining and whining: Chicago magazine's overcooked conflict." *Chicago Reader* 23: 9–10.

Montagne, Prosper. 1988a. Jenifer Harvey Lang, ed. *Larousse Gastronomique*. New York: Crown.

Morningstar, Inc. 1999. "Morningstar no-load funds." *Morningstar Mutual Funds* 13: 165. January 22.

———. 2003. *Morningstar Mutual Funds Resource Gguide*. Chicago: Morningstar, Inc.

Mukerji, Chandra, Michael Schudson. 1991. Introduction: Rethinking popular culture. Pp. 1–61 in Chandra Mukerji and Michael Schudson, eds., *Rethinking Popular Culture: Contemporary Perspectives in Cultural Studies*. Berkeley: University of California Press.

Mulkay, Michael, Elizabeth Chaplin. 1982. "Aesthetics and the artistic career: A study of anomie in fine-art painting." *Sociological Quarterly* 23: 117–38. Winter.

Mullins, Nicholas C. 1972. "The development of a scientific specialty: The Phage Group and the origins of molecular biology." *Minerva* 10: 51–82.

Neuman, W. Russell. 1991. *The Future of the Mass Audience*. New York: Cambridge University Press.

*New York Magazine*. 1968. "Between the lines." *New York Magazine* 1(26): 2 Sept. 30.

*New York Times*. 1999. "Best seller list." *New York Times Book Review* 104(1): 22. January 3.

Norton, Andrew A. 1986. "Data management capabilities of full-featured microcomputer statistical packages." *Computers and the Social Sciences* 2(1/2): 39–50.

Ohmann, Richard. 1987. *Politics of Letters*. Middletown, CT: Wesleyan University Press.

Parker, Robert Nash. 1986. "A review of regression, correlation, and ARIMA capabilities in four full-featured microcomputer statistical packages." *Computers and the Social Sciences* 2(1/2): 11–22.

Parseghian, Pamela. 2003. "Celebrated chef Loiseau's death stirs furor over ratings tension." *Nation's Restaurant News* 37(10): 1, 81. March 10.

*PC Magazine*. 1993a. "PC Magazine reviewer's guide: Statistical software." *PC Magazine*. Unpublished manuscript.

———. 1993b. "Suitability to task: Statistics software." *PC Magazine* 12(9): 228. May 11.

———. 1993c. "Summary of features." *PC Magazine* 12(9): 272–81. May 11.

———. 1997a. "A guide to graphics lingo." *PC Magazine* 16(8): 144. April 22.

———. 1997b. "Summary of features." *PC Magazine* 16(8): 155. April 22.

———. 1999. "In order to be the benchmark, you have to set a few yourself." *PC Magazine* 18(2): 90–91.

———. 2003. "The perfect PC." *PC Magazine* 22(11): 77–93. June 30.

Peterson, Richard A., ed. 1976. *The Production of Culture*. Beverly Hills CA: Sage Publications.

———. 1978. "The production of cultural change: The case of contemporary country music." *Social Research* 45(2): 292–314.

———. 1994. "Culture studies through the production perspective: Progress and prospects." Pp. 163–89 in Diana Crane, ed., *The Sociology of Culture: Emerging Theoretical Perspectives*. Cambridge, MA: Blackwell.

———. 1997a. "The rise and fall of highbrow snobbery as a status marker." *Poetics* 25: 75–92.

———. 1997b. *Creating Country Music: Fabricating Authenticity*. Chicago: University of Chicago Press.

Peterson, Richard A, David G. Berger. 1975. "Cycles in symbol production: The case of popular music." *American Journal of Sociology* 40(April): 158–73.

Peterson, Richard A., Roger M. Kern. 1996. "Changing highbrow taste: From snob to omnivore." *American Sociological Review* 61(5): 900–907. October.

Petreley, Nicholas. 1995a. "Reaching an OS impasse." *InfoWorld* 17(46): 90–116. November 13.

———. 1995b. "Seeking a comfort factor (while treading carefully) in testing Oracle Objects." *InfoWorld* 17(5): 105. January 30.

Pfeffer, Jeffrey, Gerald R. Salancik. 1978. *The External Control of Organizations: A Resource Dependence Perspective*. New York: Harper and Row.

Popely, Rick. 1997. Private interview. August 14.

Porter, Theodore M. 1995. *Trust in Numbers: The Pursuit of Objectivity in Science and Public Life*. Princeton: Princeton University Press.

Pratscher, Maureen. 1985. "Eating out." *Restaurants and Institutions* 95(25): 98–106. December 11.

Prial, Frank J. 1996. "Pierre Franey, whose lifelong love of food led to career as chef and author, dies at 75." *New York Times* 146(50,582): A18. October 16.

Ragin, Charles. 1987. *The Comparative Method: Moving beyond Qualitative and Quantitative Strategies*. Berkeley: University of California Press.

———. 1992. "'Casing' and the process of social inquiry." Pp. 217–26 in Charles C. Ragin and Howard S. Becker, eds., *What is a Case? Exploring the Foundations of Social Inquiry*. Cambridge: Cambridge University Press.

Ragin, Charles C., Howard S. Becker, eds. 1992. *What is a Case? Exploring the Foundations of Social Inquiry*. Cambridge: Cambridge University Press.

Rash, Wayne, Jr. 1994. "No editors' choice." *PC Magazine* 13(22): 203–8. December 20.

Raskin, Robin. 1994. "Binding agreements." *PC Magazine* 13(4): 30. February 22.

Reichl, Ruth. 1980a. "A little romance." *New West* 5(4): NC21-NC23. February 25.

———. 1980b. "The prime of their lives." *New West* 5(24): 135–40. December 1.

———. 1981. "Lights! Camera! Dinner!" *New West* 6 (8): 88–91, 127. August.

———. 1985. "Diary of a diner." *Los Angeles Times* 104: 3. January 27.

———. 1993. "How one place can offer two contrasting experiences depending on who you are." *New York Times* 143(229): C20. October 29.

———. 1995a. "Restaurants." *New York Times* 144(224): 24. Aug. 11.

———. 1995b. "Restaurants." *New York Times* 146: C24. October 6.

———. 1996. Personal interview. October 30.

———. 1997a. "Restaurants; Paola's." *New York Times* 146: B35. February 14.

———. 1997b. "Restaurants; A New Le Cirque, the Same Old Magic." *New York Times* 147: F1, F11. October 1.

———. 1997c. *Tender at the Bone*. New York: Random House.

———. 2001. *Comfort Me with Apples: More Adventures at the Table*. New York: Random House.

———. 2005. *Garlic and Sapphires: The Secret Life of a Critic in Disguise*. New York: Penguin.

Rice, William. 1990. "The nation's most critical foodie gives a tasteful review of some of Chicago's most popular restaurants." *Chicago Tribune* 143 (45): 1. February 14.

Richman, Phyllis. 1986. "Quirky recipe for a restaurant survey." *Washington Post* 109: N61. November 28.

———. 1996. Personal interview. October 26.

Richtel, Matt. 2003. "Court rules against Network Associates' software review policy." *New York Times*. January 18.

Rohr, Wendy. 1993. "The critic's voice: What critics look for when they review your restaurant." *Restaurants & Institutions* 103(23): 137–54.

Ross, Val. 1981. "The clout of the inscrutable palate." *Macleans* 94: 46–47. Sept. 7.

Ryan, Nancy Ross. 1984. "Restaurant critics: The poison of the pen?" *Restaurants & Institutions* 94: 166–82. March 28.

Sanson, Michael, John Mariani, Ron Davis. 1990. "Dangerous liaisons: Relationship between restaurant critics and restaurant operators." *Restaurant Hospitality* 74(9): 105.

Santoro, Marco. 2002. "What is a 'cantautore?' Distinction and authorship in Italian (popular) music." *Poetics*. 30: 111–32.

Schaffer, Simon. 1999. "Late Victorian metrology and its instrumentation: A manufactory of Ohms." Pp. 457–78 in Mario Biagioli, ed., *The Science Studies Reader*. New York: Routledge.

Scherer, Ron. 1995. "Tim and Nina Zagat tally up scores for fall's restaurant report card." *Christian Science Monitor* 87: 14. August 31.

Schroeder, John J. 1985. "Restaurant critics respond: We're doing our job." *Cornell Hotel & Restaurant Administration Quarterly* 25: 57–63.

Schudson, Michael. 1984. *Advertising, the Uneasy Persuasion*. New York: Basic Books.

Schwartz, Barry. 2002. "The new Gettysburg Address: A study in illusion." Presented at the Annual Meeting of the American Sociological Association. August 18.

Schwarz, Carl J. 1993. "The mixed-model ANOVA: The truth, the computer packages, the books." *American Statistician* 47(1): 48–59

Scriven, Michael. 1991. *Evaluation Tthesaurus*. 4th ed. Newberry Park, CA: Sage Publications.

Sewell, William H., Jr. 1992. "A theory of structure: Duality, agency, and transformation." *American Journal of Sociology* 98: 1–29.

Shapin, Steven. 1994. *A Social History of Truth: Civility and Science in Seventeenth-Century England*. Chicago: University of Chicago Press.

———. 1995a. "Cordella's love: Credibility and the social studies of science." *Perspectives on Science* 3(3): 255–75.

———. 1995b. "Here and everywhere: Sociology of scientific knowledge." *Annual Review of Sociology* 21: 289–321.

Shapin, Steven, Simon Schaffer. 1985. *Leviathan and the Air-Pump: Hobbes, Boyle, and the Experimental Life*. Princeton: Princeton University Press.

Shaw, David. 1984. "The restaurant critic." Pp. 258–95 in *Press watch*. New York: Macmillan.

Shaw, George Bernard. 1961. Dan H. Laurence, ed. *How to Become a Music Critic*. New York: Hill and Wang.

———. 1991. Brian Tyson, ed. *Bernard Shaw's Book Reviews*. University Park: Pennsylvania State University Press.

Shaw, Steven A. 2000. "The Zagat effect." *Commentary* 110(4): 47–50. November

Sheraton, Mimi. 1984. "Eating around." *Vanity Fair* 47: 39. December

———. 2004. *Eating my Words: An Appetite for Life*. New York: Morrow.

Shils, Edward. 1957. "Daydreams and nightmares: Reflections on the criticism of mass culture." *Sewanee Review* 65(Autumn): 587–608.

———. 1968. "Deference." In J. A. Jackson, ed., *Social Stratification*. Cambridge: Cambridge University Press.

Shrum, Wesley. 1991. "Critics and publics: Mediation in the performing arts." *American Journal of Sociology* 97(2): 347–77.

———. 1996. *Fringe and Fortune: The Role of Critics in High and Popular Art*. Princeton: Princeton University Press.

Simmel, Georg. 1955. "The web of group affiliations." Pp. 125–95 in Kurt H. Wolff and Reinhard Bendix, trans., *Conflict and the Web of Group Affiliations*. Glencoe IL: Free Press.

Smith, Adam. 1976 [1776]. *An Inquiry into the Nature and Causes of the Wealth of Nations*. Chicago: University of Chicago Press.

Smith, Craig S. 2003. "Bitterness follows French chef's death." *New York Times,* pp. A3. Feb 26.

Snow, David A., E. Burke Rochford, Jr., Steven K. Worden, Robert D. Benford. 1986. "Frame alignment processes, micromobilization, and movement participation." *American Sociological Review* 51: 464–81. Aug.

*Software Digest.* 1991. Statistics programs. *Software Digest Ratings Report* 8(5): 1–67. May.

Sorensen, Alan T. 2004. "Bestseller lists and product variety: The case of book sales." Unpublished paper. Available at http://www.stanford.edu/~asorense/papers/bestsellers.pdf.

Sorensen, Alan T., Scott J. Rasmussen. 2004. Is any publicity good publicity? A note on the impact of book reviews. Unpublished paper. Available at http: //www.stanford.edu/~asorense/papers/bookreviews.pdf.

Spang, Rebecca L. 2000. *The Invention of the Restaurant: Paris and Modern Gastronomic Culture*. Cambridge, MA: Harvard University Press.

Sproull, Lee, Sara Kiesler. 1986. "Reducing social context cues: Electronic mail in organizational communication." *Management Science* 32(11): 1492–1512.

———. 1992. *Connections: New Ways of Working in the Networked Organization*. Cambridge MA: MIT Press.

Steigerwald, Bill. 1992. "Dining critic's death reveals crime probe." *Los Angeles Times* 111: 5. February 5.

Steinem, Gloria. 1990. "Sex, lies & advertising." *Ms*. 1 (1–2): 18–28.

Stern, Willy. 1995a. "Did dirty tricks create a best seller?" *Business Week* 3436: 22. Aug. 7.

———. 1995b. "The unmasking of a best seller: Chapter 2." *Business Week* 3437: 40. Aug. 14.

———. 1995c. "Reengineering the best seller list." *Business Week* 3438: 4. Aug. 21.

Storch, Charles. 1993. "Palate intrigue." *Chicago Tribune* 147: 1, 2. September 21.

Swidler, Ann, Jorge Arditi. 1994. "The new sociology of knowledge." *Annual Review of Sociology* 20: 305–29.

Talley, Brooks, Holly Blumenthal. 1997. "If at first you don"t succeed, buy a big showy ad that says you won anyway." *InfoWorld* 19(15): 54F. April 14.

Timacheff, Serge, Alan J. Fridlund. 1988. "InfoWorld survey of statistics users." *InfoWorld* 10: 58. Sept. 19.

Tukey, John W. 1977. *Exploratory Data Analysis*. Reading, MA: Addison-Wesley.

Turgeon, Charles, Francis Turgeon. 1976. "The final days of a Washington restaurant critic." *Washingtonian* 12: 226–28. June.

van Housen, Alice, ed. 2003. *2003/04 Chicago Restaurants*. New York: Zagat Survey.

van Rees, C. J. 1989. "The institutional foundation of a critic's connoisseurship." *Poetics* 18:179–98.

Velleman, Paul F. 1986. "On evaluating statistics software." *Computers and the Social Sciences* 2(1/2): 81–83.

Velleman, Paul F., Roy E. Welsch. 1976. "On evaluating interactive statistical program packages." *Communications in Statistics, Part B, Simulation and Computation* 5: 197–208.

Vettel, Phil. 1989. "Avoid real work: Be a dining critic." *Chicago Tribune* 143: 3. October 1.

———. 1992. "Assessing the best requires some special ingredients." *Chicago Tribune* 146: 5, 13. November 6.

———. 1996a. "Reworked Yoshi's Cafe retains culinary excellence." *Chicago Tribune* 150(194): 36, 38. Jul 12.

———. 1996b. "A four-star treat awaits at still-dazzling, meticulous Trio." *Chicago Tribune* 150(103): 36–37. April 12.

———. 1996c. "At theme restaurants, food often just the appetizer." *Chicago Tribune* 149(147): 1,17. May 26.

Wanderer, Jules J. 1970. "In defense of popular taste: Film ratings among professionals and lay audience." *American Journal of Sociology* 76(2): 262–72.

Watt, Ian. 1957. *The Rise of the Novel*. Berkeley: University of California Press.

Waxman, Sharon. 2001. "Hated it! A travesty! No stars! What a mess!" *Washington Post* 124(168): C1, C11. June 17.

Whaples, Robert. 2001. "Hours of work in U.S. history." *EH.Net Encyclopedia*. August 15, 2001. eh.net/encyclopedia/?article-whaples.work.hours.us.

Wheaton, Dennis Ray. 1995. "Is lettuce wilting?" *Chicago* 41(3): 109–11. March.

———. 1996. "Chopstakes." *Chicago* 45(8): 33–35.

———. 2003. "Hood vibrations" *Chicago* 52(9): 52–56. September.

White, David Manning. 1964. The "Gatekeeper": A case study in the selection of news. Pp. 160–72 in Lewis Anthony Dexter and David Manning White, eds., *People, Society, and Mass Communications*. New York: Free Press.

White, Harrison C., Cynthia A. White. 1993 [1965]. *Canvases and Careers: Institutional Change in the French Painting World*. Chicago: University of Chicago Press.

Whitney, D. Charles, Lee B. Becker. 1982. "'Keeping the gates' for gatekeepers: The effects of wire news." *Journalism Quarterly* 59: 60–65.

Widder, Pat. 1993. "Fact and fantasy: Real world not nearly as simplistic as TV portrays it." *Chicago Tribune* 146(52): 41. February 21.

Wilkinson, Leland. 1985. *Statistics Quiz: Problems Which Reveal Deficiencies in Statistical Programs*. Evanston IL: Systat Inc.

Wilmington, Michael. 1998. "The editor's cut." *Chicago Tribune* 151(171): 4. June 21.

———. 1999. "Inside the National Society of Film Critics: How 'Private Ryan' fell out of sight." *Chicago Tribune* 152(20): 1, 7. January 20.

Wine, Cynthia. 1993. *Eating for a living: Food, Sex, and Dining Out*. New York: Penguin.

Woodward, Joan. 1965. *Industrial Organization: Theory and Practice*. London: Oxford.

Wuthnow, Robert. 1989. *Communities of Discourse: Ideology and Social Structure in the Reformation, the Enlightenment, and European Socialism*. Cambridge, MA: Harvard University Press.

Zagat, Tim, Nina Zagat. 1996. *1997 New York City restaurants*. New York: Zagat Survey.

———. 2002. *2003 New York City Restaurants*. New York: Zagat Survey.

Zaller, John. 1992. *The Nature and Origins of Mass Opinion*. Cambridge: Cambridge University Press.

Zaret, David. 1989. "Religion and the rise of liberal democratic ideology in seventeenth-century England." *American Sociological Review* 54 (April): 163–79.

———. 1985. *The heavenly Contract: Ideology and Organization in Prerevolutionary Puritanism*. Chicago: University of Chicago Press.

Zibart, Eve. 1996. "Tripe it, you'll like it." *Washington Post* 119: N26. October 25.

Zuckerman, Harriet, Robert Merton. 1971. "Institutionalized patterns of evaluation in science." *Minerva* 9: 66–100.

# Index

# About the Author

**Grant Blank** is Assistant Professor of Sociology at American University, Washington D.C. His special interests are in the sociology of culture, reviews and other forms of cultural evaluation, the influence of computers and electronic networks, and analysis of qualitative and quantitative data.

ML                                          3/07